William Hunt, a historian with the National Park Service, completed this historic resource study of the Wrangell-St. Elias area in 1991. This publication was originally printed by the Government Printing Office and distributed to offices and libraries throughout Alaska as a reference guide for park managers and historians. The staff of Wrangell-St. Elias National Park and Preserve and the Alaska Natural History Association felt that this book should be made available to the general public since there is so little written about this corner of the state. Over one hundred photographs have been added to the original work and editorial revisions have been made to complement the original study. Although Wrangell-St. Elias National Park is the largest national park in the United States, the written stories of this area are still relatively few. We hope this book will be a catalyst to entice other writers, storytellers, and adventurers to explore this spectacular mountain wilderness area of Alaska.

Frankie Barker
Executive Director
Alaska Natural History Association

Margie Steigerwald
Interpretive Specialist
Wrangell-St. Elias National Park and Preserve

Mountain Wilderness

An Illustrated History of
Wrangell - St. Elias National Park and Preserve, Alaska
By William R. Hunt

Rafts on the Copper River. Courtesy of the National Park Service, M. Steigerwald photo, 1993.

Previous page: Climbers on Mt. Drum. Courtesy of the National Park Service; photograph by C.J. Jones.

Copyright © 1996 by Alaska Natural History Association
Alaska Natural History Association, 605 West Fourth Avenue, Suite 85, Anchorage, Alaska 99501

The Donning Company/Publishers, 184 Business Park Drive, Suite 106, Virginia Beach, Virginia 23462

⁎ Steve Mull, *General Manager*

⁎ Barbara Bolton, *Project Director*   ⁎ Tony Lillis, *Director of Marketing*
⁎ Elizabeth B. Bobbitt, *Executive Editor*   ⁎ Teri Arnold, *Marketing Assistant*
⁎ Cynthia Dooley, *Graphic Designer*   ⁎ Dawn Kofroth, *Production Manager*

Library of Congress Cataloging-in-Publication Data
Hunt, William R.
Mountain wilderness: an illustrated history of the Wrangell-St. Elias National Park and Preserve, Alaska / by William R. Hunt.
p.   cm.
Includes bibliographical references (p.) and index.
ISBN 0-89865-971-X (softcover : alk. paper)
1. Wrangell-Saint Elias National Park and Preserve (Alaska)--History. 2. Wrangell-Saint Elias National Park and Preserve (Alaska)--History--Pictorial works. I. Title.
F912.W74H84   1996   96-24564
979.83--dc20   CIP
Printed in the United States of America

Contents

Kennicott Glacier. Courtesy of the National
Park Service, M. Woodbridge Williams photo.

Acknowledgments

The original manuscript for *Mountain WIlderness* would not have been possible without the writing and research of Bill Hunt, the research of Robert Spude, and the support of Kate Lidfors, all of the National Park Service. For this second printing I would like to acknowledge the research and editing of Geoffrey Bleakley, and the support and review of Anne Worthington, Rebecca Nelson, Frank Norris, Logan Hovis, and Melissa Hronkin of the National Park Service. The following organizations contributed photographs or other assistance to the publication: the Alaska State Library, the Anchorage Museum of History and Art, the Valdez Museum, the Rasmuson Library of the University of Alaska, the Washington State Historical Society, the Museum of History and Industry in Seattle, the Tacoma Public Library, the Cordova Historical Society, the Copper Valley Historical Society, the McCarthy-Kennicott Historical Museum, the Sheldon Museum and Cultural Center in Haines, Special Collections at the University of Washington Libraries, the National Archives, the United States Geological Survey and National Park Service. The following individuals also contributed photographs: Alfonse Nikolaus, Mike Sullivan, James McGavock, Jean McGavock Lamb, and the William C. Douglass Family. Thank you to artist Gail Niebrugge for contributing the cover artwork and to the Alaska Natural History Association for their financial and administrative support. And finally, special thanks to Jay Wells, Jon Jarvis, and Russell Galipeau for supporting my work on this project.

MARGIE STEIGERWALD
Project Coordinator
Wrangell-St. Elias National Park and Preserve

Lynx waking up. Courtesy of the National Park Service.

Evening shadows and fishwheels on the Copper River. Courtesy of the Sheldon Museum and Cultural Center, Haines, Alaska. H.A. Ives photo.

Introduction

History always concerns people but developing an understanding of the people requires an understanding of their natural environment, their use of the environment, and their beliefs about it. Of non-Natives in the region we usually ask, "What brought them to the country? What was the lure?" Of the Natives we focus on other considerations and note that their environment does not consist of a land and sea to be utilized only for its yield of sustenance.

Although experts have barely begun to examine the Wrangell-St. Elias region, their interim reports confirm its extensive prehistory. Geologists, for example, suggest that parts of its volcanic terrane formed three hundred million years ago, and archaeologists maintain that even its human occupation has continued for more than a millennium.[1] Space limitations, however, limit this study to the region's historical period, beginning with its European discovery in the mid-eighteenth century.

⁕ Establishment of Wrangell-St. Elias National Park and Preserve ⁕

Efforts to preserve the region's spectacular natural beauty began long before the park was established. Alaska Governor Ernest Gruening started lobbying in the mid-1930s to protect the area. Writing to Interior Secretary Harold L. Ickes in 1938, Gruening noted that:

. . . the region is superlative in its scenic beauty and attractiveness and measures up fully and beyond the requirements for its establishment as a National Monument and later as a National Park. It is my personal view that from the standpoint of scenic beauty, it is the finest region in Alaska. I will go further and state my belief that nowhere on the North American continent is such striking scenery to be seen.[2]

Other officials apparently supported Gruening's proposal. After touring the area, Harry J. Liek, then superintendent of Mount McKinley National Park, and John D. Coffman, the Interior Department's Chief of Forestry, wrote that:

. . . there is no question . . . that this area meets the superlative character so desirable in a national park. It is superlative in scenic features and in its presentation of glacial phenomena. . . . Among our national parks it would rate with the best if in fact it would not even excel the mountain scenery of any of the existing national parks.[3]

In response to Gruening's pressure, Interior Secretary Harold L. Ickes recommended in January 1940 that President Franklin D. Roosevelt designate the area as a National Monument. Faced with the onset of World War II, however, the president declined to act:

In view of the emergency with which we are confronted and the necessity for the preparation for total defense, with the vast expenditures which this preparation entails, I have recommended the curtailment of every possible activity not directly related to national defense. It seems to me that there is no urgency with respect to this proposal. Most of the area is now within the public domain and is accorded some protection. . . . In the circumstances, I deem it appropriate to withhold the issuance of the proposed proclamation.[4]

Little changed until 1959, its Statehood Act allowed Alaska to choose 103.5 million acres from the public domain. State efforts to satisfy that entitlement soon prompted Alaska's Native residents to file their own land claims, based on their aboriginal "use and occupancy."

On January 17, 1969, Interior Secretary Stewart Udall responded to their action by denying further state selections until the claims issue had been satisfactorily resolved. Congress eventually complied, passing the Alaska Native Claims Settlement Act (ANCSA) in December 1971.

Alaska Natives were not the only group to gain from the land claims struggle. Environmental organizations benefited as well. ANCSA authorized the Interior Secretary to withdraw up to 80 million acres in Alaska for study toward their potential inclusion in national parks or forests, wildlife refuges, or wild and scenic river systems.[5]

This provision eventually led to enactment of the Alaska National Interest Lands Conservation Act of 1980 (ANILCA), placing 104.5 million acres of the state under permanent federal protection. Among those selected were the 13.2 million acres now included in Wrangell-St. Elias National Park and Preserve.

❊ Area Description ❊

Superlatives are hard to resist when describing the great Wrangell-St. Elias National Park and Preserve. It is the largest park in the United States. It includes some of the grandest and least known physical features on the continent. Six times larger than Yellowstone National Park, it encompasses an area of 13,188,024 million acres in south-central Alaska. From the coast of the Gulf of Alaska the park extends some 160 miles to the north to enclose the country's largest glacier system. Its eastern border is formed by the boundary between Canada and the United States and extends to include the upper portion of Alaska's coastal panhandle bounded by Canada to the north. Canada's Kluane National Park and Territorial Game Sanctuary encompasses 5.4 million acres across the international boundary.

The great Copper River forms part of Wrangell-St. Elias Park's western border, along with the towering mountains of the Chugach Range. Ten of North America's fifteen highest summits lie within this region. The Wrangell Mountains of the interior enclose the nation's largest glacier system and include the Nabesna Glacier—the world's longest interior valley glacier. Other prominent geographic features are the huge glaciers flowing from the Chugach Mountains and St. Elias Range into the sea, including the Malaspina, which is the largest piedmont glacier in North America, and the 127-mile-long Bagley Icefield.

The land and marine ecosystems comprise elevations from below sea level to peaks higher than 18,000 feet. Alpine tundra covers 40 percent of the surface; glaciers and ice fields, 25 percent; upland spruce-hardwood forest, 10 percent; coastal western hemlock-Sitka spruce forest, 5 percent; wave-stirred beach, 5 percent; and other ecosystems, 15 percent. There are six hundred miles of riverine environment, ninety miles of wave-stirred beach, and ten miles of wave-beaten rocky coast.

The interior lowlands in the vicinity of the Wrangell Mountains can experience very cold winter temperatures. Gulkana and Northway often record the coldest temperatures in Alaska, sometimes to less than minus sixty-degrees Fahrenheit. McCarthy and Chitina do not get that cold, and, of course, the region near the coast benefits from warming maritime influences. From the coast to the crest of the Chugach Mountains the climate is characterized by frequent cloudy conditions and a heavy rainfall. The average annual temperature is forty degrees Fahrenheit. North of the Chugach the average temperature is colder at thirty-five degrees and the rainfall is less. Summer temperatures can reach ninety degrees in the interior and rainfall is sparse. Gulkana receives between eleven and fourteen inches a year. Promoters of mining during the Klondike gold rush era often contended that the Copper River country had the best climate in Alaska and boasted of the long growing season in summer. Of course, they exaggerated, as agricultural experiments later proved. Generally, it can be said that the climate is one of extremes from winter to summer.

The narrow coastline along the Gulf of Alaska is known for its beauty and its hazards to navigators because of occasional fierce winds of up to one hundred knots, high waves, and fifteen- to eighteen-foot tidal range. Precipitation averages from one hundred to one hundred sixty inches a year.

The land offers more than dramatic scenery. It is rich in wildlife, including moose, caribou, brown and black bear, wolves, wolverines, mountain goats, and the largest specimens of Dall sheep known. Fish and birds abound. Bird populations migrating along the coast are also particularly notable, including half of the world's trumpeter swans. The Copper River delta supports some of the largest populations of bird life known. It is the principal nesting ground of dusky Canada geese and a significant feeding area for many other kinds of migrating fowl. The coastline from Yakutat Bay to Prince William Sound is an important habitat for bald eagles, harbor seals, sea otters, sea lions, and many varieties of seabirds.

❋ World Heritage Site ❋

Wrangell-St.Elias is one of four contiguous conservation units spanning some 24 million acres that have been recognized by the United Nations as an international World Heritage Site. The original 1978 designation included Wrangell-St.Elias and Kluane. In 1993 both Glacier Bay National Park and Preserve and the Tatshenshini-Alsek Provincial Park in British Columbia were added to that designation. Altogether it is the largest internationally protected area in the world.

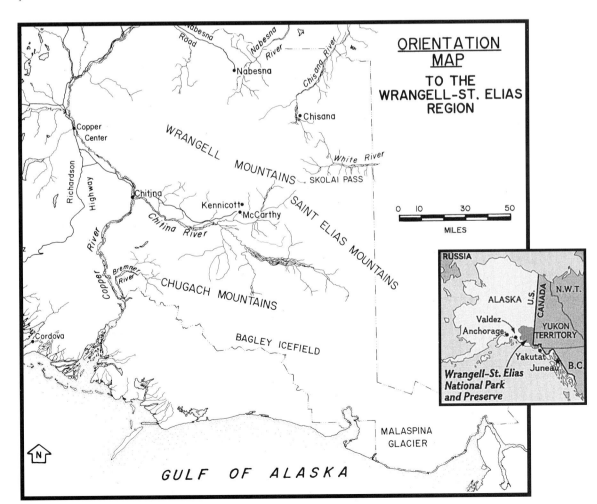

Ahtna women frequently packed heavy loads.
These reportedly exceeded 80 pounds.
Courtesy of the Valdez Museum, Miles
Brothers photo 916.

Chapter 1

＊　＊　＊

Initial Contact with Native Peoples

Much of the Wrangell-St. Elias region is a mountainous, icy world devoid of human settlement. Alaska's Native peoples traditionally occupied more hospitable, lower areas, such as the Copper River valley (called *Atna' Nene* meaning "Ahtna land"). A rolling lowland, forested with aspen, birch, and spruce, and dotted with lakes, it abounds with fowl, fish, and large animals. The headwaters of the Chisana and White Rivers resemble the Copper basin in appearance and the availability of food resources. At some time in the distant past, still disputed among archaeologists, prehistoric people ventured into these verdant lowlands and stayed. Artifacts discovered at Dry Creek and Healy Lake suggest that humans first occupied interior Alaska about 10,000 years ago. Early caribou hunters regularly visited the Tangle Lakes by 8,000 B.P. and probably entered the Wrangell-St. Elias region about two thousand years later. As glacial ice retreated and more land became available, these early residents developed social organizations, shifting patterns of settlement, and diverse languages.

Five distinctive groups inhabited discrete portions of the Wrangell-St. Elias region. The Ahtna controlled the upper Copper River and its tributaries; the Upper Tanana held the Nabesna and Chisana River Valleys; the Southern Tutchone occupied the White River drainage; and the Yakutat Tlingit and the Eyak dwelled along the coast, though both ventured inland for seasonal hunting. Interior Indians spoke various Athapaskan languages while the Tlingits and Eyaks spoke their own tongues, only distantly related to the former through a common protolinguistic family, which modern linguists call Na-Dene.

The Ahtna were the most numerous residents of the Wrangell-St. Elias region. Scholars, however, still debate just how many there actually were. While most experts now estimate their aboriginal total at about 2,000, U.S. Army explorer Henry Allen calculated that the entire Copper River Valley only contained 336 inhabitants in 1885—and doubted that its population was ever any greater.[1]

Game in the region was not plentiful enough to support large numbers; hence a pattern developed of small villages of twenty to thirty members of a familial clan, usually located where a major tributary entered the Copper River. At some point two larger villages developed: Taral, near Copper's confluence with the Chitina River, and Batzulnetas, at the start of the primary trail leading north across the Alaska Range. A *denae*, heading each village, was the principal hunter and, when the fur trade developed, the leading trapper and trader.

The Upper Tanana population was only about one hundred in early historic times, perhaps decimated by an epidemic of scarlet fever in 1851. Some people lived in villages on the Nabesna and the Chisana Rivers, but most lived in the flats of the Tanana River. The Southern Tutchone numbered only about fifty and lived on the upper White River. They were related to a larger group inhabiting the southwestern portion of Canada's Yukon Territory.

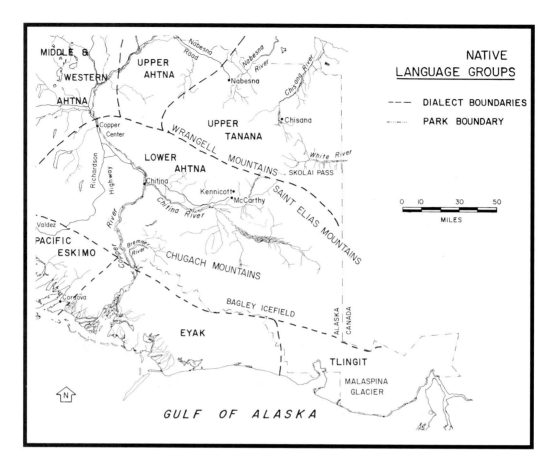

Native language groups

At the time of contact, the Tlingit were slowly expanding westward, capturing territory largely by assimilating its existing Eyak occupants. Never populous, the Yakutat Tlingit did not occupy their villages on the south shores of Disenchantment Bay until after what has been called the "little ice age," lasting from 1500 to 1850 A.D. The receding glaciers provided newly exposed land.

The Eyaks probably emanated from an interior Native group. They apparently moved down the Copper River to its mouth, then southeast across the Bering Glacier to occupy the coast between Yakataga and Yakutat. Pressure from larger groups of Chugach Eskimo and Yakutat Tlingits eventually reduced their numbers to a few inhabitants of two coastal villages, Eyak and Alaganik.

Cultural attainment levels among Alaska's Native peoples often are measured by comparing standards of craftsmanship exhibited by objects of their material culture. The cultural attainment of the Wrangell-St. Elias region's peoples in clothing, implements, and housing is distinguished. They wove close-knit baskets and spruce root hats and made useful objects of metal, stone, wood, and bone. Abundant native copper found on the tributaries of the Nizina, Kuskulana, upper Nabesna, and White Rivers made its way into weapon points and became a valuable trade item. For clothing they utilized fur-bearing animals, ornamenting articles with porcupine quills, shells, and bones before buttons and beads were acquired from traders.

❉ Tlingit ❉

The Tlingit people traditionally occupied an extensive domain, comprised of thirteen territorial divisions and stretching all the way from the northern end of Prince of Wales Island to the Malaspina Glacier. The most northerly of these divisions, the Yakutat Kwan, controlled portions of the coastal region now included in Wrangell-St. Elias National Park and Preserve.

Dimitri Tarkhanov was the first European to describe in full the Yakutat Tlingits' material culture and subsistence cycle. Noting that they were master carvers, he related that their houses were made of stout planks, possessing floors of wooden blocks and containing partitions which separated the sleeping quarters of various families. A fireplace in the middle of the house served for all cooking done by as many as fifteen families in residence. In such crowded quarters harmony reigned. They were not at all inclined to quarrel, " . . . there being no foolishness and scandal, in addition to the friendliness of greeting and love of each other."[2]

Such houses were built near streams because of the all important salmon fishery. Among fishing methods was what he called an "enclosed fishery." The Indians built traps, then they set out up the stream, from where they paddled back, striking the canoe with sticks, piercing the water with harpoons, and driving with these the frightened fish into the traps . . . they take up the traps with such a great multitude of fish, scarcely able to draw them to the shore.[3]

Tarkhanov recorded Tlingit religious practices as well, recounting, for example, the actions of a local shaman: They made a fire of logs in the middle of the barabora, all the inhabitants of that place assembled, even the small ones. On the floor they place poles, striking it with them quite often and singing their talk. The Shaman is all painted with eagle's down on the face and hair. He runs around the fire and shouts. He bends his head back, stops and embraces an Aleut [this is probably the shaman's assistant]. . . . He speaks in a furious manner. . . . Then he takes . . . [totemic images] resembling birds, fish, and otters which he carries in his hands. He puts on his head by turns [images of] different painted birds, all of which he [represents]. And he ends his shamanism.[4]

❉ The Eyak ❉

Although Tarkhanov also visited the Eyak, he devoted little effort to describing them. Neither did anyone else. Failing to recognize that they were a separate people, most early observers dismissed their culture as merely a blend of Tlingit and Chugach Eskimo. Frederica de Laguna is credited with "rediscovering" the group's discrete identity during a 1930 research trip to Prince William Sound. While investigating Chugach prehistory she learned about the people from an Eyak informant named Galushia Nelson. De Laguna soon interviewed Charles Rosenberg, who had been the first American trader to live among the group. Five years later she also met Col. William R. Abercrombie, a retired American Army officer who had visited the Eyak villages in 1884. The meeting of Abercrombie and de Laguna was a fortunate occurrence for regional scholarship. "His written report on that expedition," de Laguna said of Abercrombie:

. . . contains perhaps the most important information to be found in any published source, but it is very little in comparison to what he was able to tell in conversation. In spite of the fact that his visit to the Eyak was 51 years ago, the Colonel retains a vivid and detailed memory of what he saw. . . .[5]

The Eyak villages included Eyak, near Mile Six of the Copper River and Northwestern Railway, where at one time a Russian trading post had been established; Alaganik, Mile

Twenty-one on the railway; Fort, below Eyak on the Eyak River, another supposed site of a Russian trading post; Beach or Whelk, on the narrow isthmus between Eyak Lake and Cordova Bay, roughly the site of the old Native village of Cordova; and summer camps at Mountain Slough and Point Whitshed. Eyak populations reported by various observers beginning in 1818 never numbered more than 154. By the time University of Alaska professor Michael Krauss began his studies in the 1960s, only a few remembered the Eyak language.

De Laguna described what housing and other material artifacts remained in the Eyak villages by 1930 and tried to piece together an outline of their cultural history. Her sources indicated that the Eyak did not get along with the Eskimos. Their slaves were Eskimos, but they never adopted Eskimos into their tribe because they "had no use for them." In modern times, however, some Eyak men took Eskimos for wives. Eyaks got along better with the Tlingits and appreciated that they were closely related to them and followed the same form of moiety organization [clans organization based on matrilineal descent]. Eyaks voyaged by canoe to Yakutat for trading with the Tlingits, and they exchanged visits to attend important potlatches. Eyaks were favorably disposed to the Ahtna and traded with them on the latter's voyages downriver, but only saw the few traders who came to the delta. Despite such good relations, the Eyaks were afraid to venture into the Ahtna country and believed the Ahtna shamans to be more powerful than their own. The Eyak could not understand their neighbors languages, although their own incorporated some Tlingit words. This lack of understanding and an uncertainty about the peaceful intentions of the others contributed to the uneasiness all three Native groups felt at the time of Abercrombie's explorations.[6]

In the early 1880s the Eyaks still lived rather primitive lives despite having access to white trade items such as rifles. Changes came fast for them after the first cannery was established at what is now Cordova some time between 1884 and 1890. "By the end of the century," de Laguna noted, "the 'civilizing' of the Eyak was practically complete, and they had almost ceased to exist as a separate tribal entity."[7]

✳ The Ahtna ✳

Tarkhanov liked the Ahtnas better than any other Alaska Natives he encountered. "The [Ahtnas] are quite virtuous," he reported, "both the female and the male sex toward the other. . . . These Indians appreciated good done to them," unlike some he had seen. "If you do not give, they become angry, and told everyone that you are a bad person."[8]

From Tarkhanov we learn that the Ahtna people made brush shelters for temporary use on fishing and hunting excursions but made strong permanent houses of poles, bark, and skins. Such permanent houses were eighteen feet square, framed with spruce poles, and covered with bark. Builders also used moss to fill chinks between poles and keep the place warmer. Walls rose to nearly four feet under the eaves. A ledge, raised three feet above the ground, extending four to five feet, provided sitting and sleeping space. Storage and other sleeping areas for women, children, and dogs was provided under the shelf. Smoke from the cooking fire escaped from a large hole in the roof. Entry to the house was through a small storm shed curtained by animal skins. Natives also built bathhouses.

Marriage and kinship determined the composition of the small villages of twenty to thirty inhabitants led by a capable hunter. The leader's wealth was often measured by the number of his copper possessions. The shaman was another powerful figure, charged with conducting hunting and other traditional ceremonies and healing the sick. Little is known about the prehistorical culture because of the swift adaptation of the Natives to Christianity and other non-native ways after contact in the nineteenth century.

Village people hunted, fished, and gathered berries within a specific area. During winter small animals were snared. Early spring was known as the "starving time," the long,

Eskilida's food cache near Chitina, 1910. Courtesy of the Anchorage Museum of History and Art, B71.4.5.26.

(Above) Native girl catching salmon with spruce root dipnet on the the Copper River. Courtesy of the Anchorage Museum of History and Art, B82.51.12.

(Left)) Army Lt. Sharp meeting an Ahtna girl at Tonsina, 1906. Courtesy of the Rasmuson Library Archives, University of Alaska Fairbanks; Zug Album, 80-68-27; P.S. Hunt photo C736.

belt-tightening period as stored products of the fall's gathering diminished and before the salmon run started. Starving was less common after contact and the introduction of Western technology, notably the fish wheel, which made gathering great numbers of salmon for preservation easier. As with the Tlingit, Tarkhanov provided some details on the Ahtna's subsistence practices:

> The livelihood [they have] from the Copper River is red fish [salmon] which come from the sea [to spawn] during the month of June, and they catch [them] in nets, a gill net bound with animal sinews, and dry on racks the yukola; fresh fish they sour in pits, head and intestines they heat with stones in wooden troughs. . . . they dig roots, and hunt rabbits in fall and spring [they catch] squirrels in summer with snares.[9]

Frederica de Laguna and Catherine McClellan completed the most comprehensive ethnographic study of the Ahtna. They identified Ahtna territory as including 23,000 square miles of the Copper River Valley. The extreme northwestern part of this area (before Cantwell was founded in 1916) was hunting territory shared by the Ahtna, Dena'ina, and Lower Tanana Indians, and lacked clearly defined boundaries.[10]

A detailed description of the Ahtna culture is beyond the scope of this book, but scholars de Laguna and McClellan indicate its complexity. Their discussions of subtle relationships and qualities of behavior provide a sense of the culture's distinction:

[T]here is avoidance . . . not only between brother and sister (including parallel cousins of the opposite sex), but also between older and younger sibling and between parallel cousins of the same sex, varying in degree according to difference in age, upon which authority also rests.[11]

The authors go on to describe the various grades of reserve, respect, shyness, or shaming, which:

. . . are first exhibited about the time of puberty, to be slowly relaxed in old age. Except at Mentasta, the second-person plural pronoun . . . is used in an honorific function to call an avoidance or respect relative when absolutely necessary; but the relatives may not look at each other. A senior may use an honorific third person plural when addressing a junior, but the junior is not supposed to answer back. Circumlocutions are substituted for kin terms in referring to a dead father, mother, or oldest sibling.[12]

De Laguna and McClellan also offer a good description of shamans and the process by which one became a shaman in former times:

When shamanistic dreams begin, they might last a year or more, and should never be revealed. The novice secluded himself for at least 30 days, avoiding places where women walked. He dared not refuse the call, although another shaman might remove the new power if the novice were 'mean,' and likely to become a 'bad doctor.' The shaman could not cut his hair or change his clothing, but wore on it some of the magic things . . . he had dreamed. These magic aids might be a flag, an embroidered 'map of the world,' a beribboned cane, a little stuffed weasel that could be sent to find lost persons, a doll that could dance, an image that warned of danger, or an object that could shoot disease into a victim.[13]

Each shaman was a specialist, able to cure certain types of illness such as soul loss or object intrusion, to perform operations with a wooden knife that left no scar, to cure wounds, or to perform wonderful feats (holding burning coals in the mouth, or letting a child thrust an arrow through the shaman's body which did no hurt).[14]

Doc Billum's ferry crossing the Copper River at Lower Tonsina about 1903. Courtesy of the Valdez Museum, P1986.117.56; Miles Brothers photo 743.

The Copper River Trading Post at Lower Tonsina, 1903. Courtesy of the Valdez Museum, P1986.117.52; Miles Brothers photo 881.

The Indians divided the year into two parts, the summer beginning in May with breakup and winter, which started in November. Activities varied cyclically through the months. In spring and summer people lived first in the salmon camps, after which they moved upland to meat camps, hunting small game on the way. In fall they descended once more to the rivers, trapping and hunting, until the several families gathered in the winter houses. These were usually near summer fish camps where the salmon were stored. By late January or February, families again were scattering to secure what game or freshwater fish they could. In pre con- tact times this movement probably depended on the condition of the food caches; as fur trapping became more profitable, the Middle and Upper Ahtna bands probably dispersed more widely in winter. The Lower Ahtna, who controlled much of the fur trade, did little trapping but bought furs from the upriver Ahtna to take to the coast on winter and spring trips.[15] Each band of people had a *denae*, or chief, whose role was of economic importance. He was responsible for "feeding his people, for moral lectures, for enforcing the traditional 'law' within his own settlement, and defending his people in legitimate grievances involving another group."[16]

❊ The Upper Tanana ❊

Euro-Americans did not make direct contact with the Upper Tanana people until the early-1880s, when the first prospectors entered the region via the Fortymile River. Even then, little impact occurred before the Klondike gold rush of 1898. Robert A. McKennan was the first anthropologist to study the people, spending the winter of 1929-1930 in the area. Starting into the country from McCarthy, he crossed the Wrangell Mountains to the head-waters of the White, Chisana, and Nabesna Rivers. He traveled on foot with pack horses, then by dog team, and later by boat to visit all the Indian camps in the Upper Tanana region except the small Scottie Creek band. Although he had some help from prospectors and traders, he traveled with Natives most of the time, living their life as far as possible and accompanying them on all their activities such as hunting and trapping:

Some informants excelled in giving me information of a technological nature, others were excellent raconteurs of the Native mythology, and still others were at their best in clearing up questions in the areas of social organization or religion.[17]

The young anthropologist appreciated the uniqueness of his opportunity:
No fur traders—Russian, British, or American—had penetrated the region during the nineteenth century, and not until the short-lived Chisana stampede of 1913 had miners in any numbers found their way into the mountains of the Chisana and Nabesna basins. As a result much of the original Indian culture was still functioning in 1929, and it was my good fortune to deal with informants who were living here when the first white men entered the Upper Tanana area.[18]

What McKennan identified as the Upper Tanana area was bound on the north by an arc extending from the confluence of the Tok and Tanana Rivers to the boundary of Canada; on the east by a line extending just beyond the boundary; on the south by a line roughly following the White River and the Skolai Pass; and on the west by a line commencing north of McCarthy and bearing north to the Upper Nabesna River, Suslota Pass, and the Tanana River. McKennan found a small population, only some 152 Indians living in five different bands. Of these bands only the one located at the mouth of Cross Creek inhabited the present limits of the Wrangell-St. Elias region.

Ahtna leader Doc Billum (center) at Lower Tonsina. Courtesy of the Rasmuson Library Archives, University of Alaska Fairbanks; Capps Collection, 83-149-930.

The isolation of the region made it relatively easy for McKennan to trace the impact of white culture. The major factor, of course, was the Chisana gold boom that began in 1913. By 1916 only about two hundred miners wintered at Chisana, and the population declined rapidly from that time. Only seven whites, one of them a woman, lived in the area when McKennan visited there in 1929. McKennan observed that the Indians benefited from the rivalry among traders. These hearty entre-preneurs included Milo Hajdukovich, brother of John Hajdukovich; Ted Lowell, with stores at Tanana Crossing,

Batzulnetas George. Note his use of pack dogs. Courtesy of the Rasmuson Library Archives, University of Alaska Fairbanks; Capps Collection, 83-149-811.

Tetlin, and the mouth of the Nabesna; and Herman Kessler, near the mouth of Gardiner Creek, whose principal customers were the Scottie Creek band. Traders had to pay high prices for furs, or Natives found another buyer. Material goods, including stoves, rifles, tents, and cloth altered the Indian culture, but in ways that were "largely superficial."[19]

By the time McKennan published his study of the Upper Tanana Indians in 1959 great changes had taken place in the region. Alterations in the Native culture could no longer be described as superficial with the advent of Bureau of Education schools, highway construction, and other fast-paced changes of the World War II era and regional developments since that time.

✳ Trading ✳

Russian efforts to establish trading posts in the Copper River Valley interior are discussed in Chapter 2. Although Russian intrusions diminished after the 1848 massacre of Ruf Serebrennikov's exploring expedition, their earlier presence effectively established a trading pattern. By 1850, as Anthropologist James Ketz said:

. . . there is little question that the participation had grown to a full commitment to a dual economy by the final quarter of the century. During the nineteenth century, the Ahtna became inextricably linked to the international commodity market in furs, and the diffusion of the economic patterns of the fur trade throughout Ahtna society must be seen as the most important historical development of the early post-contact era.[20]

Ahtna Chief Nicolai told Capt. William Abercrombie about bringing copper downriver to the Russians who wanted the metal for bolts used in ship building. Trading in copper between Natives of the interior and the coast, particularly the Eyak, antedated the Russian interest. Frederica de Laguna believes that the early trade was a limited one and utilized the Keystone Canyon and Lowe River route to the coast at what became Valdez, thence across Prince William Sound to Nuchek. Abercrombie found a well-worn trail up the canyon and across to Tiekel in the Copper River Valley. He also found a shell heap at the mouth of the Lowe River which he thought was evidence of an "Eskimo village founded because of the copper traffic."[21]

Abercrombie speculated that the route was abandoned about 1868 following a particularly devastating measles epidemic or because of growing quarrels between Eyaks and Eskimos at Ellamar. In any case, at about this time the Ahtna began transporting their copper by boat, which probably prompted the Eyak to establish their village of Alaganik on the Copper River delta. Whether the Ahtna took the copper to Nuchek or commissioned the Eyak for this remains a matter of controversy.

The Alaska Commercial Company (ACC), which became the major fur trading enterprise in Alaska after the Russian American Company withdrew, did not establish any posts in the interior part of the Copper basin. In the early 1890s the company started stores at Tatitlek, a village near Bligh Island and forty miles northwest of Cordova, at Cape Martin, and at Valdez, but all these posts shut down before the 1898 gold rush. The records of the Kodiak branch of ACC, which serviced stations in Cook Inlet and Prince William Sound, only mention Copper River Indians in connection with the Valdez store. This suggests that the major portion of the interior fur trade was conducted at canneries on the Eyak River. When Frederick Schwatka's 1891 expedition reached the Copper River from the Yukon and White Rivers, the explorers traveled to the coast with Chief Nicolai from Taral. About this time Charles Rosenberg, an independent trader, established a trading post at Alaganik, a village in the Copper River delta. ACC competed, too, not by establishing a fixed post, but by sending George Fleming to one of the canneries with goods every summer from the mid-1890s.[22]

Another trade traffic route sometimes used by Copper River Natives was the overland passage to upper Cook Inlet. The ACC trader at Tyonek was ambitious enough in 1894 to send a man with $200 in trade goods to the Copper River interior from upper Cook Inlet, but apparently this experiment was not repeated. The venture may have been inspired by the arrival at Tyonek in spring 1894 of a trader named Andrew Holman who brought in Copper River furs.

For reasons that are not clear, the ACC's fur trade declined through the 1890s. With the gold rush everything changed as the company and its rivals shifted from the fur trade to provisioning miners. The Ahtna no longer had to depend upon the ACC for goods because the stampeders brought tons of provisions into the country, much of which was sold off cheaply or abandoned when the golden expectations of the '98 rushers were not met. This blow to commerce and the general uncertainty of traders in regard to the Ahtna is expressed in a lament from H. C. Turell, the ACC's agent at Knik: "There was so much goods taken in and left on Copper River last and this summer that [I] do not expect much trade from Copper River Natives, although one cannot be sure in regard to them."[23]

A new trading pattern emerged from the gold rush. Valdez and stations along the Valdez Trail, like Copper Center, emerged as the mercantile centers for both Natives and whites. After 1910,

An Ahtna family. Courtesy of the Washington State Historical Society, 41.175.

An Ahtna house at Taral, as reported by Lt. Henry Allen in 1885. Courtesy of the Alaska State Library, Alaska Purchase Collection, PCA 20–35.

with the production of copper and the construction of the Copper River and Northwestern Railway, other stations, such as Chitina and McCarthy, became important supply centers. The final evolution occurred with the Chisana gold rush of 1913. Early Chisana miners outfitted at Dawson, but as the area boomed the route by railroad to McCarthy, then overland to the mining camp, became the better established one.

⁂ John Hajdukovich and the Upper Tanana Indians ⁂

When Chisana declined, trade patterns for the northern reaches of the Wrangell-St. Elias area shifted to some extent. The field was left open for an enterprising, independent trader, John Hajdukovich, who went into the Upper Tanana district sometime between 1915 and 1922 and remained a powerful influence in the area until his death in 1965. Hajdukovich showed a real, if paternalistic, concern for Natives and aggressively protected what he perceived to be their best interests. He strived to keep liquor out of his district and achieved a political triumph in 1930 when Congress established the Tetlin Indian Reserve.[24]

The trader's region extended to include the Nabesna area, where Herman Kessler kept a store from the 1920s. Nabesna Village should not be confused with the Nabesna site of the Nabesna Mining Company that is within the Wrangell-St. Elias National Park and Preserve. Nabesna Village was located six miles southwest of the Northway Junction, which is outside the park, yet close enough to provide some focus for trade and Native history in the region.

Other stores operated or provisioned by Hajdukovich included one near Gardiner Creek on the Chisana River; the mouth of the Healy River; Tetlin; Last Tetlin; and Moose Creek. Merchandise was brought to the stores by boat in summer and dogsled in winter, and transportation costs kept prices high. The cost of freight from Fairbanks to Big Delta, ninety miles by auto, was $20 a ton; from Big Delta to Tanana Crossing, seventy river miles, cost $100 per ton; from Tanana Crossing to Tetlin was another fifty miles by river.

Trail building and maintenance in the region was the responsibility of the Alaska Road

Commission (ARC), which was always swamped with demands for more work than its budget allowed. Hajdukovich frequently petitioned the ARC for improvements in his district and sometimes won the contract for construction.

Another benefit reached the region in 1924 when the Bureau of Education established a school at Tetlin. The first teacher, Jack Singleton, was an able and dedicated man. Natives from Nabesna moved to Tetlin every summer for fishing and to take advantage of Singleton's willingness to instruct the children during the fishing season.

Matters of trade, economic prospects, Native welfare, trail and road maintenance, and education were closely interwoven. In 1927 Hajdukovich petitioned the road commission, the Bureau of Education, and the U.S. Geological Survey. From the road commission he wanted trails and roads that would encourage mineral development.

From the Bureau of Education he wanted a new school at Tanana Crossing; and from the U.S. Geological Survey he wanted a geological survey of the Mentasta Pass region. Bureaucrats responded more favorably than usual because of the work of Carl Whitham, a persistent prospector who discovered lode gold deposits on the upper Nabesna River in 1925. Within four years he began production and gave new hope for the region's commercial development.

To encourage miners, the U.S. Geological Survey commenced a program in 1929 for the investigation of mineral resources of the eastern part of the Alaska Range from the Delta River to the international boundary. Surveys were scheduled for the area between the Big Tok and the Nabesna Rivers in 1931 and 1934; the area between Suslota Lake and the Nabesna River in 1938; and the area between the Chisana River and the international boundary in 1940. During the same period the U.S. Geological Survey also conducted topographical surveys in the region from 1937 to 1939.

Among those who appreciated Hajdukovich's concern for Natives was Earl Beck of the

Ahtna Chief Nicolai. Courtesy of the Anchorage Museum of History and Art, B80.98.52.

Bureau of Education. Beck conceded that the trader benefited directly in fur trading volume by refusing to traffic in liquor: "A drunken native did not produce as much fur as the same Native would if he were sober all the time." Yet Beck believed that Hajdukovich was also motivated by concern for the Indians' well-being—as other traders were not: "The trader that does not give liquor in some form or other in Alaska is the exception rather than the rule."[25]

Robert A. McKennan, the pioneer anthropologist of the Upper Tanana Indian culture, benefited from Hajdukovich's guidance when he began his investigations in 1929. The two men traveled together and McKennan had ample opportunity to appreciate the trader's role as "the patron saint and father confessor" to the Tetlin and Nabesna Indians.[26]

Wendell Endicott, hunter and author, praised the trader as "wise, sane, and clear-thinking," observing with admiration his attempts to discourage Indians from impoverishing themselves with the potlatch, a fundamental part of Athapaskan ceremonialism. "Save something for your old age," the trader admonished. He noted that some Copper Center Indians traveled as far as Healy to attend a notable potlatch.[27]

Nabesna miner Carl Whitham was a vociferous opponent of Hajdukovich's lobbying for a Tetlin Reserve. Whitham protested "the biggest and rawest land sovereignty grabbing plan ever attempted by any autocratic bureau in Washington, D.C., and will if carried through as planned mean stagnation and decay of Alaska progress for all time to come."[28]

The Cordova Chamber of Commerce also opposed the plan as "an attack on the development of Alaska." Others saw a threat to the existing hunting situation. The Alaska Game Commission resolved "that the setting aside of large areas for the same purposes as the Tetlin Reservation is detrimental to the interests of the Territory."[29]

Boundaries of the reserve continued to be a concern of Hajdukovich even after it was created because of the liquor problem. He found that Herman Kessler, the trader at Nabesna Village, had shipped in three tons of booze and other goods in 1932 and in 1937 brought in even more and was trading to Indians from Nabesna and elsewhere in the region. He was not successful in getting the reserve enlarged so that Kessler's traffic could be policed, nor was he able to get the government to act against Kessler. In disgust he resigned his long-held office as U.S. commissioner.

Aside from the Hajdukovich trading area, there is little that is distinctive about the trading history within the Wrangell-St. Elias region. For the most part the trade was tied to highway or railroad communities and ebbed or flowed with the local currents of prosperity. Mostly, after the shutdown of the Kennecott mines and the railroad, it ebbed. There were traders like Lawrence DeWitt of Slana, who ventured away from the road in the 1930s to call at Indian villages, but their roles have not been well documented.

An exception should be made for the place of Otto A. Nelson, a Missouri schoolteacher who moved to Alaska to become a surveyor on the construction of the Copper River and Northwestern Railway in 1908, then acted as engineer on other railroad projects until retiring to become a storekeeper in about 1932. After the railroad shut down in 1938, Nelson stayed on in Chitina and eventually bought most of the buildings in what became a virtual ghost town but for his Chitina Cash Store. He trucked merchandise in from Valdez during the summer and served the needs of about seventy-five Natives and twenty-five whites who still lived in the area in the 1940s and 1950s.[30]

❋ Archaeological Studies ❋

In 1936 Froelich G. Rainey undertook a pioneer expedition to archaeological sites in the Copper River Valley, sponsored by the American Museum of Natural History and the University of Alaska. He made his initial survey traveling from Fairbanks to Copper Center, thence up the river and crossing over to the Nabesna and the upper Tanana River. Little scientific work had been done in central Alaska prior to this time, and he had to depend upon information gained from Natives living in the area in locating old semipermanent dwellings and "the focal points for the seasonal concentration of the shifting, partly nomadic population."[31]

Rainey's observations of the material condition of the Copper River Natives confirmed what he had learned in the reports of Lt. Henry T. Allen, a U.S. Army explorer who traversed the region in 1885, and in the accounts of earlier Russian traders. It was a game-poor region where Indians faced periodic famine. "Present conditions are apparently no better; we saw no game during the summer of 1936 and found the few remaining Indian groups anxiously awaiting the salmon run to allay their hunger."[32]

Though Rainey did not have great expectations for the results of archaeological work in central Alaska, he noted that prehistoric dwelling sites had been reported in the Copper River country. Allen had noted old house sites above the mouth of the Chitina River, and modern highway builders working the stretch from Gulkana to Nabesna found house sites and crude stone tools near Indian River, a tributary of the upper Copper River. Another house site had been reported near Batzulnetas.

Acting on information gathered from local Natives, Rainey found and excavated sites near Gakona, at Slana, and near Batzulnetas. Results of his investigation were mixed. The Gakona site proved to be historic, but he was pleased to find pre-Columbian pits near Batzulnetas which were probably used for fish storage. He believed that the indications there suggested that in earlier times the region must have supported a larger population than that observed by Allen and later travelers. The sparse population of the upper Copper region, however, worked against the discovery of additional sites. "A thorough knowledge of the archeological remains in this area," he concluded, "will depend upon its settlement and agricultural development."[33]

In 1970 James VanStone, the second archaeological investigator in the Copper River area, made a limited excavation at Taral Creek, south of Chitina. He believed that the site had been a Russian post. Nearby he also discovered what he assumed were Indian house pits of post-contact origin.[34]

In 1973 Anne D. Shinkwin, a University of Alaska archaeologist sponsored by the National Park Service, excavated a very interesting early-nineteenth-century site near Chitina. Shinkwin theorized that the site would represent a protohistoric settlement, a place that predated Allen's explorations but not contact with Europeans. The recovery of European trade goods and other evidence confirmed her expectations, and she placed the site in the 1816–1838 era. The people of that period had obvious trade contacts with the coast, and their material culture resembled that of another coastal village on Knight Island in the Yakutat region.[35]

Research on Ahtna historic sites done by Holly Reckord of the University of Alaska, Fairbanks, Cooperative Park Studies Unit between 1974 and 1976 lists 115 separate sites and provides a summary of the available information on each. She also completed a report which outlines the history of subsistence uses over the past 150 years.[36]

✳ Ahtna Place Names and Dictionary ✳

James Kari and Mildred Buck published a major study of 1,383 Ahtna place names in 1983. Place name studies include valuable information about the people, their views of the environment, and its resources in addition to geography. A number of Ahtna elders assisted the authors. Kari gives an example of the importance of annotations in interpreting place names with a story about Tahneta Pass, at the head of the Matanuska River. According to a story long told by elders, people used to carry a handful of soil from their homes when they took the river trail to Cook Inlet. The Ahtna name for Tahneta Pass, "Nekets'alyaexden," means

Elaborate Ahtna shelter, made of spruce bark, at Taral about 1903. Courtesy of the Anchorage Museum of History and Art, 32.1.152.

"where we turn around." It was the place where they looked back at their homeland before venturing into the little known country, scattered the soil from home they carried, and "made a prayer for a safe journey."[37]

In 1986 Kari published a collection of narratives of the Upper Ahtna titled *"Tatl'ahwt'aenn Nenn'*: The Headwaters People's Country." The stories are written in Ahtnan and translated into English giving the reader an opportunity to learn much about the Ahtna culture through the words of a few elders including Katie John, Fred John Sr., Adam Sanford, Huston Sanford, Jack John Justin, and Nicholas A. Brown. In 1990, after years of linguistic research, Kari published the first dictionary of the Ahtna language.[38]

❊ The Ahtna Regional Corporation ❊

Ahtna, Incorporated is one of the regional corporations created by the Alaska Native Claims Settlement Act (ANCSA) of 1971. The corporation owns more than one million acres of the Copper River Valley. Eight villages, including Cantwell on the upper Nenana River, qualified as village corporations under terms of ANCSA. Total Ahtna enrollment recorded in 1973 was 1,038, making it the least populous corporation area in Alaska. The corporation is unique, however, in the historical unity of the villages assigned to Ahtna, Inc. As ethnologist Holly Reckord noted:

. . . the Ahtna shareholders trace their historical roots to a single cultural grouping, the Ahtna. In aboriginal times their ancestors were the sole inhabitants of the Copper River Valley above Wood Canyon. They spoke several dialects of a single Athapaskan language and shared cultural values, social traits, and technological inventories. Ancestral unity means that the selection of historical sites should not be hampered by the politics of tribalism or regionalism.[38]

Ahtna individuals participated in Alaska Native organizations and contributed some leaders to the Alaska Native Brotherhood, founded in 1954, and to the thrust that resulted in the passage of ANCSA. Ahtna, Inc. was involved in several joint ventures with Alyeska Pipeline Service Company, and Ahtna individuals worked on the construction of the trans-Alaska pipeline.

Ahtna leaders have a sophisticated understanding of political and economic power. They opposed enrolling their children in public schools during the 1950s, but nevertheless were forced to do so. Considerable cultural disruption followed, as many families were forced to move from subsistence villages to Copper Center, Glennallen, and Gulkana to comply with government edicts. The Ahtna people have begun reviving their traditional culture. Elders have encouraged respect for story telling and old ceremonies, including the potlatch. Interest in Native dancing, singing, foods, and language has grown.

❊ Conclusion ❊

Natives of the region had distinct cultural identities, beliefs, and languages for thousands of years before non-natives entered the region. Although the fur trade changed certain subsistence and travel patterns and brought more imported goods into the community, the effect on traditional Native cultures was minimal at first. During the gold rush era (1898–1914), changes were more marked and came faster. In time there were schools, roads, non-native communities, and other forms of contact that accelerated the assimilation process. The variety and complexity of traditional Native cultures is only hinted at here, but interested readers may refer to books cited in the notes and bibliography.

Mt. St. Elias from Point Manby, near
Yakutat. Courtesy of the Alaska State
Library, Kayamori Collection, PCA 55-177.

Chapter

Russians and other Explorers

❋ ❋ ❋

Fog surrounded the ship until clearing around noon. Yet the day remained gray and
drizzly, and the Russian voyagers aboard *St. Peter* had only a few glimpses of the sun
as winds occasionally parted the clouds. The voyagers believed that land was near.
Suddenly the fog lifted to reveal a magnificent and welcome sight—a towering peak arising
from a chain of snow-covered mountains. It was July 16, 1741, the feast day of St. Elias on
the Orthodox Church calendar, so according to legend Vitus Bering named the lofty peak for
the saint. This was the Russian mariner's first glimpse of Alaska. A few days later, landing on
what later came to be called Kayak Island, Bering gave it the saint's name as well. Actually,
the circumstances of the name St. Elias were somewhat different. From the narrative of
Sven Waxell, one of Bering's officers, we have a more accurate report:

> *On this day we sighted land in the direction of* N *by* W *and at a distance of about 25 German miles [120
> nautical miles]. This land consisted of huge, high snow-covered mountains. We attempted to sail in closer
> towards land, but, as we had only light and shifting winds, it was not until 20th July that we let go our
> anchor in the neighborhood of an island of considerable size, lying at no great distance from the mainland
> . . . . On our map we called the place Cape Elila, since . . . it was on Elila's day that we had anchored there.*[1]
> At the pleasant sight of land, the sailors expressed their jubilation, embracing each other, and crying with joy. They had
> found North America and would surely be richly rewarded by the Tsar. Actually, the initial discovery of Alaska had been
> made on July 15 by the second ship of Bering's command, St. Paul, under Capt. Alexei Chirikov. Weather conditions had
> forced a separation of the two ships the previous month. Thus, Chirikov's earlier sighting probably was of Prince of Wales
> Island in the Alexander Archipelago.

According to Georg Steller, scientist of the expedition, the discovery did not lower Captain
Bering's anxieties. "A great discovery no doubt," he said as his officers congratulated him,
"but who knows where we are, when we shall see Russia, and what we shall have to eat in the
meantime?" Bering had good reason for concern. The voyage had been hard and would grow
harder. He was among the many mariners who did not live to see Mother Russia again.[2]

The exploration of Alaska and the first scientific investigations of its resources began when
Steller landed on Kayak Island. His brief stay on Kayak Island did not allow him much time for
scientific work, but he made the most of his few hours ashore, collecting plant and animal
specimens. Obviously, and understandably, the young scientist was dazzled by the unique
opportunity presented so tantalizingly to him. A huge new land awaited the discoveries of
the first trained observer to land there—but there was little time to utilize the unparalleled
opportunity. In this study it seems important to report Steller's observations in some detail
as he recorded them in his journal entry for July 20, 1741:

*As soon as I was on land with the protection and assistance of one man, and realized that time was all too
precious, I made the best of the situation and with all possible speed immediately headed for the mainland to get as
close as I could to discover people and habitations.*[3]

Very soon he did discover evidence of Native people. Steller eagerly scrutinized every
sign: "Under a tree I found an old piece of log hewn as a trough in which a few hours earlier

the savages, lacking kettles and dishes, had cooked meat with glowing stones." Judging from the scattered bones, the Natives had been eating an animal similar to a reindeer, although Steller did not observe any such animals. He also saw portions of dried fish and numerous very large scallops and blue mussels similar to those found in Kamchatka. He also noticed sweet grass (cow parsnip) completely prepared for eating in Kamchadal fashion with water poured on it to extract the sweetness.

Rather swiftly Steller concluded that the Alaskans and Kamchadals either had trade connections or they were one nation, and the Alaskans had emigrated from Asia. Although the Russians had not yet encountered the Aleutian Islands stretching across the Bering Sea, Steller further conjectured that the similar customs of Alaskan and Kamchatka Natives suggested that America extends farther westward and, opposite Kamchatka, it is much closer in the north.

Steller walked a couple of miles farther along the beach, then followed a path into a deep woods. He encountered an underground hut and examined it and its contents closely, noticing utensils made of tree bark, arrows, and bales of thongs. He sent his helper back to the beach with samples of these things and continued to search for people until he spotted smoke from a campfire: "I now had the certain hope of meeting people and learning from them what I needed for a complete report." He hurried back to the beach with more of his plant specimens and "dead tired, I made . . . descriptions on the beach of the rarer plants which I was afraid might wither and was delighted to be able to test out the excellent water for tea."[4]

Steller, beside himself with excitement, dispatched a sailor to Bering aboard ship, asking for "the small yawl and a few more men for a couple of hours" so that he could get around easier for specimen collection and possible contact with the Natives. The response from Bering dashed his expectations: "In an hour or so I received the patriotic and gracious answer: I was to get my butt on board pronto, or without waiting, they would leave me stranded."[5]

In a bitter mood Steller did what he could "to snatch together everything possible before our flight from shore, and because it was already toward evening, I went once again on a tour to the west." After returning to the ship with various observations and collections, he noted more conclusions about the new land. There were several indications that the climate was warmer than that of Kamchatka. As he was aware that his sponsors might be more concerned about his observations on valuable minerals than anything else, he explained his lack of data: "My failure to have much to report is not attributable to my carelessness or laziness. Therefore, I freely admit that I noted nothing but sand and gray rock."[6]

In observing another kind of valuable resource he was more successful. He found the excrement of otters everywhere along the shore. This was a promising find because it suggested that taking fur animals would be comparatively easy in contrast to Kamchatka, where the hunter-shy animals never came ashore. Of land animals Steller was able to report sightings of black and red foxes and did not find them particularly shy.

He was pleased to report on ten different kinds of birds along with the familiar raven and magpie. The new birds were easily distinguished from the European and Siberian by their particularly bright coloring. Among these, of course, was what was later called Steller's jay. His assistant brought him a specimen which excited him. He recalled having seen the same bird in a book about the Carolinas. The find was further evidence that he was in America. Bering was anxious and impatient, fearful of the safety of his men. Science had to be his secondary consideration, and he ordered his unhappy scientist to board ship once the crew had filled their water casks. Steller lamented the decision but could not alter it. "Why spend ten years getting to America for ten hours," he wondered.

Bering's apprehension was not misplaced. His ship was wrecked on one of the Commander Islands off the coast of Kamchatka. He soon died, as did many other crewmen who were stranded on Bering Island over the winter. The survivors managed to get away in spring, Steller among them, carrying the specimens he had leisure to collect over the enforced stranding on the island.

Other Europeans Explore the Gulf of Alaska

The rugged mountains guarding the coast allow only a few entries from the Gulf of Alaska, but Icy Bay and Yakutat Bay are prominent. Yakutat Bay offers a magnificent inlet, twenty miles wide at its capes. Its shore is also hospitable, wooded lowland extending twenty-five miles to where the foothills begin. Searchers for the fabled Northwest Passage hoped that this great bay would provide the long sought passage across North America that would give Europe easy access to the wealth of Asia.

There were no further approaches to the region until 1778. That year the greatest of Pacific Ocean navigators, Capt. James Cook, sailed past the entrance to Yakutat Bay. Thinking that Bering had anchored there rather than off Kayak Island, he named the inlet Bering's Bay. The weather was clear enough for Cook's men to see Mount St. Elias and other peaks, but they did not linger long enough to enter the bay or otherwise examine the immediate coastline.

Eight years later a French navigator—Jean F. Galaup de La Pérouse—was the first to bring a ship into the bay. After a long voyage from Hawaii, La Pérouse approached the coast in the fog, which lifted on June 23 to expose the mountain Bering had named earlier. La Pérouse took in the view with a sense of foreboding: The view of "masses of snow covering a sterile, treeless soil was painful. The mountains appeared close to the sea, which breaks against a shelf of land." He observed black rocks, which appeared as if calcined by fire, which had no plant covering and formed a striking contrast to the whiteness of the snow in the background. The French officer attempted to find an anchorage but failed.[7]

La Pérouse named the inlet "Baie de Monti," after one of his officers. The astronomer of the expedition calculated that Mount St. Elias was only 12,660 feet in elevation, far short of its actual 18,008 feet. Sailing west out of the bay La Pérouse reached Icy Bay, which he called Bering's Bay, confusing it with Yakutat Bay so named by Cook. After failing to enter Icy Bay the Frenchman proceeded southeastward to discover Lituya Bay, where he remained for some time after several crewmen drowned.

In 1787 Capt. George Dixon, a British fur trader, became the first European to explore Yakutat Bay. Dixon gave us our first chart of the bay and a member of his crew provided the first description of its inhabitants:

They are of a middle size, their limbs straight and well shaped, but, like the rest of the inhabitants we have seen on the coast, are particularly fond of painting their faces with a variety of colors, so that it is not an easy matter to discover their real complexion. [8]

Face washing was important to Dixon, and he induced a young woman to try it: *Her countenance had all the cheerful glow of an English milk maid, and the healthy red which flushed her cheeks was*

Captain-commander Vitus Bering.
Courtesy of the Alaska State Library,
Alaska Purchase Collection, PCA 20-1.

even beautifully contrasted with the whiteness of her neck; her eyes were black and sparkling; her eyebrows the same color, and most beautifully arched; her forehead so remarkably clear that the transparent veins were seen meandering around even in their minutest branches—in short, she was what would be reckoned as handsome even in England.

Dixon was less impressed with the Native housing: " . . . the most wretched hovels that can possibly be conceived: a few poles stuck in the ground—without order or regularity, recrossed and covered with loose boards . . . quite insufficient to keep out the snow and rain." What the captain saw, of course, were the temporary summer hunting shelters. Later visitors saw the substantial spruce plank buildings that served for permanent housing. These were large structures, usually supported on the inside by four huge carved and painted posts, with an opening in the roof to allow smoke from cook fires to escape.[9]

Driven by the quest for the Northwest Passage, European cartographers toyed with the geography of the north Pacific throughout the eighteenth century. Late in the century interest focused on an alleged earlier voyage by one Lorenzo Maldonado, who was said to have discovered the Strait of Anian, or the Northwest Passage connecting the Pacific and Atlantic Oceans at about the latitude of Yakutat Bay. Maritime rivals of Spain believed that the Spanish had suppressed information about Maldonado's geographic discovery, fearing that other Europeans would covet their New World holdings. But, as the Spanish were themselves fooled by rumors of this voyage, the government ordered Alejandro Malaspina, then in Mexico on a voyage of discovery, to investigate the Maldonado entry.

Malaspina reached ice-choked Yakutat Bay in June 1791 and explored the eastern shore. Its glacier-fed waters did not open into the interior by way of the legendary Strait of Anian, and Malaspina named the inner body of water Disappointment Bay. Subsequently, the Hubbard and other glaciers receded, but even their disappearance did not reveal an entry into the continent.

The Spanish established an observatory on shore to fix the location of the place. From June 26 to July 6, 1791, they also gathered wood and water and bartered with the Indians for sea otter skins. The Indians were curious and pleasant to the visitors but there was some tension when thefts occurred. "This was told to one chief," wrote Tomas de Suría, "who regretted it very much." Though the stolen items were returned, tensions grew. "We began to see them armed with bows and arrows, knives and lances." Violence was avoided, and the mariners finished their work after a few days.[10]

Aside from describing the appearances of the Indians, their habitations, and some social customs, de Suría speculated on their religion: "We could not find any trace of their religion although to me it appears that they bestow some worship on the sun."[11] The Spanish were quite curious about leadership among the Natives. Incidents they observed suggested that supreme command vested in the chief and that his position is hereditary in his family. The visitors also noted that other ranks existed in the society, creating an inequality of rank. It seemed odd to find differences in authority among men who seemed so equal in their limited needs and their means of satisfying them.

The Natives apparently preferred the establishment of fixed abodes, where hunting and fishing provide abundant subsistence, to wandering. They did not seem to have the need to invade the territories of others but did have to defend their own. Consequently, they were warriors. Their customs, their music, and their dances reflected a warlike character, and they seemed proud of their military reputation. The Spanish were impressed by the Natives' foot-long knives made of iron and wondered where they got the metal. They knew that Dixon had traded there prior to their visit but doubted that he traded the Natives enough iron for their needs.

Among the necessary formalities charged to Spanish explorers was that of making a ceremonial claim to the territory. Officers gathered on July 2nd, built a small pyramid of rocks, and placed at its base a formal claim document secured in a bottle and supported by a coin. The notice read: "The Corvettes of His Majesty *Descubierta* and *Atrevida* commanded by Don Alejandro Malaspina and Don Jose Bustamente discovered this port on the 20th of June, 1791, and called it Desengaño [Detection], taking possession of it in the name of His Catholic Majesty."[12]

Though Malaspina may have been disappointed that the bay did not lead to the Northwest Passage, he expressed a sense of accomplishment in extending Spanish sovereignty to the far north of America. He had not seen any signs of gold or other precious metals or jewels, but they might be discovered later. Meanwhile, he had added territory and done important scientific work. After planting the claim notice that was supposed to alert other Europeans to Spanish priority, there was little more to do except to gather up a few rocks for later scientific study and sail on.

Three years later, in 1794, the British were back under the command of Capt. George Vancouver, who surely earns credit for the first careful investigation of the southern Alaska coast. Vancouver's narrative shows that the search for water passages into the interior had not abated. He was no more successful than Malaspina in finding a navigable opening. By the end of his survey of the Northwest Coast from the Columbia River to the Bering Strait, Vancouver believed that he had been able to "remove every doubt, and set aside every opinion of a north-west passage, or any water communication navigable for shipping, existing within the north Pacific, and the interior of the American continent, within the limits of our researches."[13]

❊ The Russians Settle at Yakutat ❊

Russian fur traders first reached Alaska in the early 1760s, some twenty years after Bering's discovery voyage. They gathered furs along the Alaska Peninsula, then explored and occupied parts of the coast both above and below. The fur trade was very profitable to the fur merchants and to the tsar, whose tax equaled 10 percent of the sales on the lively Chinese market. As the Russians developed their bases and extended their range, relying on Aleut hunters, they were aware of the interest of other nations—Spain, England, and France. Only the Russians established permanent colonies, initially on the Aleutians and at Kodiak. The tsar encouraged further traders to enter the field until 1799 when Grigorii Shelikov's company was given exclusive rights to Alaska.[14]

Russian exploration and trade in the Wrangell-St. Elias region began in the 1780s. During a period of considerable expansion the Russians sought new fur sources, moving from their bases on the Aleutians, Kodiak, and Kenai to the east and southeast along the mainland coast. Yakutat had been viewed favorably as a post from the time of the first Russian visit in 1788. In 1791 Shelikov had planned an agricultural granary there and expected to eventually establish the colony's capital at Yakutat. In June 1792 a trading party of 180 baidarkas, with Native hunters from the Alaska Peninsula and Chugach led by Russian promyshlenniki, called at Yakutat to trade with the Tlingits. The next year an even larger party, some 500 baidarkas, arrived to trade.

Traders Egor Purtov and Demid Kulikalow of the Shelikov-Golikov Company advised their employer on their progress: "We made them [the Yakutats] to understand that we wanted their friendship and to prove their feelings the chief presented us with Yakutat Sound and the small islands that are in it." As prospects looked good for furs, Alexander Baranov, manager of the firm that would later become the Russian American Company and hold a monopoly on fur trading in Alaska, decided to establish a permanent post in 1795. This was significant as the only Russian effort to bring permanent settlers, as distinguished from fur traders, to Alaska. Shelikov recruited a party of serfs, including some former convicts, for the pioneering community.[15] He sent full instructions to Baranov:

In case it cannot be avoided and some foreign ship comes, let them see that the Russians live in a well organized way. Don't give them reasons to think that Russians live in America in the same abominable way as in Okhotsk. Please, dear friend, for your own pleasure and satisfaction, plan the new settlement to be beautiful and pleasant to live in. Have public squares for meetings and gatherings. The streets must not be very long but wide, and must radiate from the squares. If you choose a place in the woods, leave the trees on the streets in front of the houses and in the garden. The houses should be well separated, which will make the settlement look bigger. The vegetable gardens must be separated from the street by good fences. For God's Sake, don't do things in the small village style. . . . In time, this small settlement will become a big city.[16]

Shelikov advised on the treatment of Natives:

If possible, invite the peaceful natives to live closer to the settlement. From them you can always obtain required information, and you can use their labor, though not, of course, without pay or favor of some kind. Coming often to the settlement, they will get used to our way of living. They will bring berries for sale, and other products.

The Russians should be in close contact with the natives, but one important rule must be observed. At night, there should be very few natives in the settlement, and the sentries should let nobody in. They also should have signals, and beat iron plates at regular intervals, by hourglass. Have skilled workers make a bell, which would be useful also for the church. I shipped to you 20 pounds of copper. It wouldn't be a bad idea to try to get some from the Copper River. To make it easier for the Russians, I suggest that half of the sentries can be Americans devoted to us. The monastery and church should be constructed in such a manner that the monks will not see what the laymen are doing, and the laymen will not see what the monks are doing.[17]

Shelikov was a stern leader: *The settlers, hunters, and the Americans should be under strict surveillance. Devise police regulations for them. If a settler becomes turbulent, punish him by sending him to work for the company in some other place, give his job in the settlement to one of the hunters, and drag him from job to job for about a year so that the others will know what will happen if a man becomes troublesome.[18]*

The trader's concern for foreign competition was manifest: *Two or three batteries should have high turrets, and on them a big Russian crest. Over the wharf, if you have one in the same place, should fly a merchant flag. Everything must be impressive and look important, especially when a foreign ship arrives. . . . We are very much astonished at your unconcern about the visit of the English ship. You knew, even before you got the new regulations, that visits by foreign vessels cannot be tolerated. . . . In the future, please act according to instruction of His High Excellency, and be bold enough to tell the foreigners that they have no right to trade.[19]*

On a spring voyage from Kodiak that year Baranov did not land his settlers because of the hostility of the Tlingits. The party returned to Kodiak, but Baranov tried again in August. This time, after negotiations with the Native chief secured his son as a hostage, the Russians left a number of settlers. The settlers were not very good prospects as pioneers. They were not accustomed to self-reliance and were terribly afraid of the Indians. Nor was Yakutat as promising a place for agriculture as the Russian fur traders had hoped.

The Russian settlers ran out of food and suffered from hunger over the winter of 1795–1796. As the Indians were also short of food, they were not able to help the Russians. The arrival of a Russian ship in the summer saved the lives of the settlers. Despite the suffering, the colony accomplished the first wintering by Russians among the Tlingits (the colony near Sitka was not established until 1799). Friendly relations had been established between the two races, although the Russians only gained freedom of movement by

Captain George Vancouver. Courtesy of the Alaska State Library, Alaska Purchase Collection, PCA 20-25.

giving gifts when their compatriots arrived.

With the landing of stores and construction materials in 1796, the Russians located a site for a permanent fort. Work commenced on a log structure surrounded by a ditch for greater security from attack. Buildings included a barracks, two storehouses, a smokehouse, a cache, a blacksmith shop, and a steambath, all enclosed by a log fence protected by cannon.

✳ The Russian Colony at Yakutat ✳

The settlers at Yakutat did not fulfill the expectations of their employers. In 1799 the Russian American Company was chartered to end the competition among Russian traders in Alaska. As field manager Alexander Baranov and other members of the dominant company of Shelikov-Golikov held their places in the new company, policy changes were not drastic. That year Baranov answered the unending chorus of complaints from the Yakutat colony to voyage to New Russia, as Yakutat was named, and investigate the administration. Among the charges against manager Ivan Polomoshnoi was that he showed too much sensitivity to complaints from Natives about the Russians' maltreatment of them. Polomoshnoi was subsequently replaced with a new arrival named Nikolai Mukhin.[20]

New Russia was not so far from the colony at Old Sitka so as to be unaffected by events there. Panic spread in the colony when the Russians heard that the Tlingits at Sitka had massacred the traders there, but the local Indians remained peaceful. New manager Stepan Larionov was ordered to build ships for the company and responded with the *Alexander Nevski*, fifty-five feet long and of one hundred tons burden, and the slightly smaller *Catherine*. Another new vessel, the *Yermak*, also was launched at the Yakutat colony. All of these vessels with Russian crews from the colony participated in Baranov's successful expedition in 1804 to retake Sitka from the Tlingits.

In 1805 the Yakutat Tlingits became aroused by a dispute over interference with their fishing grounds. They attacked the Russian fort and slaughtered most of its forty residents. The report of Ivan Repin to Baranov described the disaster:

I venture to report to the Most Honorable Aleksandr Andreevich or, if by Grace of God he has not yet arrived in Kadiak, then to Your Honor Ivan Ivanovich: I beg you, My Dear sir, not to be alarmed by my letter. On the evening of August 26th a three-man Aleut baidarka arrived from Yakutat and brought sad news: our enemies, the Native workers, and part of the Yakutat Natives have massacred all the Russians and our late chief Stepan Fedorovich Larionov. All were slain, to the last man. Only the children of the Russians were spared. I am afraid to report to you, Dear Sir, these sad tidings. I asked several times: "Is this really true?" And I was told that it was all too true. The Chugach Natives from the village of Kanikhliut fled last year from Sitka and were kept at Yakutat temporarily. Six of the Chugach and four Kadiak Natives were sent by the late Larionov to pick berries and when they returned home all in the fort were dead. They saw the dead lying everywhere in the fort. Not waiting for their comrades they took a baidarka and went in the bay. They were shot at three times but nobody was killed. On their way from Yakutat they stopped overnight five times and from this I gather that the massacre took place about the 20th. I asked also if they had heard any news as to how things were at New Archangel. They replied that they heard from the inhabitants of Akoi that not a single baidarka is to be seen there now but that they heard nothing about the Russians there. There was no ship at Yakutat this summer.

So here is my news for you, My Dear Sirs. Men were alive at home in the fort and were at work making a gate and were all killed right there.I venture to report further. On August 18th, a baidarka arrived from Copper River and toion Matvei with twelve men brought the murderer of the interpreter Aleshka and also two escaped native workers: Mikheika and another. He found them up the Atna. He promised to bring also the murderers of Galaktionov and the escaped workers. He assured me that he will serve the Most Honorable Collegiate Councillor Aleksandr Andreevich Baranov faithfully and promised to come again in the latter part of September. Other toions promised to come also. This toion Matvei brought a few garments: four martin skin kamleikas, seven sewed kamleikas, three fur parkas made of young deerskins, one parka made of deer-skins and 13 river beavers. He says that he did not see the up river natives and that it was on account of that he brought so little. The murderers of Galaktionov were not at home but went hunting up the Chetitna [Chitina?]. He promises to bring these murderers and escaped workers, but asks his son to be taken to Nuchik and wants him to be looked after by you, My Dear Sirs. I wonder if they have some other thoughts on their minds, that they promise to come this fall. They see how few men we have and I beg you to send men to rein-force us. Even a small reinforcement will help, because we are in grave danger.

I have dispatched a baidarka to make fish traps in the creeks for catching our winter supply of salmon. Sixty thousand humpback salmon were prepared this summer. At the other fishtrap, twenty thousand red salmon. God will help us to catch some silver salmon yet. Duck hunters provided us with 142 parkas made of bird skins. This is counting Nuchik, but not counting last year's 55 parkas. This year the hunting of birds was not very good—there were very few of them.

I am sending at the same time with this letter the murderer of the interpreter. When his accomplices are brought in, I will send them immediately. As we do not have a blacksmith, I am sending a rifle to be repaired. Some were sent before for the same purpose. Please send company tobacco; that which we have is fast being used.[21]

Stirred by the ease of their victory, Natives planned an attack on Port Etches on Hinchinbrook Island, but one of their Chugach Eskimo captives warned the Russians. The Chugach Eskimos, friendly to the Russians and traditional enemies to the Yakutats, invited the visitors to a feast. The Yakutats, perhaps assuming that the Chugach wished help in removing the Russian yoke, were foolish enough to attend. During the festivities the Chugach killed most of their guests.

The Yakutats did not succeed in spreading their revolt, but neither did the Russians try to reestablish their post. For a time the Russians considered retaking Yakutat essential to control of their trading network, but other priorities, such as the Yukon trade and establishing agricultural colonies elsewhere, became more important. As the years passed the Yakutats had nothing to fear from the Russians and may have sometimes missed the trading opportunities the Europeans offered. At any rate, they were receptive to the first American traders to appear after the Alaska purchase. Oral tradition says that the community suffered a disastrous smallpox epidemic in 1836–1839. The population estimate for 1835 was only 150. By 1861 the estimate had reached three hundred, and this number was also given in the first U.S. Census in 1880.

✳ The Tarkhanov Voyage of 1796 ✳

With a base on the mainland coast, Russian expansion, or at least exploration of the interior, was certain to follow. Farther north along the coast, the great delta of the Copper River suggested an obvious route for penetration. The discovery of the mouth of the river had been made by Leontii Nagaev in 1781 but without any immediate results. Apparently, four expeditions had been launched but all were turned back before making much progress because of the difficult navigation and Native hostility.[22]

Though the Yakutat colony was not particularly well located for exploration of the interior by way of the Copper River, it did serve as a base. Some years after the first abortive ventures in the 1780s it was the starting point for a successful expedition into the interior. We know about this expedition because of the recent discovery of a manuscript journal in the Russian archives. Prior to the surfacing of this document, it had been assumed that the Russian knowledge of the middle Copper River had been deferred to the 1819 investigation made by Afanasii Klimovskii (discussed later in this chapter).

The forgotten expedition was made by Dmitri Tarkhanov. Tarkhanov was not a fur trader but a mining engineer who had been in Alaska since 1794. After Baranov gained permission from the Natives for a venture upriver, Tarkhanov set off from Yakutat for the Copper River on snowshoes in September 1796. An important expedition goal related to the legendary Northwest Passage. Tarkhanov was instructed to go up the Copper River to reach a sea bay of large lakes which was connected to the sea via Hudson Bay. Baranov probably had greater hopes for an economic goal more likely to be discovered than the Northwest Passage. Copper deposits had long been rumored to exist upriver.

Tarkhanov initially did some local traveling, including a visit to Chief Eltekh of the Eyak village located on upper Yakutat Bay. Among his traveling companions was Fyodor, the son of the Tlingit chief who had been in Kodiak as a hostage over the winter. He probably was baptized that year with Baranov as godfather and thus became the first Tlingit converted to Orthodox Christianity. From the Eyak village the Russian set out with Chief Eltekh and others for the northwest and the Copper River. The Yakutat Tlingits and Eyaks had established a trade relationship, so travel through the Eyak country was not dangerous.

Two months of travel took the party from Yakutat to Icy Bay, then to the principal Eyak village called Kaiiakh. Tarkhanov found the travel hard because the Tlingits except for Chief Eltekh would not help carry his baggage. He was relieved to reach the Eyak village and rested there for some months, well-fed and cared for by the hospitable villagers. When the Russian moved on to the region of Controller Bay, Tarkhanov took Eyaks along, but most refused to travel into Ahtna country with him. They feared the climate, the long distances involved, and the hostility of the Copper River Indians. Tarkhanov's last effort at persuasion was made at a village that later became known as Chilkat.

The Russian and three Eyaks eventually reached the first Ahtna village, and he distributed gifts of beads and tobacco, noting that the family kept two slaves. His hosts accompanied him farther, but hunger forced their early return. In a fresh attempt the party got lost in the maze of the Copper River delta. Slaves dispatched by the local Ahtnas saved them from death by finding them and guiding them back to the village in March 1797. The Russian touched the conscience of the Ahtnas in discussing slavery and gained the use of one slave for the river voyage, after exchanging suitable gifts.

It was either March or April when Tarkhanov and his companions reached the Copper River and started up over the ice. Soon they ran out of food and were reduced to eating boiled pieces of fur seal skin and fir bark. They were in bad shape when they dragged into the village of Takekat, which was on the Kenna River tributary of the Copper. Tarkhanov was viewed as a sensation because he was the first European these people had seen. People gathered from miles around to look at the strange man, and his hosts, honored by the presence of such a curiosity, treated him very well.

Tarkhanov was intrigued by the presence of Natives from the upper river, probably from the Gulkana River area, who offered to take him along when they finished their trading. They told him that they traded in the neighborhood of Tazlina Lake each year with Indians from Cook Inlet who

knew about Russians and could make the sign of the cross. These Dena'ina people, as we now understand, traveled up the Matanuska Valley and crossed over to the Copper country. But Tarkhanov, too ill to take advantage of the opportunity, was forced to retreat to the mouth of the Copper for rest and recuperation. As his health worsened he had to give up plans to return upriver and eventually returned to Kodiak. He was unable to recover from the effects of his arduous journey and returned to Russia as an invalid in 1798. Although Tarkhanov did not succeed in his travel goals, his expedition was invaluable. He was the first European to visit the Ahtnas (see Chapter 1).[23]

❊ Other Russian Explorations ❊

Afanasii Klimovskii led a 1819 expedition upriver to either the mouth of the Chitina or the Gulkana, becoming the first Russian to visit the village of Taral and the first to describe Mt. Wrangell. His party established a trading post, but neither its precise location nor its duration is known. Other evidence suggests that the post was maintained for many years before inter-ethnic disputes finally forced its closure.

The Russian American Company tried to reestablish trade and explore the remaining portion of the Copper River with Ruf Serebrennikov's expedition of 1847–1848. Serebrennikov's party wintered over at Taral, near the mouth of the Chitina River, then continued upriver in May 1848. After reaching the mouth of the Tazlina, they briefly left the Copper River to explore Tazlina Lake. They soon returned to the river, however, and continued upstream. About a month later, the leader and most of his party were killed by the upriver Ahtna, probably at Batzulnetas.

According to information derived later from Chief Nicolai, there had been three massacres of Russians by Indians during this period—one above Taral and two below. These mishaps discouraged attempts to expand the Copper River trade. The Russian post at Taral closed in 1850, when the Ahtna confiscated its goods. Although it reopened briefly in 1858, four years later it closed for good.[24]

The oral tradition of the Athapaskan people of the upper Copper River includes an account which may explain the killing of Serebrennikov's party. The story, as related by Katie John of Batzulnetas and Fred John Sr. of Mentasta, provides further details of the event:

When the first Russians came up the Copper River and up this way they were mean, they were hungry for blood. Those Russians were probably after fur or something like that. At every village they ask who the chief is and kick him and whip him with a whip with knots on the end. They took everything from the Indians. The Russians come up Slana River to Batzulnetas. The story start in Batzulnetas.

In Batzulnetas village they had a big chief. And the chief went down to the Russians and they grab him, tie him to a stump and whip him right there. The chief he had a knife, a knife right in his mukluk. The chief reached for his knife but one Native says no there is too many there. Just watch. We might do something after. He would have killed four or five Russians right there. And the chief he says, 'People like you people red-headed do me like that.' Then the Russians ask what he said and this Aleut came up with the Russians—said, 'He said, Oh he hurt.' And the Russians laughed. The chief gave up and never pulled his knife. Then the chief went back and said, 'Let's go, as far as I am going I will kill myself anyway.'

Batzulnetas was a big village and had many places. But the Russians took the women and chased out the men from their homes. The Russians killed the dogs and made the women tan the hides. This was something they had never done before. The women had never tanned one dog hide. They took everything: the spears, stick guns (bows), arrows and all those things the Russians took away. They try to make the Indians starve to death. However, out in the woods the Indians have cache and everything. They just go to the cache and eat the stuff there.

But the Russians don't know there is another village seven miles up from Batzulnetas on Suslota Creek. The chief sent a young fellow up to the Suslota to tell them how they were chased out of the village. The people from Suslota send down a lot of clothing, blankets, and things. So the people move up, way up the creek and make the spruce tree winter camp. The people from Suslota came down and they got everything and everybody start making arrows and like that right there.

They start training for war. We get there and start training ourselves for war. The Batzulnetas people, Suslota village people and some from Mentasta. We all got down there. October I think the Russians came up. That October, November, December and January we train. It lasted until January. Well those days when they train like that they have to get up early in the morning and go out. Went out and jumped to the top of spruce trees and rip them down. They run, cut wood and all those things. Try to run faster than the other. They used to train themselves.

After they were training three months they send down some boys to Batzulnetas to tell the women, all the Indian women, to pack up the Russians' guns with sticks and to put water in their muzzle loaders. And all the women did that. A lot of Aleuts came up with the Russians and all those Aleuts understood the language. This Indian chief came up and told them it's going to start early in the morning; they are going to attack the Russians in the village. And they tell the Aleuts when we start, just sit still. The Batzulnetas chief talk to the Aleut chief and said we clean that building out [the Russian blockhouse] at night time by the morning. Don't sleep; get up at midnight. All the Russians will be sleeping in the building. And the Aleut chief told his men to sit still.

Early in the morning the people in Batzulnetas heard all kinds of animal noises. That's what they used to do when war, make all kinds of animal talk. And the village people started to get excited. They attack. The Russians get up and try to shoot their muzzle loaders but nothing fires. An Indian jumps in with arrow giving and giving, killing and killing. The Russians try to go out the roof and they got that spear. And all that spearing out there. The Indians cleaned everyone out. All the Russians.

The Aleut boys they were all safe and all the Indian women. The Russians killed only one Native. At the end a big building full of Russians was ankle deep in blood. They burned up that building; when I was a child I saw the place where they burned the bodies in Batzulnetas. That building was packed full of Russians.

After the Russians were killed, one Aleut half-breed—his daddy a Russian—they ruin him. The Aleut chief said, 'I will take him back. 'He knew his family; they were Eyak. The Aleuts went down the river about twelve miles and the Aleut half-breed try to kill them with a spear. He said that they helped the people there kill the Russians. Every time he get up tried to kill the other Aleuts with a spear. The Aleut chief sent up a boy to the Batzulnetas Indians to tell them they better come down and kill that fellow. They came down and speared him.[25]

The full account has been quoted here to give a sense of the oral tradition on the Copper River. What we know of the incident from other sources is not at variance with what has been passed along by Indian storytellers.

✳ Conclusion ✳

Despite its early start as the first Russian fur trading post on the mainland, the Yakutat region was not influenced by the Europeans for long. Neither was the impact of the Russians on the Copper River interior of lasting duration, and there was no implantation of institutions such as the Orthodox Church. The Russians penetrated a portion of the Wrangell-St. Elias region to trade and gather furs, encountered considerable hostility that discouraged their enterprise, and withdrew. As there was little Russian presence within the Wrangell-St. Elias region after the late 1840s, the transfer of Alaska to the United States and withdrawal of the Russian American Company had no immediate effects on the area.

Captain William R. Abercrombie at his
headquarters in Valdez. Courtesy of the
Anchorage Museum of History and Art,
B62.1.406.

Chapter

❅　❅　❅

U.S. Sponsored Expeditions 1867-1923

From the first intrusions of Western man, the Wrangell-St. Elias region has excited explorers and scientists. Initially explorers concentrated on geography, pinpointing locations of inlets, and determining the coastal configuration. Later, they sought to fix the elevations of great mountains, the dimensions of glaciers, the locations of mineral and other resources, and establish travel routes into the interior. Practical and economic considerations stimulated some scientific work. This chapter describes some of the more significant, but little-publicized, explorations and scientific investigations in the region.

❉ Coastal Surveys ❉

Congress authorized a geological and geographical survey of the nation's newly acquired territory in 1867. This was not easily accomplished, and, in fact, inland explorations were not even attempted until fifteen years later. Maritime commercial interests pushed for navigation studies, and the U.S. Coast Survey under George Davidson and others worked at the survey task when the departmental budget allowed. In 1870 William H. Dall, later acknowledged as the dean of Alaska scientists, joined the coastal survey. Dall had been on the Yukon with the unsuccessful Western Union Telegraph Expedition to unite Siberia and Alaska. Dall's first book, *Alaska and Its Resources*, covered his telegraph experiences and provided basic historical, geographical, and resource information.

Dall and his colleagues accomplished much with little. The survey budget for Alaska work, as historian Morgan Sherwood noted, fluctuated from $8,000 to $15,000 between 1881 and 1895. "By 1885, the USGS had surveyed 1,000 miles of coast, or about 5 1/2 percent of the total," and by 1888 had published forty-five charts of Alaska anchorages. Dall's contribution to science in the Wrangell-St. Elias region was not as distinguished as the general high level of his work. After triangulating the height of Mount St. Elias from three land and one sea station his estimates varied up to 2,000 feet. He fixed on 19,500 feet, plus or minus four hundred, which was a thousand feet too high. With less evidence he also concluded incorrectly that the Copper and Alsek Rivers, the latter southwest of Yakutat Bay, shared the same headwaters.[1]

Dall's accomplishments and many useful publications far outweigh his few miscalculations. He encouraged survey men to collect natural specimens and arranged the shipment of shells, fossils, plants, Native cultural materials, and varied zoological specimens to Washington's museum for study. After leaving the survey he became associated with the Smithsonian Institution and there had opportunities to pursue his varied scientific interests. Later he joined the U.S. Geological Survey, an agency whose work in the interior was of the same practical benefit to miners that coastal survey work had been to sailors.

In 1874 Dall and Marcus Baker of the U.S. Coast Survey worked the Yakutat Bay-Mount St. Elias coastline, calculating mountain heights. Their geological and glacial observations were published in the 1875 *Pacific Coast Pilot*. Information gathered by the scientists from their observations and the published literature provided an "exhaustive compilation," as Israel C. Russell noted in the *National Geographic Magazine*, ". . . a valuable summary of what was known . . . of the history and physical features of the country." Among their achievements was accurately describing for the first time in scientific literature "the true character of the Malaspina Glacier."[2]

Dall and Baker added to impressions gathered on their 1874 visit to the glacier on another trip in June 1880. "For the first time the real and most extraordinary character of this plateau was revealed," Dall noted. In the absence of seasonal snow they could examine the glacier more closely. It was "one great field of buried ice. Almost everywhere nothing is visible but boulders, dirt and gravel." But the thaw during the 1880 season had opened a space of several square miles between Point Manby and Nearer Point to reveal:

. . .a surface of broken pinnacles of ice, each crowned by a patch of dirt, standing close to one another like a forest of prisms, these decreasing in height from the summit of the plateau gradually in a sort of semicircular sweep toward the beach, near which, however, the dirt and debris again predominate, forming a sort of terminal moraine to this immense, buried, immovable glacier, for it is nothing else.[3]

Between Disenchantment Bay and the foot of Mount St. Elias the scientists counted seventeen glaciers, all of them relatively small. The two investigators believed that these glaciers lacked the mass and great bulk necessary to form the plateau. This and other mysteries concerning the great glacier remained, but the pioneer scientists made a good start and also provided the name of Malaspina, "in honor of that distinguished and unfortunate explorer."[4] Several nineteenth-century government agencies shared responsibility for gathering and disseminating information about Alaska. They were required to make commercial considerations a priority. The demand for surveys and geological information grew as research funds diminished.

❋ Abercrombie Explores the Copper River ❋

Brig. Gen. Nelson A. Miles, the Civil War soldier and commander of the Department of the Columbia and a famed Indian fighter, was not content to see the U.S. Army excluded from Alaska. In 1868 the navy took over administration of the territory from the army, but Miles decided that exploration was still his responsibility. Accordingly, Miles sent Lt. Frederick Schwatka to the Yukon in 1883 and Lt. William R. Abercrombie to the Copper River in 1884. Miles ordered Abercrombie to ascend the Copper River, then explore the Tanana River Valley. To justify the expeditions, Miles directed his explorers to investigate the alleged hostility of Natives—a proper matter of concern for the army. As Abercrombie put it: "The conflicting interests between the white people and the Indian of the Territory were likely in the near future to result in serious disturbance, hence it was deemed important that all possible information as to the facts should be obtained for the guidance of the military branch of the Government."[5]

Abercrombie's party landed at Nuchek, site of a trading post, on June 16, 1884, and reached the Copper River mouth five days later. With the help of local Indians the soldiers tried to paddle their small boats upstream. When this failed, they commenced the arduous job of pulling their boats against the current and soon wondered if the river were a serviceable route to the interior. Abercrombie described their travails:

The water had now grown so cold that it was impossible to make any headway against it. Wading deeper than midway between the knees and trunk, one would be paralyzed after submersion for fifteen or twenty minutes so that all draft power was gone for a time, forcing the men to let go the towline and run up and down the bank to warm themselves. The water was running off a bank of ice of many thousands of acres in extent, and its effects were beginning to show themselves upon the men, whose members were becoming more or less rheumatic and swollen.[6]

As Abercrombie ascended the river, he saw other evidence that navigation of the river would be perilous even for larger, well-powered boats. The presence of two great glaciers gave the officer an opportunity to flatter his patrons (he named one for General Miles and the other for George Washington Childs of Philadelphia) but was otherwise threatening. The glaciers' movement sheared off leading edges of ice and rock into the river: "The water fairly hissed, carrying with it boulders, some of them two feet in diameter, the impetus of which would break a leg or rip the bottom out of a skin boat."[7]

As Abercrombie watched, the glaciers provided an even more exciting display of nature's force in calving great slabs of ice into the rushing current. Abercrombie estimated that some of the slabs were 500 feet long, 250 feet wide, and eighty feet thick and that they carried a surface burden consisting of tons of dirt and rock. Sometimes the ice movements provided scenes of unworldly splendor:

On the night of the morning in question I beheld one of the grandest spectacles ever witnessed by living man. First, bergs came majestically sailing down stream, passing and repassing each other as the force of water backed up by their united presence became sufficient to force them through the sandy bottom of the river. . . . These monsters differ in color. Some are white, others black, and yet others (the latter predominating) are of an aquamarine color. As they backed and filed they somewhat resembled the maneuvers of a fleet of men-of-war.[8]

Progress was slow and discouraging. The coastal Indians soon gave up, but upriver Indians, bound for the trading post at Nuchek, helped the soldiers. After several weeks the explorers only managed to get to the rapids, later named for Abercrombie, above Miles and Childs Glaciers. This obstacle proved the last straw: Abercrombie gave up and returned downriver.

✳ The Allen Expedition of 1885 ✳

The next year Lt. Henry T. Allen received the same assignment. Allen, who was to have a brilliant career in the army, had looked after the provisioning of Abercrombie's expedition from Sitka and Nuchek in 1884 and was eager to make his own mark as an explorer. He was a recent graduate of the U.S. Military Academy, tall, handsome, cultivated, and determined. He had read all the available literature about the country and talked to anyone he could find in Alaska who knew something about it. Only then did he present his exploration plan to Col. H. Clay Wood, adjutant of the U.S. Army's Department of the Columbia, and to Gen. Nelson Miles. Allen argued that the headwaters of the Copper could be reached in one season with an early start in March. He believed that there was nothing to fear from Indian hostility. He also pointed out that the large Abercrombie expedition had been unwieldy and stated his preference for a three-man party.

Eventually General Miles approved of the young officer's proposal. With instructions to gather information about the Natives and the country and a very modest budget of $3,500 for salaries, transportation, and provisions, Allen was ready for the field. He took two enlisted men, Pvt. Fred Fickett, who had been with the Signal Corps at Sitka, and Sgt. Cady Robertson. The soldiers were landed at Nuchek from the U.S. Navy's Pinta along with their provisions. At Nuchek, Allen conferred with George C. Holt, a trader of the Alaska Commercial Company. He learned that the Ahtna Indians of the Copper River had not yet reached the post on their annual fur trading expedition, but were at the Eyak villages in the river delta.

Holt's relationship with the Indians was interesting. They seemed to fear him as one who commanded the awesome force represented by the armed tug *Pinta*, which made occasional calls. Holt's supposed power reminded the Indians of "Russian chastisements," which they sought to avoid from the Americans. Upriver Indians had never seen *Pinta*, but the story of its visible might when landing the exploration party followed Allen upriver and was:

. . . the indirect cause of much respect shown us by the natives. The farther we ascended the river the larger became this vessel and its guns. At one place its length, as estimated by a man, was equal to the distance between two islands, approximately half a mile, and the bore of its guns was expressed by the greatest partial enclosure formed by the arms, tips of fingers widely separated.[9]

Allen added prospectar Peder Johnson and several Eyak and Ahtna Indians to the party and started for the Copper River mouth in rowboats. His equipment included the necessities for navigation and map making: a sextant and artificial horizon, a Howard-movement watch, a barometer, a pocket sextant, aneroid barometer, psychrometer, and prismatic and pocket compasses. He also hauled along the rather cumbersome photographic equipment of the day, including the hard-to-handle glass plates used for exposures. This form of documentation turned out to be of little use.

Allen found negotiating with Indians at the river's mouth difficult. The Eyaks of the coast and the Ahtnas had come downriver for trading. Indians promised to help him get upriver, then some backed out. Allen, exasperated by their reluctance, wanted to start off at once. The Ahtna even used the rain as an excuse to postpone their departure. In his report Allen quoted Abercrombie's comments on the coastal Indians in a context that seemed to embrace all of those he had encountered so far. "Lieutenant Abercrombie says of the coast people: 'These natives are inveterate liars, and were they not cowards we would stand a very indifferent prospect of exploring the country with their aid to any extent."[10]

Allen was never as harsh as Abercrombie in describing the Indians' manner. Later, he concluded that maliciousness did not lie behind their widely varied opinions of ice conditions and other concrete matters. They were simply unable to "make proper deductions. They tell the most wonderful stories about parts of the country with which they are unacquainted, and doubtless believe very much of what they say."[11]

Once Allen finally got away from the coast in late March, he felt better. Before many weeks passed he was pleased to revise his sour opinions of the Indians. But for their help, he would not have achieved very much. Allen started with canoes, carrying sleds to be used where needed. Private Fickett was left behind with most of the stores, charged with joining the first party at Taral in May or June. By then he could voyage upriver with the main body of Ahtnas returning from their trading venture to Nuchek. Allen got two Ahtnas and three Eyaks to accompany him.

After ascending the river only six miles they encountered ice. Allen decided to switch to sleds and sent Fickett back to bring up more sleds and all the provisions he could convey. Traveling on the soft snow was difficult for heavily laden sleds. Allen had to abandon half of their ammunition, cooking outfit, food, and clothing, and even their tent. They started off again with limited provisions, only 150 pounds of flour, one hundred pounds of beans, forty pounds of rice, two sides of bacon, fifteen pounds of tea, some extract of beef, deviled ham, and chocolate.

By April 2 they reached the gorge Allen named Abercrombie Canyon. Progress was slow and painstaking, and the weather was bad. By the time Allen reached the Tasnuna River on April 6 most of the party was suffering from snow blindness. Allen nonetheless pushed on, reaching Taral on April 10. At this village, consisting of two dwellings, they found Peder Johnson's

Start from Alaganik (Lt. Henry Allen's exploration party). From Lt. Henry T. Allen, "Report of an Expedition," Plate No. 7.

prospecting partner, John Bremner, who had ascended the river the previous summer.

Bremner had survived a hellish winter. While he was away from Taral the previous summer on a prospecting trip, Indians had stolen his three hundred pounds of provisions. For some months rabbits had been his only food, and he was delirious with joy when Allen and Robertson arrived. He even fired his last rifle ammunition to announce his presence. "John," noted Allen, [was] "certainly the most uncouth specimen of manhood that I had, up to this time, ever seen. . . . He was shortening his belt one hole every other day."[12]

Allen was not in very good shape himself, considering his ambitious exploration goals. His provisions consisted of 230 pounds of food, "with which to subsist a party of five white men and a number of natives until the Yukon River was reached." As ice conditions impeded further upriver travel by sled, Allen set out to explore the major Copper tributary, the Chitina River. "I was unwilling to pass such an important tributary of the Copper River as the Chittyna without learning something about it and the supposed store of minerals existing thereon."

The minerals Allen referred to were, of course, the great copper deposits reported to be somewhere on the great river or its tributaries. No one who observed the uses Indians had made of copper for utensils could doubt its presence in the country, but its location was uncertain. Had the vast copper wealth of the region been better known, American prospectors, who had already established Juneau as the starting point for investigation of the Yukon country, might have been more active.

Allen sent the Indians who had accompanied him back downriver with some trepidation: *"I considered their return perilous on account of the condition of the ice, a fact they realized. In speaking about it their faces would assume a pitiful expression; their worn-out moccasins and bloodshot eyes were alluded to." Allen managed to buy some dried fish—twenty-five salmon only, although he offered precious tea and tobacco in exchange. With some of this salmon the coastal Indians had to be content and set off for their return journey. Fortunately, the Indians made it downriver safely.*[13]

Allen cached most of his provisions at Taral and followed the Chitina River. The five whites and a single Indian trekked into the unknown territory, each carrying some food, a sleeping blanket, a share of the equipment, rifle, and ammunition. "From this time," Allen wrote: *. . . we began to realize the true meaning of the much-used expression "living off the country." The provisions* *with which we started could easily have been consumed by us in four days, but they were held as a reserve. Our main dependence was on rabbits, the broth of which was thickened with a handful of flour.*

Everyone wore "native boots," mukluks Allen had secured in trade to replace worn boots. By this time most of the snow was gone, and they had to walk over "granite boulders and pebbles." In the soft boots the way was hard. On April 13 they came upon Skilly, one of the Indians who had traveled with them from the coast. He had found portions of a moose killed by wolves during the winter. The soldiers were not fastidious, as Fickett's journal recorded:

They [the Indians] had left a few scraps lying around, and these, that neither they nor their dogs would eat, we were forced by hunger to gather up and make a meal on. This is Lieutenant Allen's birthday, and he celebrated it by eating rotten moose meat.[14]

The Indian Allen called Skilly was the brother of Chief Nicolai, whom the explorer was seeking. He had hoped to find "the proprietor of Taral, Tyone of Chittyna, and chief trader among the natives," at Taral. In fact, Allen's travels on the Chitina were as much to find the chief as to explore unknown territory, as the young officer had concluded that Nicolai's assistance was essential to his hopes of further passage up the Copper River.[15]

As the soldiers slogged along the river some thirty miles southeast of Taral, travel difficulty increased as they encountered various channels of the river, some beds of which were a mile wide. "Near the end of the day's march," Allen noted:

. . . found us with a deep, impassable water to our front and right, and a very high, rugged point to our front and left. To climb this when in good physical condition, without packs or guns, would have been a difficult task. To cross it under the circumstances severely tested both the courage and strength of the party.[16] Worse yet, they had the necessity of hunting for their supper at the end of each day's march. By April 17 they could no longer delay their hunting until the end of the day.

Allen quoted Fickett's journal in his report: "*Rotten moose meat would be a delicacy now. So weak from hunger that we had to stop at noon to hunt. All so weak that we were dizzy, and would stagger like drunken men.*" At this point they got some relief when the mother of one of their Indians, who was traveling with a hunting party in the vicinity, came into camp with "a small piece of meat and a moose's nose, which, with the rabbits we killed, considerably strengthened us." She had brought the meat on her son's orders but had done so reluctantly, crying on behalf of her younger children who were also near starvation. She was not exaggerating. Allen met the hunters, four adults and a number of children, and their hunting luck had not been good. The hunters were able to tell where Nicolai's dwelling place could be found near the headwaters of the Nizina River, but gave conflicting reports on his hunting success.[17]

With an Indian guide Allen and his men traveled about thirty miles to reach Nicolai's camp. They were relieved to find him and rejoiced to see a large pot of meat stewing on the fire. Each traveler consumed at least five pounds of meat and plenty of broth. Allen was fortunate in meeting Chief Nicolai for a number of reasons. He needed food, a boat for transport back to Taral, and information about the country, or, better yet, Nicolai's personal guidance upriver—and all this was provided. With Nicolai's help Allen got back to Taral on May 4. Although he remained ambitious about further exploration, his thoughts turned to friends in the states. Allen named local features for several acquaintances, including Dora Creek for his fiancee, Miss Dora Johnson of Chicago.

At Taral Allen rested for a day and considered the geography he had observed. He found it hard to determine, because of the ice, whether the Chitina (or Chittyna as he spelled it) was larger or smaller than the Copper. Since Indians told him that Chittyna meant copper, he considered calling Chittyna the Copper on his official map. "Subsequent events showed the western tributary to be much larger, and on this account I have continued it by the better known though improper name."[18]

Soon he was off for the passage upriver, towing a boat filled with provisions and baggage from the bank with the help of Nicolai and three other Indians. Going against the swift current was hard, and he realized why Natives did not travel on the river by canoe. *The usual communication of the natives is afoot in ascending and by raft in descending. The baidara is used for transportation to the trading station, Nuchek, and when an extended descent of the river is made. If it is used in ascending, it is always cordelled.*[19]

Progress upriver was steady and not too unpleasant as the days became warmer. Two days above Taral Allen enjoyed the sight of the green vegetation filling the "natural terraces" above the river banks.

These terraces present the same appearance as would the front of a huge earth fortification. The uniformity of the two slopes, one above the other, the uniform height of each parapet for several hundred yards, would seem to indicate the work of man rather than that of nature.[20]

Four days above Taral, Allen stopped at a village of thirty inhabitants, headed by a chief called Liebigstag, who seemed nearly equal in rank to Nicolai, "though not nearly such a diplomat."[21] Allen described a feast given them by Liebigstag in his house on the bluff. *"Never have I known lines of caste to be so rigidly drawn as with these people. I was considered the chief and in ascending the bluff, natives had come down to escort us up and carry my bed."* Each person was seated for eating in the "spruce-bough tepee" according to rank. Nicolai and Allen sat to the right and left of the host while Private Fickett *"was assigned a place with the 'oi polloi.'"*[22]

Allen's democratic senses were offended by the Native customs in regard to rank: "I did not have time nor was it in my instructions to attempt any reform in their social and political customs; yet had we been less dependent on the natives I should certainly have let them understand that the ablest worker was the chiefest man." It pained Allen that chiefs would not do any physical work and took rewards he tried to give willing underlings for themselves.[23]

From the chief's place the travelers had a wonderful view, "one of the finest views I have ever seen," Allen wrote. He saw towering mountains to the east and north of the river, including Mount Wrangell; Mount Blackburn, which he named for U.S. Senator J. C. S. Blackburn of Kentucky; Mount Drum, which he named for Brig. Gen. Richard C. Drum; and Mount Sanford, which he named for his grandfather, Reuben Sanford.[24]

Allen moved upriver with increasing style as Liebigstag and his retainers joined the party. They had plenty of moose meat and expert guidance into the main channel of the river with the local chief's help. On the twelfth they reached the largest village yet encountered, one with about forty-seven inhabitants. Everywhere Allen asked his hosts to draw maps of the region and even distant places they might know such as Cook Inlet. Results varied, and he was unsure of the best route to the Tanana country.

Traveling with Nicolai became irksome as the chief counseled other Indians to demand the highest prices for food. The soldiers had also become very weary of the ceremonies and rank consciousness of their companions. "None of the natives would sell us any food without consulting him, and he advised prices that would make a commissary in civilization shudder."[25]

At the mouth of the Tazlina, Nicolai left the expedition to return downriver. From this point on the soldiers would be traveling in country about which they had no knowledge. On May 15 Allen entrusted the chief with letters to be taken to Nuchek. Nicolai was also asked to carry a number of photographic plates and equipment that had been cached below the Tazlina River. Unfortunately, the Indians opened the box of plates, exposing and ruining them.

As they ascended the river the group encountered very little game. For this reason and because

An 1885 *engraving of an Ahtna cache and sled. From Lt. Henry T. Allen, "Report of an Expedition," Plate No. 8.*

of the uncertainty regarding the trail to the Copper's headwaters and beyond, the explorers' mood was dismal:

No *buoyancy of spirit characterized the party as it left the mouth of the Tezlina [sic], entirely in ignorance of what was in store for it: and, wearied with hunger and other hardships, there was just cause for melancholy. The party had scarcely been dry day or night since leaving Taral.*

On the first day above the Tazlina River they had a serious accident. Their skin boat struck and grounded on a large boulder in midstream. "The dogs were thrown out of the boat, the sides of which were crushed in, and for a few minutes general consternation prevailed until we were again safe on land. Had the boat upset our bedding, guns, and instruments would have been lost, and doubtless the lives of some of the party." Their loss had not been great as the boat could be repaired, but the incident further depressed the explorers.[26]

The many channels of the Copper River often forced them to wade. The water was shallow enough to permit them to pull their boat in this fashion, but it was cold. Even at night they could not shake the effects of their chilling work: "Improper circulation of the blood and frequent discharge of urine at night was the cause of much sleeplessness," Allen said.[27]

Hunting prospects remained poor, although they did manage to kill a few geese and find a few of their eggs. On May 24 they met the first Natives they had seen since the 15th: "They were the thinnest, hungriest people I have ever beheld. The children were slowly wasting away. Their only support had been a few small fish, rabbits, and roots." Thanks to their sidearms, the army party considered themselves far better off, despite their limited food supplies. "I shudder to think," Allen wrote, "of the subsequent condition of those poor women and children, unless the salmon-run quickly followed us."[28]

The necessity of continual wading in a hunger-weakened condition made progress slow. Six miles was the best Allen could do most days, and the boat was getting too heavy for them. As they no longer needed so large a boat, Sergeant Robertson and Bremner remodeled it on a smaller scale. A crippled, starving Native joined the party, claiming knowledge of a distant trail over the Alaska Range and a family relationship to a "big Tyone of the upper Copper." Allen tried to leave the Native behind as a useless drain on their small resources, but he persisted in tagging along and, as his skill in root digging and other survival talents became obvious, Allen was happy to adopt him as a mascot and "valuable assistant . . . without whose services we would undoubtedly have suffered much more than we did."[29] Rabbits were now hard to come by, and they had to use the little rice and flour they had been saving for emergency. Allen quoted Fickett's journal on their travails:

May 28.—Had a little paste, rotten and wormy meal for dinner; rotten goose eggs and a little rice for supper. Each meal about one-fourth of what we needed. . . . Whole party played out.

May 29.—Party nearly played out for want of food. Can just crawl. Had to stop in the middle of p.m. to make a flap-jack for each and a little beef tea. Decided to abandon the boat at the next Indian house.

May 30.—Temperature of water 43. Course NE. by E. Arrived at an Indian house at 11 a.m. hungry. Decided to abandon boat. Indian gave us a dinner of boiled meat, from which he scraped the maggots by handfuls before cutting it up. It tasted good, maggots and all.[30]

On May 28 they passed the mouth of the Chistochina. As this river seemed as large as the Copper, Allen considered following it. He decided against it because his Indian mascot said that no Indians lived on the Chistochina but that villages would be encountered on the Copper. A few miles farther on Allen reached a village of twenty-three Indians, who were about to head downriver for fishing at Taral. Just upriver was another village where they left the boat. On June 2 they found a well-marked trail to the village of Chief Batzulneta. Allen was pleased to learn that Tanana Indians had arrived at the camp to await the salmon run, so he got a better fix on the region's geography.

Batzulneta was the largest Indian the explorers had ever seen, standing six feet, four inches, "clad in a blouse of red scarlet flannel, obtained from a trading station on the Yukon River." His hair, three feet long, could not be cut or combed, as Allen understood the situation, because he was a medicine man. "Altogether he was the most picturesque character we had met, yet his face showed neither courage nor cunning. His ascendancy had doubtless arisen from a superstition concerning his unusual stature."[31]

One Tanana Native drew Allen a map, showing the Tanana and Yukon Rivers, "which is inserted to show how great is the geographical knowledge of these primitive people." The Native said that he had visited the trading station of Jack McQuesten on the Yukon—a fact Allen confirmed when he later met the famed pioneer trader.

The Indians feasted the explorers on arrival, as was the custom, but could not be induced to sell any food as their stores were meager. Everyone eagerly awaited the great day that brought life and hope back to the Copper River country—the return of the salmon. It came while Allen was preparing to leave camp. "A series of loud shouts was heard, proclaiming the first salmon of the season. It was a rather small silver salmon, which was placed in a conspicuous place on one of the spruce-bough tepees, where all visited it with great singing and glee."[32]

Allen did not wait for the expected run before starting for the Slana Valley and Lake Suslota at the foot of the pass he named for Gen. Nelson Miles. Enough fresh fish for the first couple of days on the trail did not make enough difference to wait around. He had managed to hire four Indians as packers and expected to find caribou in the valley and fish at the lake or elsewhere. Crossing the low mountain pass he saw high mountains to the east and south, which he assumed contained the headwaters of the Tanana, Copper, and White Rivers. At Lake Suslota he knew that he had not far to go before crossing to the headwaters of the Tanana. It seemed odd that the two great rivers, Copper and Tanana, headed so near each other, and he considered it "one of the most interesting discoveries of the expedition."[33]

From an elevation a thousand feet above the lake he saw Lake Mentasta to the north. A few miles farther on they reached a stream full of salmon. They enjoyed the first feast they had eaten in a long time. One man ate three salmon, "including the heads of all and the roe of one, from the time of going into camp until retiring."[34]

On June 9 Allen stood on a divide 4,500 feet high and recorded his excitement: "From this the most grateful sight it has ever been my fortune to witness was presented . . . the 'promised land' . . . the extensive Tanana Valley with numerous lakes and the low, unbroken range of mountains between the Tanana and Yukon rivers." He exulted at his success.

On this pass, with both white and yellow buttercups around me and snow within a few feet, I sat proud of the grand sight which no visitor save an Ahtna or Tanana had ever seen. Fatigue and hunger were for the time forgotten in the great joy at finding our greatest obstacles overcome.[35]

Allen went on to complete his passage to the Yukon and the Koyukuk before finishing his adventures at St. Michael. No other Alaska explorer ever accomplished so epic a journey and achieved such significant geographic results. Allen, Fickett, and the others of the party richly deserved their fame.

One of the greatest achievements of the Allen expedition was recording the lives of Copper River Indians more fully than had been done earlier. He was the harbinger of a tide of whites whose impact would disrupt the traditional cultures to a large extent, although everywhere he traveled he saw signs of the long-established trade patterns dating from the Russian presence on the Copper and the British and American traders on the Yukon.

By Allen's calculations he had traveled 160 miles from Nuchek on the coast to Taral, then 90 miles from Taral to Nicolai's village, 240 miles from Taral to Lake Suslota, then after crossing the pass, some 550 miles to the junction of the Tanana and Yukon. During the journey he had covered some 1,500 miles, much of it through wilderness.

The public was not generally aware of Allen's achievement. He was not an engaging writer, and his official report moldered on the shelf. By contrast, the work of another army explorer, Lt. Frederick Schwatka, who ascended the Chilkoot Pass and charted the Yukon River in 1883, became widely known. Schwatka had traveled over familiar ground but wrote popular articles and a book on his adventures in a lively style. Regardless of writing ability, Allen's achievements clearly stand out as much more significant. As historian Morgan Sherwood has noted, Allen's greatest achievement was in geography. He tried to be a scientific observer in other fields, but he lacked the opportunity to gather natural history specimens or make extensive geological observations. His mapping and descriptions of physical features were excellent, and his map was relied upon until the gold rush era.[36]

❋ Schwatka and Hayes ❋

Frederick Schwatka's 1891 expedition explored the region north of the St. Elias Mountains that included the first reconnaissance of the White and upper Nizina Rivers. Their reason for focusing on this area was obvious: "So far as can be learned it had never been penetrated by white men, and the lakes, rivers and mountains which may appear on any maps are products of the geographer's imagination."[37]

Schwatka, geologist C. Willard Hayes, and prospector Mark Russell initially entered Canada via the Taku River, later traversing to Teslin Lake and descending the Teslin River to old Fort Selkirk on the Yukon. From there, the party crossed overland to the lower White River. Here their difficulties intensified. Schwatka's Native packers abandoned the expedition near the present international boundary at Kletsan Creek, claiming that it was impossible to cross Skolai Pass in the summer. Despite this setback, the party decided to proceed:

It was something over two hundred miles back to Selkirk, and although an unknown country a considerably shorter distance to an Indian village on the other side of the mountains. Trusting in our ability to reach the latter inside of two weeks, a period for which we had provisions, we decided to push forward.[38]

The explorers abandoned all non-essential gear, reducing their loads to about eighty pounds apiece. Constant rain slowed their progress, and owing to their lack of a tent, also compounded their discomfort. Nevertheless, four days later the trio crossed Skolai Pass and soon reached the headwaters of the Nizina River. Travel, however, remained difficult.

Forcing our way through the dense growth of alder and spruce which covers the steep slopes at the base of the canyon walls was extremely slow and painful work. A mile in four or five hours was counted fair progress.[39]

Compelled to ford the river frequently, the party decided to build a boat.

Our tools consisted of a very dull axe and our pocket knives, but with these we hewed out a keel and gunwales from spruce saplings and fashioned ribs from willow poles, lashing the structure together with twine ravelled from our pack ropes. Over this frame was stretched the canvas in which our bedding had been wrapped and finally the covering was smeared liberally with spruce gum. In this craft our progress was more rapid and not without excitement.[40]

After running the remainder of the Nizina, including its treacherous canyon, the group descended the Chitina River to Taral, which they reached exactly fourteen days after leaving Kletsan Creek. There they met the renowned Ahtna Chief Nicolai, who provided them with a "most hospitable reception,"as well as transportation to the coast in a "large skin boat manned by ten of his vassals [sic]."[41]

The explorers realized the significance of their accomplishments. "Between Yukon River and the St. Elias Mountains lies a large area, embracing the whole of the White River and its tributaries, as well as the headwaters of the Copper and Tanana, which has been geographically a blank." That hole was now filled: Schwatka's party had successfully connected the explorer's 1883 Yukon survey with Allen's 1885 chart of the Chitina and the Copper Rivers.[42]

Prospectors lining a boat up the Copper River. Courtesy of the Washington State Historical Society.

※ The U.S. Geological Survey ※

A U.S. Geological Survey party consisting of William J. Peters and Alfred H. Brooks was the first to ascend the White River entirely by boat. Conducting a general reconnaissance of the Yukon region in 1898, the pair found the ascent feasible, "though exceedingly difficult." They lined, poled, and pushed their canoes while wading against the swift current. "We were much hampered," Brooks wrote, "by the many quicksands which occur along the river, and which sometimes almost threaten to make further progress impossible." Much time was lost in repairing their canoes which sometimes swept against snags and were damaged. Snags "were often difficult enough to avoid when they could be seen, but when buried in the opaque, muddy waters they proved exceedingly treacherous."[43]

Peters and Brooks were keen to gather information on overland routes to the Tanana. From the White River, they ascended Snag Creek. Conditions were easier for poling because of the creek's hard bottom—yet it took two weeks to make fifty miles, reaching Mirror Creek, a tributary of the Chisana River. The broad valleys of Snag and Mirror Creeks form "good routes of communication between the White River and the Upper Tanana," Brooks wrote in 1900. "Indian portage trails are said to exist from both Ladue Creek and Katrina River to Tanana waters; these routes probably reach the main river by Scottie and Gardner creeks."[44]

Although the pair did not explore the headwaters of the Chisana River in 1898, Peters and Brooks returned a year later for another reconnaissance. From the upper White River they traveled with prospectors E. J. Cooper and H. A. Hammond, said to be the first men to bring a pack train through the Cooper Pass-Chisana route to the White River Valley. After reaching the glacier "in which the Tanana River heads," they followed the Chisana River down to cross over to the Nabesna Valley via Cooper Pass.[45]

Geologist Oscar Rohn was also active that season. He ascended the Chitina River, naming McCarthy Creek for prospector James McCarthy, who had earlier lent him some horses. Joined by prospector Arthur H. McNeer, Rohn made the first recorded crossing of the Wrangell Mountains, via the Nizina and Chisana Glaciers, before returning overland to the Copper River at Batzulnetas.[46]

Following additional USGS expeditions in 1900 and 1902, in which such notable geologists as Frank C. Schrader, Arthur C. Spencer, and Walter C. Mendenhall participated, the region could no longer be considered a "geographical blank." Spencer, in fact, just missed his shot at immortality. Although prospectors Clarence Warner and Jack Smith first discovered Kennecott's fabulously rich Bonanza lode, Spencer independently located the same ore body only a few weeks later.[47]

With railroad construction in 1908 promising to spur interest in prospecting, the U.S. Geological Survey sent Fred H. Moffit, Adolph Knopf, and Stephen R. Capps to further investigate the Nabesna-Chisana-White River region. They focused on the Nabesna and White River Valleys because they were less known and because copper seemed rare on the Chisana except for around the head of Cross Creek. While making a close survey of mineral prospects, geologists did not overlook other regional characteristics. They estimated that there were only forty-five to fifty Natives living in the area between the headwaters of the Copper and White Rivers, located mostly in villages at Batzulnetas, Cross Creek, and Notch Creek, all of which lay along a major trail. The trail, originally described by Ahtna people to

Lieutenant Allen, carried from the present-day Slana area through Cooper Pass, down Notch Creek and Cross Creek to the Chisana River.[48]

This route served many of the miners of the Chisana region years later. Because there were no new mineral developments or other kinds of major economic development within the Wrangell-St. Elias region after the decline of Chisana, the old routes remained the key ones of the area. In 1923 Fred Moffit of the U.S. Geological Survey described "certain well-established routes of travel" within the district.[49]

The route followed a depression between the Nutzotin and Wrangell mountains between Copper River Valley and the Chisana and White Rivers. From above the mouth of Copper Creek it ascended to Cooper Pass at 5,000 feet, the highest point along the way. Heavy snow necessitated winter and summer trails. The summer trail swung northeast of the northwest-trending mountain range, and the winter trail wound around the southwest side of the ridge. "The two trails," Moffit noted, "are nearly parallel for about 8 miles and nowhere are more than 1/2 mile apart." The winter trail has easier grades but was avoided in summer because of numerous large boulders in stream bars. "The summer trail necessitates a steep climb by south-bound travelers of more than 500 feet on the north side of the summit, and for more than one mile just north of the summit it follows a smooth mountain slope . . . where footing is uncertain."[50]

The reports of the U.S. Geological Survey reveal something of a proprietary spirit about Alaska. Reporters project a sense of purpose and accomplishment. They knew that people relied upon their work and that their service was not transitory. If the job did not get finished in their season of work, they or others would return to complete it. And, if important mineral discoveries occurred in any region, they would follow hard on the heels of the prospectors to evaluate the new information.

Thus Stephen Capps, reporting on the Chisana-White River district in 1916, began his report by reviewing all the previous explorations and geological investigations before the current one, including Alfred Brooks's brief report in 1914 on the Chisana strike. The Chisana gold excitement in 1913 encouraged the U.S. Geological Survey to undertake a major effort by two field parties in 1914: "It seemed advisable to extend the topographic mapping northward into the unsurveyed portion of the region, to extend also the aerial geologic mapping, and examine the conditions under which the placer gold deposits occur."[51]

As usual, the geologists did their work capably and made certain cautious forecasts regarding the possibilities of other strikes like that at Chisana. As summarized by Brooks in the preface: "The outlook for finding other placer deposits in this intensely glaciated region is not very favorable." As always, lode mining in remote areas required good transportation and would be feasible only if the region "is made accessible by a railroad." Hope of a railroad extension had dimmed but not died. If prospects or world mineral market prices improved it would have looked a bit better.[52]

As elsewhere, U.S. Geological Survey work in the Wrangell-St. Elias region profited from its continuity. No other government or private agency has had such a sustained record of consistent activity in Alaska. Scientists concentrated on geology but also reported on wildlife, the people of the region, and other features. The published reports of the survey, still widely available in libraries, have provided an indispensable source of regional history.

Float Copper
Nugget-Nizina

Three-ton copper nugget found in the bed of
Nugget Creek, 1903. The fourth man from
the left is James McCarthy, for whom the
town of McCarthy was later named. Courtesy
of the Anchorage Museum of History and
Art, B62.1.573; Miles Brothers photo 697.

Chapter

Gold Mining

✳ Early Mining in Alaska ✳

Economic exploitation of Alaska by Russian traders and their early American era successors, primarily in the fur trade, did not dramatically change much of the territory. Mineral prospecting and mining was a far greater catalyst to change, although its development was gradual. Northern gold excitement began with a modest stampede up the Stikine River to Cassiar in 1862, followed by a much larger development there in 1871. Just one year before the second Cassiar strike, gold was discovered at Sumdum Bay. In 1872 gold was found near Sitka, and in 1873 prospectors began moving into the Yukon Valley. A major strike in 1880 led to the founding of Juneau and established a base for subsequent penetration of the interior.

Leroy N. "Jack" McQuesten and Alfred Mayo were the first prospectors on the Yukon River. They reached Fort Yukon from the Nelson River region of Canada, then established a store at Fort Reliance for the Alaska Commercial Company. The vast interior did not look very promising for the fur trade or for anything else in the 1870s, but other prospectors began coming into the country from the coast in the 1880s, and an air of expectancy developed. Most prospectors entered the interior over the Chilkoot Pass at Dyea, the historic Indian trade route that had been long dominated by the coastal Chilkats. Evidence indicates that George C. Holt was the first prospector to use the Lynn Canal entry.

At the time of the first U.S. Census in Alaska in 1880 the white population was estimated at 430 and the territory's Native population was thought to be about 33,000. The number of whites soon increased rapidly, however, after the decline of the Cassiar excitement and development of mining in the Juneau area. A few hundred prospectors crossed Chilkoot Pass in 1883, and several reported making good money mining river sandbars. Several prospectors examined the Copper River country, as well, but that region was not considered as promising as the Yukon Valley.

The first substantial interior gold strike was made in the Fortymile River country. The river's headwaters lie within Alaska, but the river's northeasterly course crosses the Canadian border before reaching the Yukon River. The border created some confusion because most of the diggings were in Alaska, while the town of Fortymile where most miners lived was within Canada's Yukon Territory. It was at Fortymile where the miners, mostly Americans, followed the mining frontier tradition to carry out the necessary governance through formal meetings. This primitive system of keeping order worked reasonably well while the population was small, but gave way when the Canadian government dispatched the Mounties to Fortymile for the proper administration of law.

A few years after the Fortymile strike another wealthy gold field was discovered on Birch Creek, and the town of Circle developed on the Yukon near the diggings. Circle was the first

A prospector is welcomed to the Copper River Roadhouse, 1902. Courtesy of the Valdez Museum, P1986.117.51; Miles Brothers photo 868.

Alaska mining town in the interior and the most important center in the Yukon country until the Klondike discovery.

The long anticipated event—the discovery of huge quantities of gold—occurred on August 16, 1896, when George Carmack, Skookum Jim, and Tagish Charlie followed a suggestion made by Robert Henderson and found gold on a tributary of the Klondike River. As a result of their find the new town of Dawson was established and boomed over the winter of 1896–1897 with miners rushing in from Fortymile, Circle, and elsewhere along the Yukon. From this time the pace of Alaska exploration and development quickened dramatically. As might be expected, the history of mining in the Copper River country dates from the Klondike gold rush era of the late 1890s.[1]

☀ Copper River Basin ☀

The Copper River basin and adjacent parts of the Yukon basin contain two mineral-bearing zones on the southern and the northern slopes of the Wrangell Mountains. U.S. Geological Survey people called the southern belt, which contained the great copper deposits, the Kotsina-Chitina region, and labeled the northern belt the Nabesna-White River region.

Prospecting and mining in the northern belt was inhibited by its remoteness. As late as 1909 Alfred Brooks of the U.S. Geological Survey observed that travelers to the area were forced to use "a rather circuitous route, between 200 and 300 miles in length," from tidewater. Exploration and mining travel into the southern belt had not been easy either, but construction of the Copper River and Northwestern Railway in 1911 eliminated most of the difficulties.

☀ Early Prospectors ☀

George Holt's distinction as an interior traveler is well documented. Addison Powell's narrative, *Trailing and Camping in Alaska*, however, suggests that Holt may have been preceded in the 1880s by a mysterious prospector named I. N. West. West told Powell about his earlier interior Alaskan prospecting expedition, and claimed to have discovered gold somewhere in the upper Copper basin. Powell, then preparing to join the '98 stampede, believed West's story and acted in accordance.

West maintained that he had entered the country from Yakutat, traversing the mountains between the Bering and Malaspina Glaciers before following the Tana River to the Chitina. After ascending the Nizina River, he crossed a pass south of Mount Wrangell to reach the White River, crossed another to the headwaters of the Tanana and the Copper, then ascended the Chistochina before returning to the coast at Valdez via the Copper, Klutina River and Lake, and the Valdez Glacier.

West remains an enigma. If he did even half of what he alleged, he deserves recognition as one of Alaska's most distinguished explorers. And if he found the gold he claimed, the publication of it at the time might have changed the pattern of the northern stampedes. At the time he "confided" in Powell, he was seventy-two years old. Before agreeing to pay Powell's expenses to Alaska and giving him a share of his gold, West wanted a pledge of secrecy. "He inquired also whether I had been bewildered; what I would take with me on such a trip; the kinds of guns and ammunition, and even what kinds of matches I would take along."

Powell guessed that West's discovery had been made at the headwaters of the Chistochina, but, wherever it was, West insisted that he and his Indian companion panned $600 in only a little time. "Gold! Why, man—come up there and I'll pay you, not only for your trouble, but you shall have an interest with me, for there is gold enough for all of us."[2] Powell was convinced. He agreed to travel with the U.S. Army's trail-blazing Abercrombie expedition and would be available when West got word to him of his claim's location. Powell headed north, but never heard from West again. Later, Powell learned that West had tried to reach the interior, but had become too sick to continue. Without further corroboration, however, it remains difficult to credit West's amazing story.

❋ Valdez Glacier Trail ❋

In 1897–1898 many stampeders succumbed to the apparent logic of the Valdez route to the interior despite the army explorers reports that it was not a good entry. By choosing a port closer to Seattle than St. Michael (the point for upriver Yukon River voyaging) that did not require hiking the fearsome Chilkoot or White Passes, they reasoned that they would accomplish a quick journey to the gold fields. More importantly, the route attracted stampeders because its difficulties were not known and because rumors of mineral wealth in the Copper River region

The Miles Brothers' camp near the future site of Kennecott. Courtesy of the Valdez Museum, P1986.117.86; Miles Brothers photo 686.

Future territorial delegate Tony Dimond (on far right) at an unidentified mining camp in the Chitina district. Courtesy of the Valdez Museum, P1987.132.5.

were persuasive. Most of those who chose the Valdez entry rued the day because, except for the Canadian overland routes, it was more arduous than the others. Many of those who wintered in the interior over 1898–1899 were ravaged by scurvy. Some of the afflicted died, and many others returned to the coast, resolving to leave gold
hunting to others.

On the map it did not appear that the route to the interior would be so difficult. Although the several thousand stampeders who started landing at Valdez in March had few accurate particulars of the country from the terminus of the glacier, they pushed on. Crossing the Valdez Glacier, often several times to bring along all necessary provisions and equipment, was none too easy. In the face of spring blizzards and some intense cold spells, it was downright hazardous. Keeping warm in camp when fuel cost a dollar a pound to transport was costly. And hoisting freight by rope and tackle at some high points along the glacier could be an exhausting, even terrifying duty.

Stampeders generally agreed that travel would become easier once they succeeded in crossing the glacier. In fact, the hard part lay ahead of them in most cases. The Klutina River (usually spelled Klutena then), which was reached from its headwaters at Klutina Lake, afforded no serene passage to the Copper River. A fiercely coursing stream, broken up by sandbars, it is barely navigable in its lower stretches by powerful river boats. For many of the boatmen who tried to use its waters, the Klutina was a destructive force which cost them all their gear and sometimes their lives. Most stampeders did not get beyond the mouth of the Klutina, where the new boom camp of Copper Center sprang up, and many of them did not

get beyond the glacier. Stampeders who went on from Copper Center were mostly heading for the Yukon via Mentasta Pass and the Fortymile River, either by cordelling boats up the Copper River or overland along the foot of Mount Drum to the mouth of the Slana River on the Millard Trail. These routes converged at the mouth of the Slana and went on across the pass.

Travelers were too busy for much prospecting along the way except in the immediate vicinity of their routes and along the Copper River from Copper Center to the sea. Some attention was given to the short Copper River tributaries coming out of the Wrangell Mountains, but the major tributary, the Chitina, was investigated only along its lower stretches. The lone reported mineral discovery was that on Quartz Creek, a southern tributary of the Tonsina, and it caused an areawide stampede late in the '98 season.

✳ Stampeders' Experiences ✳

The 1898 experience of Charles A. Margeson and his party typified that of other stampeders after crossing the glacier. Before moving on to Klutina Lake, the next stage of travel, the men spent a week prospecting the headwaters of the Klutina River. All they found was color and a little "flour gold," but it was enough to encourage them about prospects farther into the interior. On July 4, after the camp of one hundred prospectors paraded and watched a baseball game and other events to celebrate the "Glorious Fourth," Margeson's group boated downriver sixteen miles to the lake.

After establishing a camp, Margeson and others in his company stampeded to a reported strike nearby in "Robinson's Gulch." They found color, built sluice boxes, and worked down to bedrock, though they never recovered enough gold to justify a couple of weeks' work. By late summer, Margeson noted the steady exodus of men leaving the country. He figured that many of those afflicted with "cold feet" had never dreamed that hardship would attend their fortune-seeking or had believed that the work of a few weeks would make them rich. Others had received bad news calling them home or were simply homesick. Once the number of "home-seekers" exceeded that of the "gold-seekers," the latter were in a good position to buy provisions cheaply. Margeson bought pork and bacon for two cents a pound and a hundred pounds of beans for seventy-five cents. He felt very good about his bargains as winter neared, then suddenly he, too, got "cold feet" and left the country before winter.[3]

Despite more sickness and discouragements than those experienced by any other aggregation of prospectors, the situation was not totally bleak for the Copper River argonauts. Over the winter of 1898–1899, they focused more on local mineral prospects rather than on the region's access to the Klondike. Prospectors located the Nikolai copper deposit in 1899, foreshadowing what would be the greatest of all regional mineral developments and also made more modest placer gold discoveries at Chistochina.

The Chistochina discovery was made by George Hazelet, whose northern career encompassed the historical trend of mining from individual entrepreneurship to corporate organization. Hazelet's future interests were to include mining at Chistochina and elsewhere in the Wrangell-St. Elias region, trail building from McCarthy to Chisana, townsite speculations, and, as mining field boss for the Alaska Syndicate, the direction of corporate strategies and management policies. All this grandeur was far from view of the school teacher-turned-prospector who crossed the Valdez Glacier in '99 with his partner, A. J. Meals. Hazelet's diary of that time catches the mood of one man who committed himself to a hard struggle in hope of improving his family's well-being. He was no daring, reckless adventurer risking a year or two in careless disregard for the future.

Hazelet reached Valdez in March on the Pacific Steam Whaling Company's *Excelsior*. There was no wharf, but, because of the deep water, ships could run close to shore for unloading. Hazelet and Meals wasted no time before hauling their freight to the glacier. It was strenuous work: "I have now learned," said Hazelet, "what it is to make an ass of myself in earnest . . . harness yourself up to a six foot sled, put 200 pounds on it and strike for the foot of the glacier which is five miles away. Repeat this twice a day for a week and you soon have long ears." The glacier trail was crowded with about 2,200 footsore men and women. Hazelet counted about twenty women and admiringly observed one who "helps her husband pull every load and seems as happy as if she were presiding over a nice little home." Enterprises on the trail included the quack medical practices of several suspicious characters. "If I had a sick dog that I wanted to get rid of I would call them in but not otherwise," said Hazelet.[4]

Men represented all nationalities, shape, and ages, from boyhood to old age, "a fair representation of the average middle class Americans." Observation of divergent types amused Hazelet, "Some pulled their sleds with all the horrors depicted in their countenances, others go along quietly with a Good morning or a How do you do, seemingly happy or pretending to be. Still others will whistle or sing some old familiar air, but there are few of that sort. The sled really seems to develop the worst side of a man, for most all are ready to 'scrap' on the least provocation."

One woman was concerned that one of the lakes of the interior, where a boat building camp rose, commemorated her name. This is "Lake Blanche," she announced to all new arrivals. Some stampeders knew the lake as Sheppard's Lake, yet Blanche had a chance because no name had been firmly established. But it is not easy to insure such matters, as Hazelet noted: "She had it written on board and posted upon the ice, but some careless cuss tore it down and now, like the women, the name must die."[5]

Hazelet prospected on the Klutina and other streams while learning the country. Several encounters with Indians impressed him favorably with their good qualities, especially when a party of them recovered a load of blankets from the river and held them for the owner's return: "this act of the Indians shows plainly they are not of the same blood of our Nebraska Indians."[6]

On July 1 Hazelet ascended the Chistochina, one of the Copper River tributaries. Indians had told him that the river showed gold signs. Later that month the miners sank a shaft about four miles from the river's mouth but were flooded out before bedrock was reached. But color signs were good. Moving upriver, they worked a sandbar and gathered some promising gold specimens. In September the miners voyaged down to Copper Center for welcome mail and provisions. Hazelet met Captain Abercrombie there and let Frank C.

Margaret McGavock operating an hydraulic giant on Dan Creek. Courtesy of the Jean McGavock Lamb Collection.

Gold mining on Chititu Creek. Courtesy of the Rasmuson Library Archives, University of Alaska Fairbanks; Capps Collection, 83-149-1012.

Schrader of the U.S. Geological Survey examine his samples of placer sand and lode rocks. Schrader's conclusions brought joy to Hazelet: "He says that if we can get to bedrock, we will surely find good paydirt." Ore samples were also promising, and Schrader agreed to gather larger samples and ship them to Washington, D.C., for a full assay.[7]

Though the Chistochina district lies outside the Wrangell-St. Elias Park and Preserve boundary, the development bears on the park's history because it encouraged other prospectors in the region. Eventually, the Chistochina in the northwestern part of the Copper River basin along the southern foothills of the Alaska Range proved to be the richest placer producer in the Alaska's south central region.[8]

❈ Trails of '98 ❈

In one sense, the U.S. Geological Survey was an information agency, providing facts on the various routes into the country as well as mineral prospects. Pulling together and publishing such information from prospectors and other travelers was an extremely valuable function. The following summary from a report on geological investigations in 1898 gave interested miners all the most essential facts on reaching the gold district from Copper Center in concise form:

From Copper Center to the Tanana, Yukon, and Fortymile rivers, the best and shortest route is the Millard trail by way of Mentasta Pass. This trail, crossing the Copper, bears northeastward somewhat near the base

Table 1
Klutina Trail Guide

PLACE	MILES	ELEVATION
Valdez	0	0
Foot of Valdez Glacier	4	210
Top of third bench	8	830
Twelvemile Camp (foot of fourth bench)	16	2,750
Foot of summit	22	3,800
Foot of Klutena Glacier	29	2,020
Onemile Camp	30	1,960
Twelvemile Camp	33	1,930
Sawmill Camp	35	1,740
Head of Lake Klutena	46	1,673
Cranberry Marsh	64	1,673
Foot of Lake Klutena	79	1,670
Amee Landing	85	1,370
Coxe Landing	90	1,320
Cook Bend	95	1,240
Boulder Spring (on bluff)	97	1,590
Copper Center (at mouth of Klutena)	112	1,050
Mentasta Pass (by Millard trail)	205	2,300

of Mounts Drum and Sanford, over the high ground of the big bend of the Copper, and is said to be a good, cut horse trail from Copper Center to near the Copper River below the mouth of the Slana. From Copper Center another route leads along the northwest side of the Copper River to the mouth of the Slana; this trail, however, is much longer than and not so good as the Millard trail.

From the northwest bend of Lake Klutena at Cranberry Marsh a trail branches off up Salmon Creek Valley and leads by way of Lake Lily northward to the Tazlina River, thence down that river to the Copper. This route seems to have been started chiefly by prospectors before the snow disappeared in the spring of 1898, after which the marshiness of the country over which it ran led to its disuse. That part of it down the Tazlina, however, is an Indian trail, and is said to be pretty fair and to continue westward down the Matanuska and Knik Rivers to Cook Inlet. Long ago it was in use by the Russians in traveling from Cook Inlet to Copper River. Schrader noted that earlier maps had reported a good trail from Taral northward on both sides of the Copper:

This is a mistake, for although portions of a trail are here and there met with, they are liable at any time to run out, usually extending but a short distance from the native villages. The Survey party, in coming down the Copper to Taral, found it necessary to cut trail most of the way.[9]

Schrader did not hesitate to make route recommendations. A proposed route from Valdez into the Copper River country via the Lowe River Valley, led north to cross the headwaters of the Tonsina and, descended Manker Creek Valley, to strike the Klutina River and trail below the lake. "It runs over some unexplored country, but seems to be by far the most suitable of all for railroad and pack train purposes." Another feasible route, noted by Schrader, would be from Valdez "up Lowe River, across the divide (which is only 1,800 feet high), and down the Tasnuna River to the Copper, whence the transportation up the Copper would be by boat, preferably a light-draft steamer of special power." Schrader provided a useful mileage and elevation table to guide prospectors.

❊ The Nizina District ❊

The Nizina District is drained by the eastern tributaries of the Copper River between Chitina and Miles Glacier, but most miners concentrated on Dan and Chititu Creeks and their tributaries. U.S. Army explorer Henry T. Allen and other early white travelers in the region had written of their interest in Dan Creek. Chief Nicolai, who had a camp at the mouth of Dan Creek, was persuaded to show them copper lodes nearby.

From its development in 1901, Dan Creek was mined continuously until recent times. This distinguishes it from virtually all other regions of Alaska for its long, sustained activity. Gold has been the chief yield, although about forty tons of copper nuggets also have been produced. Dan Creek is famed as the discovery site of a nearly three-ton copper nugget, which has become a museum piece. The history of Rex Creek, a tributary of the Chititu, has been similar to Dan Creek except for the lack of copper mining. Golconda Creek is the only other stream in the district where successful placer production occurred. Most of the gold was mined at Golconda between 1901 and 1916.

Clarence Warner and Dan Kane, grubstaked by Stephen Birch, originally located Dan Creek (named for Kane) in 1901. The Dan, which flows into the Nizina River four miles north of Chititu Creek and four miles south of the Chitistone River, drains an area of forty-five square miles. After a strike on Chititu Creek the following year, a modest stampede into the region occurred in 1902 and 1903.[10]

In 1902 Robert Blei grubstaked several prospectors to search for copper prospects in the Nizina district. Instead of copper, the prospectors found gold on Chititu Creek. News of the discovery caused a small influx of miners, but did not prevent Blei, Frank Kernan, and Charles Kopper from gaining control of most of Chititu, Rex, and White Creeks. Production in 1903 involved 135 miners hired by Blei (lower Chititu), Kernan (upper Chititu), and Kopper (a small section between the others' claims). The base camp for the Chititu, Young, and Dan Creek diggings was at Sourdough City, located on the south bank of the Nizina River at the mouth of Young Creek, about eight miles southeast of McCarthy. The smaller camps of Kernanville and Kopperstown were built on the Kernan and Kopper claims.[11]

Walter C. Mendenhall and Frank C. Schrader of the U.S. Geological Survey reported on the new district in 1903. Their short published description of the discovery, geography, and current mining was the only official information available to eager readers of government reports. The government men used a map of the district given them by miner George M. Esterly and were cautiously optimistic about future prospects.

In June and July 1902, reports reached Valdez to the effect that coarse gold had been found on the upper Nizina. The reports were sufficiently definite to cause considerable excitement in the town, and many who were free to go promptly stampeded to the new district, only to find that through the abuse of the power of attorney practically all of the available property had been staked.

The Nizina field includes the drainage basins of three southeast tributaries of the upper Nizina River—Young Creek, Chititu Creek, and Dan Creek. . . . In the present embryonic state of development it is not possible to predict with any definiteness the future of these creeks as gold producers. It is thought, however, that a district may be created here which will yield as well as the Chistochina. More than this is scarcely to be expected.[12]

In 1903 mining engineer L. A. Levensaler voyaged to Alaska with Horace V. Winchell who had options on Nizina and Chititu Creeks. After Levensaler reported somewhat favorably on the properties—placer ground consisting of benches—Winchell sold out to the Marcus Daly estate. The new owners of the options sent Levensaler back in February 1904 to make a complete survey "and a contour map from which yardage could be computed." The party included "an experienced placer man" and some Butte, Montana, miners who were to run prospect tunnels to bedrock.[13]

George Hazelet conducted the party from Valdez in horse sleds. Unfortunately, the early breakup of a lake impounded by the Kennicott Glacier caught them on the Chitina River. They lost six tons of food and horse feed and had to push on overland with pack horses. Their investigation was a major effort involving twenty men for the summer, but the ground did not prove valuable enough to take up the options.

Levensaler returned to the region in 1908. His employer, Stephen Birch, the Kennecott copper developer, wanted the creek prospected and mapped. In 1909 Levensaler was dispatched to Kennecott to prepare the Bonanza and Jumbo claims for mining and remained with the copper operation for many years. Birch sent James Galen to Dan Creek for further testing, then in 1910, turned over his properties to his brother, Howard Birch, an engineering graduate of the Columbia School of Mines.

Mining was confined to pick-and-shovel methods until 1907–1908, when the first hydraulic plant was installed. Birch and other miners were encouraged by the construction of the Nizina Bridge in 1914, which gave them the use of an all-season haul road. The vicissitudes of mining included the destructive force of nature. Birch's $70,000 hydraulic plant had been in operation for only three days in September 1913 when swiftly rising water tore through the valley, sweeping dams, pipelines, sluice boxes, cabins, and huge trees downstream in a rampaging flood. For an area of three miles the turbulent stream altered the landscape. As a newspaper noted, "The creek had taken on the appearance of a glacial moraine." Within a month, Birch and his twenty-five-man crew managed to repair the damage and reestablish operations on safer ground. A similar mishap had occurred in 1911, and this time Birch relocated on ground high enough to prevent further flooding.[14]

Dan Creek's development as a well-paying district had come slowly. In the early years of the century individual miners did poorly, lacking the machinery to remove the scattering of large boulders. It took a corporate organization to acquire seven hundred acres from the original holders and finance a hydraulic operation. In 1918 Birch invested in an extensive hydraulic system that enabled miners to attack a hill lying over the ancient creek bed. Birch sold out to John J. Price in 1924, and Price, H. A. Ives, and L. A. Levensaler formed the Dan Creek Hydraulic Mining Company. The company improved Birch's hydraulic system on the lower creek.

Despite such intensive mining of the limited area, speculators became interested in the Dan's prospects again in the 1930s. The Nicolai Placer Mines Company, successor to the

Fred Stevenson panning along the Chitina River. Courtesy of the Valdez Museum, P1987.132.3.

Dan Creek Hydraulic Mining Company from 1928, was reorganized in 1934 as the Partners Mine Corporation. New equipment was brought in, and a dam and reservoir were constructed just below the canyon, connecting it with several hundred feet of wood flume and a mile and a half of pipe to a water source. The company mined with a work force of seven to fourteen men until 1940 (although the name changed back to the Nicolai Miners Company in 1937). In 1940 the claims were leased by the Joshua Green Association, but the closure of the railroad and subsequent war-time restrictions on mining ended large-scale mining.

Chititu had a sawmill and, from August 1902, a road tramway connecting the camps to the diggings. Charles Bridges designed the system, which used local spruce logs for rails and ties for its five-mile length. Gold production was $135,000 in 1903 but, unfortunately, this nice yield was not a harbinger of a bright future. Subsequently, production dropped. In 1906 Blei's Chititu Development Company was bankrupt, and George Esterly purchased the property for $10,000.

Esterly built another sawmill, a lighting plant, machine shop, pipeline, and a telephone line from the camp to the diggings. About 1907 Esterly sold to J. D. Meenach, but remained to manage what was called the Nizina Mining Company. By 1909, between Esterly and Kernan, the creek's hydraulic operations employed fifty men. Production was $40,000 in 1910. Most of the Chititu activity from 1910 to 1920 consisted of the movement of paper as various parties gained and then relinquished control of claims. Even the completion of the Nizina Bridge in 1914, which made it easier to haul in heavy equipment, did not immediately revive mining. Technology had advanced by 1922, and installation of a hydraulic plant on Rex Creek gave the area its highest production since 1907.

For the new owner, the Hanover Bank and Trust Company, Hamlin Andrus expanded the Nizina Mining Company (or Rex Creek Mining Company) operation in 1924, employing thirty-five men. He also improved the hydraulic plants on Chititu and Rex Creeks in the early 1930s. It was during this period that the superintendent, C. H. Kraemer, moved the camp from Nizina to the present and well-preserved Chititu at the confluence of Chititu, Rex, and White Creeks.

Production continued between 1930 and 1950, although the yield was modest. Thanks to Tony Dimond, once the underpaid U.S. commissioner at Chisana in 1913 and a hopeful

Carl Whitham's Nabesna gold mill. Courtesy of the Anchorage Museum of History and Art, B71.X.5.14.

miner on Young Creek earlier, the Chititu mine was exempted from war-time restrictions on mining. The influence of Dimond, then Alaska's delegate to Congress, did not ensure prosperity, however. The mine was shut down in 1952, and the Hanover Trust employed Walter Holmes as caretaker until his death in 1964.[15]

❊ Miners of Note ❊

Among the Nizina miners Edward H. Stroecker typifies the restlessness of the typical gold hunter. Stroecker, a young San Francisco accountant, resisted the Klondike lure until 1900, when he joined a group heading for the Kuskokwim. The venture showed no success, and Stroecker returned to San Francisco after a few months. Within weeks he headed north again with a companion, landing at Valdez from the *Excelsior* in January 1901. In March they crossed the Valdez Glacier, sledded up the Copper and Chistochina Rivers to Slate Creek, prospected over the season, then rafted back to Valdez. In 1902 Stroecker mined for wages on Slate Creek, wintered again in Valdez tending bar at the Montana Saloon, then stampeded to Nizina in 1903. After a few weeks on Chititu Creek, he joined a group of miners grubstaked to prospect at the head of the White River. En route, the party crossed three glaciers, the Nizina, Frederika, and Russell, then prospected on Horsfeld Creek without success. Stroecker returned to Chititu Creek for the spring 1904 mining season. In early fall they joined a party traveling to the head of the White River and over the divide to the head of the Chisana, thence down the Tanana to Fairbanks by boat. From this time Stroecker's adventures lie outside the Wrangell-St. Elias region, but more years passed before he chose a settled life and eventually became an important banker in Fairbanks.[16]

Anthony "Tony" Dimond left mining for distinction in politics. In 1905 Dimond and his partner, Joseph H. Murray, traveled from Valdez to the Nizina River. Murray led Dimond to prospects he had investigated a year earlier, including Young Creek and Calamity Gulch, both tributaries of the Nizina. The men worked through the summer and fall, returning to Valdez in January to file on their claims. Though they told people they had found "good prospects," their claims were only mildly encouraging—and they were broke. Murray got the city magistrate's job, while Dimond supported himself with odd jobs and made summer excursions to the Nizina for prospecting and some work on his claims. In 1909 he prospected the Chitistone River and located a copper claim there. After a few years of divided interest, Dimond commanded work as a miner for others. He was a powerful, two-hundred-pound six-footer, and the Houghton Alaskan Exploration Company hired him in 1909 and 1910 to oversee the assessment and improvement work on its copper claims on McCarthy Creek in the Kennecott area.

The Young Creek claims held by Dimond and Murray began to look promising as Dimond started working them during the 1911 season. A reporter for the *Chitina Leader* was pleased to predict that a rich strike was coming: "There are veritable mountains of pay gravel in many places, while the creek shows good colors in almost every pan. Numerous holes have been sunk and some tunneling has been done by the owners, and in every instance the most flattering results have been obtained."[17]

Dimond tried to sell an interest in his properties to investors capable of doing hydraulic work, but nothing came of it. The uncertainty of mining was one reason for Dimond's pursuit of a legal education during these years, first through study on his own, then by clerking for Murray and Tom Donohue in Valdez after an accident left him with a badly shattered leg. When Dimond became a member of the bar, he was eligible to receive an appointment as U.S. commissioner for Chisana in 1913. Later he was to hold the most important of Alaska's elected offices, that of delegate to the U.S. Congress.

Nizina had a post office from 1903 to 1926 during its existence as a mining camp. The camp was actually located on Chititu Creek, five miles southeast of its confluence with the Nizina River, and served diggings on Dan, Young, and Chititu Creeks. Later, Sourdough City, on the south bank of the Nizina at the mouth of Young Creek, was active from 1908 to 1911 when McCarthy became the region's trading center. During the Nizina's heyday of 1902 through 1905, the boom and building bustle was of modest proportions. Though the usual exaggerations of great wealth spread abroad, it was obvious to the first miners that the gold-bearing areas were relatively insignificant.

By 1906 George Esterly and his principal (lower creek) and Frank Kernan (upper creek) held virtually all the claims. Miners hired Outside soon learned that their work place was remote. When Harold Smith left Oregon in 1909 he voyaged to Valdez to join several other men hired by Kernan. In late March the men left snowbound Valdez over the military trail, hauling a hand sled. After five days, they reached Tonsina and took the Copper River-Chitina trail, leaving the comforts of roadhouse stations behind. Another five days brought them to the mouth of the Tonsina and a halt of three weeks. News from the mines indicated no hurry since everything there was snowed in, too. Fortunately, the miners were able to bunk with a freighting outfit bound for the mines.[18]

When the miners finally reached Chititu, they mucked out one of the many empty log cabins and settled in. There was only one business in the community, a store-roadhouse operated by John Fagerberg. Fagerberg's contribution to the camp's economic amenities was an important one. More information exists on Fagerberg's affairs than for other storekeepers because his wife Anna sued him for divorce in 1912. They had married in 1907 at Seattle, but Anna made only two short visits to Alaska because of a disagreement over her role. He claimed that she wanted a separate dwelling and no roadhouse duties, and he thought she should run the roadhouse and be content living in it. "She is a woman," Fagerberg complained, "who insists upon having her own way or will in all matters of marital interest." When thwarted, he alleged that she grew hysterical and threw herself on the floor. Anna denied all this. She had been keen to run the roadhouse, but John wanted her to remain with her parents in Seattle. When she came to Nizina, John put her out of the house, then hired a housekeeper who was lodged in two rooms furnished more splendidly than those Anna had occupied. The judge believed Anna and allowed her alimony. It appeared that Fagerberg's frugality had caused the domestic problems. He was channeling income from Nizina and properties owned in Seattle into a venture involving the shipment of cattle to Alaska. As a meat provider, Fagerberg took advantage of Alaska's natural wealth in cold storage facilities, caching his meat in a cave carved into the Kennicott Glacier until needed.[19]

Mining could not commence until Smith and others removed fourteen feet of ice—frozen floodwater that covered the diggings. With dynamite, pick, and drill they cleared the obstruction by June 1 and were joined by other miners who had worked on railroad construction over the winter.

The sixteen-man crew utilized a hydraulic "giant" to tear away the overburden and wash the soil into the sluice box. Cleaning away large rocks was a major part of the work. The weekly cleanup required the pulling of riffles and lining boards from the sluices and the direction of a light head of water to separate the gold from the gravel. Copper nuggets found with the gold were discarded because separate handling of them was uneconomical. Copper and silver were much more plentiful on Dan Creek, where the annual cleanup of copper yielded about a ton of nuggets which were sacked and transported to the rail head at McCarthy.[20]

Although the community of Nizina retained its post office until 1926, most of its trade activity shifted to McCarthy in 1911. As the terminal of the Copper River and Northwestern Railway, McCarthy's advantages as a regional hub were obvious. McCarthy was laid out on John E. Barrett's homestead. Barrett, once holder of Mother Lode and Green Butte copper claims, sold the Mother Lode to Kennecott in 1919. His efforts to develop Green Butte were aborted because of declining copper prices in the 1920s.

❋ "The Feudal Barons" ❋

Mining operators were reputed to be hard-working fellows of no particular romantic distinction, but a federal judge considered two of them akin to greedy medieval aristocrats. One of them, Frank Kernan, who employed Smith at Nizina, was no stranger to litigation. Lawsuits were one hazard of mine ownership, and some of Kernan's were particularly interesting. On one occasion he destroyed a cafe building next to the Vienna Bakery owned by Charles Malander at Nizina. Malander, aggravated by Kernan's removal of a building he thought he had purchased from two women who ran the cafe, wanted damages. But Kernan prevailed because he owned the ground and structure. No one could complain when he decided that the cafe building had to go because it sat over potentially rich bedrock.[21]

As might be expected, there was strife between Kernan and George Esterly, the two dominant operators in the Nizina. Esterly, who managed the claims of John E. Andrus and some of his own, was a mining engineer who had stampeded north in 1897. As pick-and-shovel miners exhausted the gold they recovered with primitive methods and moved along, Esterly acquired their claims for hydraulic operation. From 1907 to 1910 Esterly spent about $250,000 for improvements. Kernan followed the same practice in his section of the diggings, and the two operators cooperated on some ventures. For a time Esterly held an appointment as U.S. deputy marshal while Kernan was the U.S. commissioner, so the major property owners had the advantage of some official authority in dealing with outsiders. Esterly used his authority to have a jail built, specifically—as he told friends—to lock up a claim jumper who challenged his rights on a particular claim.

The two operators benefited through cooperation, such as arranging their outfitting together. But cooperation gave way to bitterness and litigation when the men disagreed about payment of their shares of the shipping costs. A more serious dispute occurred over water rights. When Kernan diverted water from White Creek to his claims, Esterly destroyed his flume. Kernan got an injunction against Esterly's interference, so Esterly retaliated by suing for recovery of Emma Bench claims allegedly jumped by Kernan. Such litigation was no small undertaking for the parties involved or for the court. After years of legal wrangling, a disgusted district judge decided that the claim-jumping suit illustrated feudal barons or, in more modern terminology, financial barons exploiting their domains, relying on the tacit acquiescence of neighboring barons not to invade their territories except in cases of falling out. Plaintiff and defendant had absorbed all individual claim owners and were alone and in conflict. The court decided for Kernan, concluding that Esterly's suit was more retaliatory than substantial.[22]

The water dispute case brought by Kernan against Esterly was decided about the same time as the "feudal baron" claim-jumping case described above and Kernan won. Former miner Tony Dimond was his attorney. Aside from the legal issues involved, litigation sometimes produced documentation on famous characters. In this case testimony established that Charley Anderson, the famed "Lucky Swede," worked a claim at Chititu in 1903 with three other men who had worked for him on his rich Klondike claim.[23]

⁂ Early Days on the Nabesna ⁂

North of the great Wrangell and St. Elias ranges lie two extensive glacier-fed river systems, the Nabesna and Chisana. Jacksina Creek forms the headwaters of the Nabesna, and the Chisana heads directly at the Chisana Glacier. At Northway Junction, the Nabesna and Chisana converge to form the 440-mile-long Tanana River, a major tributary of the Yukon. The Nabesna Valley was not carefully investigated until 1899, when Alfred Brooks and William Peters of the U.S. Geological Survey and Oscar Rohn and A. H. McNeer of the U.S. Army conducted separate expeditions. The explorers had reports of prospectors traveling through earlier, but none had found anything of note. Early prospectors were looking for placer gold; those of the post-Klondike era sought copper; but the region's chief resource proved to be in quartz—and that in limited quantities. Of the routes used by prospectors, Brooks wrote:

In the past the few prospectors who penetrated this region limited their journeys chiefly to the larger waterways. In the open season they followed these in boats, or more often in downstream trips on rafts, and in the winter traversed their frozen surfaces with dog teams. The Indians also use cumbersome rafts for navigating the rivers, which they construct very ingeniously without the use of tools. When they are unprovided with axes, they use drift timber or burn off dead trees, and fasten them together with withes [tough, flexible twigs]. They also construct well-shaped birch-bark canoes, which are decked over in the kayak fashion and are usually only large enough for one or two persons.[24]

Also during their 1899 expedition Brooks and Peters met two prospectors, E. J. Cooper and H. A. Hammond, while examining copper prospects on Kletsan Creek, a tributary of the White River. Cooper and Hammond are credited as the first to have taken pack animals through Cooper Pass on the old Indian trail.[25] The army explorers, Rohn and McNeer, who had perused the Chisana and Nabesna Valleys, entered the region after crossing the Nizina Glacier. The traverse proved treacherous. They spent fifteen days traveling just forty-seven miles to reach the Chisana. Once there, the explorers were uncertain about their location and the relationships of the region's rivers, but they learned more after pushing on to the Nabesna:

During the trip over the glacier the storms which are almost constant on the summit at that time of the year, the difficulties of traversing glacial ice, and snow-blindness absorbed our attention and left us no time to speculate on what drainage we were reaching. When, however, the glacier had been crossed, the latter became the all-absorbing question. After following the stream which headed in the glacier for a distance of 12 or 15 miles in a northeasterly direction, and finding that it led out of the mountains in a direction almost due east, we became convinced that it was the Tanana River, and we decided to make a portage through a gap in the mountains to the west, by which we hoped to reach what we felt sure was a branch of the Tanana, called by the natives Nabesna.[26]

The first quartz gold discovery was made on Jacksina Creek at the headwaters of the Nabesna River in 1899. Because quartz mining required heavy equipment, including a stamp

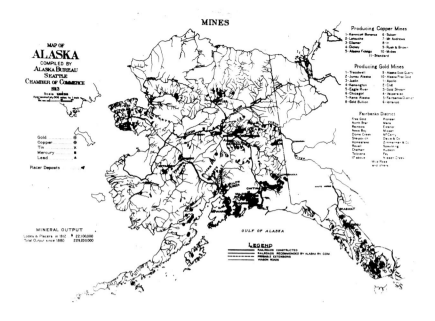

1913 map of mining activity in Alaska. Courtesy of the Museum of History and Industry, Seattle, No. 10312

mill, the strike generated little excitement. During stampedes, quartz might be noted and, if convenient, located, but the prospectors quickly moved on, looking for placed deposits offering an immediate return from their pick-and-shovel efforts. It was not until 1903 that the 1899 discovery was reported by a Valdez newspaper in an interview with K. J. Field:

In 1899 a party of prospectors were camped on the Jacksina and were looking for placer gold. Mr. Field was one of the party and during his prospecting he discovered that a certain slide which came off the mountain contained much fine gold though not sufficient to pay. He concluded that this gold came from a quartz ledge which could be plainly seen above the slide but as in those days quartz in that locality was considered worthless he continued his search for placer.[27]

In 1902 the U.S. Geological Survey again investigated the Nabesna country, looking particularly at quartz finds reported on Monte Cristo Gulch, California Gulch, and Orange Hill and at the head of the Nabesna River east of the Nabesna Glacier. They found only low-grade gold quartz of uncertain economic potential. A small stampede surged briefly in 1902 from Dawson to Beaver Creek near the international border. Beaver and its tributaries were staked far and wide, but the few holes put down did not yield anything very valuable. Rumors of a placer discovery had triggered this stampede, but subsequent prospecting centered on the search for lode deposits, particularly copper. Copper seemed more promising than gold in the Nabesna region, particularly after the discovery of the great Bonanza claim at Kennecott. Optimistic miners reasoned that the north side of the mountains would be as rich as the south side. One prospector told awed folks in Valdez in 1902 that he had discovered a ledge of copper 500 feet long between the Chisana and Nabesna Rivers and could see a million dollars worth of exposed copper.[28] Though exaggerated, this report stimulated prospecting activity in 1902. Benjamin F. Millard of Valdez grubstaked W. A. Dickey, who staked forty-one copper claims on the Nabesna and carried out ore samples for testing. Dickey's prospects did not amount to anything, but he found a fame of sorts later by suggesting the name adopted for Mount McKinley.

Prospecting continued in 1903 and 1904, but most of it was done by Nizina miners who were en route to the gold strike at Fairbanks. The Nizina men crossed the Skolai Pass to White River, thence to the head of the Nabesna or Chisana and down the Tanana to Fairbanks. K. J. Field, who had located gold quartz on Jacksina Creek in 1899, returned in 1903 with other miners to stake gold and copper claims. Field and Paul Paulson formed the Royal Development Company (originally the Royal Gold Mining Company) in 1905 for development of twenty-eight Jacksina Creek gold claims.

Another interested prospector was Henry Bratnober, an Englishman considered a quartz mining expert who first saw the country in 1898 on an expedition with Jack Dalton. Bratnober and Dalton took a mule pack train into the Upper Tanana in 1903 looking for copper prospects. On reaching Valdez, Bratnober told newsmen that he found nothing exciting and saw hundreds of starving prospectors at the head of the Tanana. Such disparaging remarks were not considered in good form. "This pot-bellied old reprobate," declared the *Valdez News*, "has some object in spreading these slanderous reports aside from the mere pleasure which some people take in lying."[29]

The *News* might have been right because Bratnober visited Jacksina Creek the next season. Although he refused to invest in the Field claims, he returned again in 1905 with a small steamboat. The 120-foot *Ella*, a gas-powered sternwheeler launched at Whitehorse, had trouble reaching the Nabesna on the Tanana waters, but finally succeeded in late July. Bratnober returned to Fairbanks, then dispatched *Ella* with men and an outfit for wintering on the Nabesna. On leaving the country this time, Bratnober talked like a booster; his expedition would open up "a good district." He did hedge somewhat on his expectations by insisting that a railroad was needed. He hoped that the Copper River and Northwestern Railway would be extended to the Yukon.[30] Bratnober did not persist in developing properties in the region. The Royal Development Company, unlike Bratnober, did work its claim.
In 1907 a three-stamp mill was brought in to process sixty tons of ore, but the yield was disappointing—a mere $12 in gold per ton of ore—so the company ceased operations.

Prospecting in both the Nabesna and Nizina districts dropped sharply when men from these districts stampeded to Fairbanks from 1903 to 1905. The Chisana strike in 1913 revived interest in the Nabesna, which developed because miners passed through the Nabesna District as they dashed toward Fairbanks. Bratnober and others knew that development of any kind in the Nabesna would require an effective transportation network, and that meant railroads: "It is no use to build wagon roads for what would you do with them when built." Roads would not get ore to the coast cheaply enough. Bratnober hoped for an extension of the Copper River and Northwestern Railway to the Nabesna and the Yukon.[31]

The Alaska Syndicate did not extend the railroad, however, nor did the government provide the rail service Nabesna miners wanted. In the end the district proved unproductive, so a railroad would not have been justified. The U.S. Geological Survey continued its mineral investigation in 1908, but mining activity was minimal. The Royal Development Company had shut down its stamp mill after processing only six tons of ore, and few hot prospects remained.

✳ Nabesna: Carl Whitham's Mine ✳

The good fortune of Carl Whitham gave pleasure to veteran Alaska miners. He had been one of the party led by K. J. Field that discovered a valuable gold lode on Jacksina Creek in 1899, the property worked by the Royal Development Company from 1905 until its shutdown in 1908. After mining at Chisana, Whitham started prospecting in the Nabesna in 1922. His investigations of the abandoned quartz mine convinced him that the Royal Development Company had given up too soon; he restaked the claims in 1924. In 1925 an "accident" of the kind much favored in mining lore excited Whitham. A bear trying to dig a ground squirrel from a moss-covered outcrop exposed a promising vein. Whitham named it the Bear Vein, noting that it was only a thousand feet from the old Royal Development Company diggings. For the next three years Whitham and three helpers trenched the outcropping and sank a thirty-foot shaft to recover ore for testing, which confirmed the lode's value at various levels. In 1929 Whitham formed the Nabesna Mining Corporation and took in enough capital to build an aerial tramway from the mine to the mill site and to install a thirty-five-ton-per-day mill.

Getting equipment to the mine site proved difficult. Much of it was freighted in during the winter of 1930–1931 on sleds pulled by a thirty-horsepower tractor from Chitina. Whitham even had his own sawmill to cut local timber for his mill buildings. The mill was operational in July 1931, and twenty-two men were hired, living in tents on the property during the work season. In 1932 Whitham had a twenty-five man crew. Gross production yielded $175,000 in gold during those two years.

Whitham's persistence paid off. He became something of a local folk hero. Other miners admired the man who managed to retain control of his properties and develop them. With some pride Whitham wrote to President Franklin Roosevelt in August 1933, applauding the president's support of higher gold prices and the construction of mining roads. "There was not even a blazed trail connecting the valley of the Nabesna with the great Richardson Highway," Whitham told Roosevelt, "and in order to get supplies in here it was necessary to wait for winter snow and bring in necessities with dog team." Now, thanks to government road funding, he would provide the country with new gold. Whitham praised the work of the Alaska Road Commission, then working on a winter road into the Nabesna that he felt certain would lead to other developments.[32]

The winter road meant ore could be shipped overland to Cordova year-round. Before the Nabesna Road, pack horses carried the ore to Nabesna Bar six miles away. From there bush pilots Harold Gillam and Bob Reeve flew the ore 120 miles to Copper Center. From Copper Center it went by truck fifty miles to Chitina, then by rail to Cordova, and on to the Tacoma smelter by ship. To establish a year-round operation, Whitham needed a pumping plant, a 2,600-foot pipeline to a spring, and a heating plant capable of serving his buildings. The road to the mine was completed in the autumn of 1933, allowing trucks to transport the ore to the railroad at Chitina during the winter or directly to Valdez in summer. In 1934 Whitham started working through the winter, and annual production accelerated. From 1931 through 1937 he shipped ore valued at $965,000 to the Tacoma smelter. By 1940 the mine had shipped 73,000 tons of ore valued at $1,869,396. Since investors put up only $175,280, the return was considered favorable, indeed.[33] By 1939 the veins were virtually worked out, and no new ore deposits had been discovered. War-time restrictions closed down the operations until 1945, when Whitham tried to get started again but his health failed. Whitham's death in 1947 led to permanent closure of operations.

⁎ The Bremner River ⁎

The Bremner River region lies in the Chugach Range about eighty miles south of McCarthy and includes the area south of the Chitina River to the Bremner River and west from the Chakina River. In 1902 prospectors rushed to Golconda Creek, a tributary of the North Fork of the Bremner River. Access to the remote area was not easy. Originally, prospectors traveled from Valdez via Marshall Pass, crossed the Copper River, thence to the Bremner drainage. Miners found some gold, but most left after hearing news of gold discovery on the Nizina. The few who remained produced modest quantities of gold until 1916. With completion of the Copper River and Northwestern Railway in 1911, supplying camp became somewhat easier. Miners traveled over winter trails from McCarthy to the mouth of the Nizina River, then up the Chitina and Chakina Rivers to Monahan Creek and on to the several mines. The trails had been improved by individual miners even before the railroad's completion, and in 1914 the Alaska Road Commission worked on a trail from McCarthy to Golconda Creek.

The area's remoteness discouraged development of lode deposits until the government raised the price of gold from $20 to $35 per ounce in 1933. The Bremner Mining Company quickly built a mill and tram and hauled ore to the railroad with Caterpillar tractors. The company also built an airstrip so planes could support the mine. Another lode mine, the Yellow Band, was developed by Asa Baldwin in the 1930s. Baldwin, a mining engineer, had been a consultant to the Kennecott Copper Company, a surveyor for the U.S. Coast and Geodetic Survey, and helped survey the international boundary with Canada from 1910 to 1913. But it was not to last. All the lode mines shut down during World War II and never reopened.

✳ Summary ✳

Mineral development within the Wrangell-St. Elias region did not follow the pattern set in the Klondike or such other Alaska districts as the Tanana Valley or Nome. The stampede of some four to five thousand adventurers in 1898 proved unfortunate for most of them as they were seeking a route to the Klondike to bypass the Yukon River route and Chilkoot-White Pass options from Dyea and Skagway. Most of the stampeders had heard rumors of copper wealth in the region, and some who journeyed there decided to stay on and prospect in the Wrangell-St. Elias region rather than join the crowd at Dawson. No one knows how many stampeders got to the Klondike from Valdez, but it was not many. Most stampeders gave up and returned home, some remained in the Valdez region, and a few headed for the Copper River country. The big bonanza proved to be in copper, and it fell first into the hands of a few individuals and then to a large corporation. The major gold strike at Chisana was not of the duration or magnitude that prospectors had hoped. Some prospectors succeeded in the Nizina where pockets of gold could be efficiently mined.

Activity by separate geographic section of the Wrangell-St. Elias region may be easier to describe. Miners and investors who expected a great strike in the northern part of the Wrangell-St. Elias ranges were disappointed. Gold production continued in the south for decades, but the output was always modest compared to other major mineral districts in Alaska. Copper was the great wealth of the southern range, and its exploitation comprises one of the grand stories of industrial development in Alaska's history.

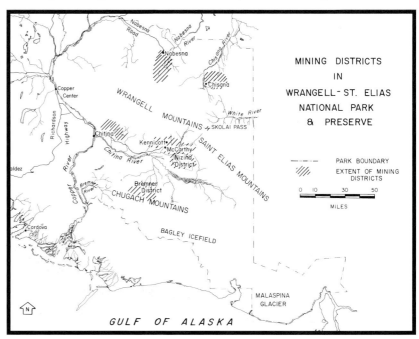

Mining Districts in Wrangell-St.Elias National Park and Preserve

75

*Men riding an ore tram. Courtesy of the
McCarthy-Kennicott Historical Museum,
No. B7-8.*

Chapter

❋ ❋ ❋

The Wonder of Kennecott

❋ Discovery ❋

Kennecott Copper Company (also known as the Alaska Syndicate) dominated mining in the Wrangell-St. Elias region, but its influence transcended copper. Kennecott's role in Alaska's political history stirred great controversy from 1905 through 1938. A party formed in 1898 by R. F. McClellan located several major copper deposits in the region. After failing to find anything worthwhile along the Copper River tributaries that first year, the Minnesota men reorganized for another expedition. In late August 1899 E. A. Gates, acting for the McClellan party, and James McCarthy and Arthur H. McNeer, representing other parties, located the Nikolai group of copper deposits on the right limit of the Nizina, a branch of the Chitina Fork of the Copper River about 180 miles east of Valdez. Subsequently, the Chittyna Exploration Company organized more exploration, which in 1900 culminated in discovery of the Bonanza deposit some twenty miles from the Nikolai mines.

Controversy erupted over the Bonanza discovery because it was not clear whether prospectors Jack Smith, Clarence Warner, and others were acting for the Chittyna Exploration Company or other individuals who eventually formed the Copper River Mining Company. Litigation started in 1902. A year later Judge James Wickersham ruled in favor of McClellan and his partners of the Chittyna Exploration Company, clearing the way for development.[1]

From 1900 to 1902 Stephen Birch, a bright, determined young man, purchased the fabulously rich Bonanza copper claims with backing from capitalist H. O. Havemeyer. He saw the advantage of merging rivals and in 1905 formed the Alaska Syndicate. Syndicate parties included banking houses of the Guggenheim brothers and J. P. Morgan, but because of their mining experience, the Guggenheims directed development of several mines located on tributaries of the Copper River. Reorganized as the Kennicott Mines Company in 1908, the enterprise emerged in 1915 as the Kennecott Copper Corporation with Birch as president. The spelling of the new company's name was an unfortunate error that still confuses people today.

In August 1900 Smith and Warner, the Bonanza discoverers, had been searching for the source of the copper float reported by Oscar Rohn of the U.S. Army in 1899. Rohn found rich pieces of chalcocite ore in the glacial moraine on the Kennicott, so the prospectors moved upriver to National Creek near Kennicott Glacier, where they staked claims. Every great mineral discovery spawns its legend, and the Bonanza was no exception. According to their stories, Smith and Warner had stopped for lunch when they spotted a large green spot on a mountain across the gulch from them. "A good place for sheep," observed Warner. "Don't look like grass to me," said Smith. They argued over whether it made sense to climb up for a look. The conflict evaporated when they found of piece of rich-looking chalcocite on National Creek. They scrambled up to the "green field," which revealed a sensational discovery.[2] After cursory examination of the lode, near the Kennicott Glacier, they returned to Nikolai to alert the other nine members of their Chitina Mining and Exploration Company.

Kennecott's mill and townsite, circa 1911. Courtesy of the Rasmuson Library Archives, University of Alaska Fairbanks; Schrock Album, 84-80-101N.

Soon after, Arthur Spencer of the U.S. Geological Survey made an independent discovery. The claims located extended a mile in length along the limestone-greenstone contact at 6,000 feet elevation. The mass was in the limestone from the contact to a height of 150 feet along the slope of the hillside at two to seven-foot widths. Spencer confirmed that "the ore was practically pure chalcocite with solid masses exposed from two to four feet across, fifteen or more feet in length and their depth not apparent." A sample showed 70 percent copper, a good measure of silver, and a trace of gold.[3]

✳ Railroad Development ✳

From the outset those interested in developing the rich mines pushed for a railroad from the site of the deposit to the coast. The story of the Copper River and Northwestern Railway, the railroad constructed to serve the mines, will be told in Chapter 11. Builders of the 120-mile line faced severe natural obstacles during construction from 1907 to 1911. Though costly by any measure, the railroad proved its value to the extractors.

✳ Evaluating Copper Ore ✳

According to legend, the visible signs of the copper lodes developed at Kennecott had been obvious for years before mining. Determining the lode's value, however, was not easy. W. E. Dunkle, a mining engineer employed by Kennecott in the earlier years, struggled to reach realistic estimates. Company experts later made a microscopic study of the Kennecott chalcocite—the main ore body—which resulted in inaccurate assessment of its value. Their investigation "seemed to show that the copper glance was secondary after bornite." By 1912 the only mining accomplished on the Bonanza fissure and the rich cliff outcrop ore body of glance pinched out at three hundred feet. Little work had been done on the parallel Jumbo fissure, and nothing on the surface indicated the enormous ore bodies yet to be found there. Kennecott's management endorsed the conservative estimate over Dunkle's. The company concluded that the copper was secondary. Deeply in the red because of railroad construction costs and only beginning to ship ore, Kennecott passed up the chance to buy the Mother Lode Mine at a modest price. Eventually, Dunkle's prognosis proved correct, and Kennecott paid dearly for a joint mining agreement with Mother Lode owners.[4]

＊ Kennecott Production ＊

Pack horses and sleds had transported equipment for a 400-ton mill, the tramway, the power plant, and other structures from Valdez long before completion of the railroad. The syndicate's big investment in the railroad began to pay off immediately after completion in 1911. Mining and milling had proceeded apace, and the loading dock at the mill was full of ore. The first mining tunnels were driven into the Bonanza and Jumbo Mines, and each had its own aerial tramway. To reach the main adit [a level entrance into a mine] level of the Bonanza Mine at 5,600 feet, workers either hiked a four-mile trail or rode the bucket tramway. The Jumbo tramway, extending 16,000 feet, began operation in 1913. Though riding the aerial tramway could be dangerous, miners much preferred it to walking.

High prices during World War I spurred production, and the mines and mill operated around the clock. Each tramway carried roughly 400 tons of ore every twenty-four hours. The larger percentage of ore was low grade, averaging 7.5 percent copper, but the Jumbo Mine's output of 70 percent copper was almost half of its yield. In 1916 William Douglass compared Kennecott's production with the famed Anaconda Mine of Butte, Montana. Thirty shafts down to 4,000 feet at Butte moved ore out of the ground with fast, modern hoists. Anaconda employed 15,000 men to produce thirty million pounds of copper each month. By contrast Kennecott's two small mines operated:

. . . through single compartment incline shafts. Its hoisting equipment was of modest scale and low-powered. The total payroll of mines, mill, and surface staff was only 550 persons, yet Kennecott produced 10,000,000 pounds monthly—one-third of Anaconda's output.

Kennecott reserves had fallen. Bonanza was fading, but the Jumbo ore was wonderfully rich "solid chalcocite for a stope [the excavation needed to reach the ore from the mine shaft] length of 350 feet, with a width of 40 feet and a height of 40 feet." That block produced 70,000 tons of 70 percent ore, which also included twenty ounces of silver per ton.[5]

Maintaining year-round operation of the railroad, mine, and mill taxed abilities to cope with the challenge. Heavy snows sometimes blocked trains despite use of the largest rotary snowplows made. Heavy storms sometimes hindered mill-mine operation, as in spring 1919 when a slide wiped out telephone lines, demolished tramway towers, and closed the trails, cutting off communication between the mines and the mill. Slides at the Mother Lode threatened bunkhouses and forced miners to live in mine tunnels for several days. Passageways from the Mother Lode to the Bonanza and Jumbo mines facilitated movement of miners no matter what the conditions.[6]

In 1919 the company formed the Mother Lode Coalition Mines to extract and mill valuable ore between McCarthy Creek and Kennicott Glacier. The Bonanza tramway conveyed ore from the Mother Lode to the mill. Some high-grade ore left for the coast unprocessed but most passed through the mill for concentration. Further processing of mill tailings followed in the leaching plant, which treated six hundred tons per day.

The Erie was the fourth mine of the Kennecott group. Perched in cliffs high above the Kennicott Glacier four miles north of the mill, it connected with the Jumbo by a 12,000-foot crosscut. Erie's production did not compare with volumes at the other mines but it helped maintain production after Jumbo reserves dwindled. Also, its development helped justify expansion of the tramway and mill in 1920. Tramway capacity rose to 600 tons and mill capacity increased to 1,200 tons per day.

Production statistics from 1901 to 1940 summarize the history of the industry. The following production statistics include output of all Alaska copper mines. Kennecott's mines and those of Prince William Sound, however, contributed 96 percent of the total production, amounting to 214,000,000 pounds from 1904 to 1930.

Table 2
Copper Produced by Alaska Mines, 1901–1920

YEAR	POUNDS	VALUE	YEAR	POUNDS	VALUE
1901	250,000	$ 40,000	1921	57,110,597	$ 7,354,496
1902	360,000	41,400	1922	77,967,189	10,525,655
1903	1,200,000	156,000	1923	85,920,645	12,630,335
1904	2,043,586	275,676	1924	74,074,207	9,703,721
1905	4,805,236	749,617	1925	73,855,298	10,361,336
1906	5,871,811	1,133,260	1926	67,778,000	9,489,000
1907	6,308,786	1,261,757	1927	55,343,000	7,250,000
1908	4,585,362	605,267	1928	41,421,000	5,965,000
1909	4,124,705	536,211	1929	40,510,000	7,130,000
1910	4,241,689	538,695	1930	32,561,000	4,244,600
1911	27,267,878	3,408,485	1931	22,614,000	1,877,000
1912	29,230,491	4,823,031	1932	8,738,500	550,500
1913	21,659,958	3,357,293	1933	29,000	1,900
1914	21,450,628	2,852,934	1934	121,000	9,700
1915	86,509,312	15,139,129	1935	15,056,000	1,249,700
1916	119,654,839	29,484,291	1936	39,267,000	3,720,000
1917	88,793,400	24,240,598	1937	36,007,000	4,741,000
1918	69,224,951	17,098,563	1938	29,760,000	2,976,000
1919	47,220,771	8,783,063	1939	278,500	30,000
1920	70,435,363	12,960,106	1940	122,369	13,800
TOTAL	**1,373,764,701 Pounds**				**$227,419,199**

The Kennecott Copper Corporation's Bonanza Mine. Courtesy of the Rasmuson Library Archives, University of Alaska Fairbanks; McKay Collection, 64-75-7.

❊ Peak and Decline ❊

Historian Melody Webb Grauman described 1923 as the "pivotal year" for Kennecott—the year that its slow decline truly commenced. Production rebounded in the early 1920s as the post-World War I slump caused by overproduction and low prices finally ended. The high level could not be maintained, however. Production fell sharply between 1924 and 1929 as high-grade ore sources were depleted. The Bonanza and Jumbo Mines steadily declined after 1918 but the Mother Lode continued to produce, and another ore body was discovered on the Jumbo-Erie crosscut.[7]

Superintendent William C. Douglass pursued a higher yield by aggressively mining the Glacier Mine and installing new technology. Technological innovations included construction of an ammonia leaching plant in 1922–1923. Developed at Kennecott by E. Tappan Stannard in 1915, the process involved using chemicals to dissolve the mineral from low-grade ore, then precipitating it into a concentrate. The leaching process was completed in flotation tanks "when oil or grease was used to separate, through a bubbling action, the mineral from its host rock."[8] Litigation between the process patent holder and other western mining companies had delayed construction of Kennecott's leaching plant. The process worked well there, allowing a recovery rate of 96 percent, but the scarcity of water over the winter restricted its use.[9]

A detailed statistical breakdown for the company operation exists for the year 1924. when 550 men were employed. Of the 321 working in the mines, 146 were in the Mother Lode. Highest wages ($5.50 to $5.75 per day) went to electricians and machinists. Skilled mill men earned up to $5.50, miners got $5.25, and laborers got $4.25.[10]

Douglass, like many other superintendents, would not tolerate union activity at the mines. All new employees were required to swear that they were not union members and to

The Kennecott Copper Corporation's Jumbo Mine. Courtesy of the Alaska State Library, Barquist Collection, PCA-164-13.

promise that they would not join a union while employed by Kennecott. A 1923 employee contract stipulated $4.60 daily wage, less board of $1.45 daily and eight cents hospital dues—not bad for the 1920s. Employees hired in Seattle were advanced the $37 charged for the voyage to Cordova, which could be gradually repaid from wages. Even the train ride on the syndicate's railroad was only conditionally free. The $23.40 fare was advanced and deducted from wages until completion of six months satisfactory employment. Once initial deductions were repaid, no others were taken.[11] The company took advantage of its isolated location to protect against contagious diseases. All new employees spent several days at a camp outside town to reduce the risk of importing disease.

In 1923 the 570 employees (249 in the mill and 321 in the mines) earned a monthly total of $86,337. It cost 8.23 cents a pound to process the ore for copper (aside from the gain from the silver extracted from the ore), and reserves were dwindling. High-grade ore originally had assayed at 75 percent but had dropped to 52 percent in the Bonanza-Jumbo and 60 percent in the Mother Lode. Copper prices averaged fourteen cents a pound from 1924 to 1928 and rose to twenty-four cents in 1929, but Kennecott's limited reserves did not enable the company to take full advantage of the boom.

⁂ Life at Kennecott ⁂

The company town of Kennecott lies four miles from McCarthy at an elevation of 2,200 feet beside the Kennicott Glacier. The different spelling of the glacier/river and town/ company is an irritating memorial to careless spelling (modern maps show "Kennicott" as the townsite name; on earlier maps it was spelled "Kennecott"). Kennicott was the name given to the glacier and the river by U.S. Geological Survey geologist Oscar Rohn as a tribute to Robert Kennicott, leader of the scientific corps of the Western Union Telegraph

Expedition of 1865–1867. At its peak in 1920 Kennecott had a population of 500, although most of the miners lived in buildings near the mines high above the town and mill.

Documentation on the society of Kennecott is plentiful, including memoirs of school days in the 1920s by Supt. William Douglass' son. Students from the twenty-odd families of the community attended a two-room school through the eighth grade. They were sent to Cordova or Outside for secondary education. The two teachers worked students hard, although a winter carnival in March provided some relief. Ice skating and hockey were the chief school recreations. The teachers, like the town's two nurses, were usually young, single women "who lived in the staff house—and were almost always married during that year, requiring replacements, because there were lots of single men."[12]

Residents enjoyed many activities and some amenities year-round. Movies were shown on Wednesday and Sunday nights in the town hall. New Year's Eve and other special occasions would bring out the musicians, and people would dance. In summer baseball was popular, as was fishing. Summer fun also included the Fourth of July celebration, the biggest festival of the year, which was held in McCarthy. Almost everyone hunted in the fall. Religious services were conducted in the schoolhouse whenever a priest or minister appeared from Cordova. Reading was popular. A lending library supplied the latest fiction and many residents subscribed to magazines which they usually passed on to others. Most shopping was accomplished by thumbing through the popular mail-order catalogues of the day. Orders, supplies, and imported foodstuffs arrived by train. A few vegetable gardens and the company's dairy supplied some fresh produce, butter, and milk.

Life in the bunkhouses was more restricted than for families living in the small company houses, but it was not unpleasant. Mining engineer Ralph McKay recalled the long winter evenings in the bunkhouse at the Bonanza Mine in the 1920s as serene. Though the men were of mixed nationalities, "they weren't restless and arguments were few. Some played poker while others were busy at blackjack." They pored over catalogues and newspapers and listened to an old hand-crank phonograph. Radio signals could not be heard at Kennecott.[13]

Emil Goulet, who also wrote of his experiences, walked most of the way from Cordova to Kennecott in winter of 1930–1931 because heavy snow blocked the railroad tracks. He got a job at the Jumbo Mine, which was four miles and 4,000 feet above the mill at Kennecott. Before taking the forty-five-minute ride by tramway, he had to waive any claim against the company for accidents. The two Jumbo bunkhouses housed eighty men each in two- to four-man rooms. A small gym and pool table were leading recreational features. Goulet liked his fellow workers but quit when company economy measures dictated a 10 percent wage cut.[14]

Fred Hoff went to work as an assayer in 1935. He was one of the lucky bachelors there to find a bride—a company nurse. The couple moved from staff housing to an apartment above the company store. Life was not too bad, but job security was a worry during the depression. The Hoffs hoped to save money, but food costs were high. Ice, however, was free from the nearby glacier.[15]

Opinions about the company and its management differed. Some miners liked working at Kennecott because, unlike most jobs, it provided work for the full year. Others used their wages to stake their own prospecting or mining. The company provided rudimentary medical care, recreation, and education for the town's children, but all its policies stemmed from self-interest, not benevolence. It met the standards of the day and achieved its corporate goals.

* Accidents *

Accidents related to Kennecott's hazardous enterprise occurred with alarming frequency. Some were acts of nature, like avalanches and landslides, but more common were accidents in the mines, the mill, and on the tramway. Injured workers often sued Kennecott. The company usually fought back and was not known for its generosity. When Ernest VandeVord, a line repairman, was thrown from the moving bucket line running from mine to mill, he fell forty feet to jagged rocks below. He ended up with a permanently stiff wrist and back. Company lawyers argued that workers assumed all risks in riding the buckets. VandeVord's attorney argued that a defect on the line caused the accident. Jurors awarded the twenty-five-year-old machinist (who had earned $90 a month) $750 rather than the $20,000 he asked. The company tried unsuccessfully to have the award set aside. When VandeVord asked his foreman about wages, he was told:

There is a new rule existing here. When a man gets hurt, his time stops and as soon as he gets out of the hospital, he has to pay board. In your case Mr. Emery will see you—and make some kind of settlement.[16]

Cases generally were litigated in Cordova, where the third district court, based in Valdez, periodically convened. Cordova jurors usually favored the company in disputes with employees. Occasionally an employee requested a change of venue, as did Daniel S. Reeder, who was injured in a railroad tunnel cave-in in 1913. The company successfully resisted the change, arguing that the absence of other employees needed as witnesses would hamper operations.[17] James Heney, another railroad worker injured in a tunnel cave-in as he dug out a previous one, asked $25,000 for the permanent crippling of his hip when timbers crushed him. His award was only $2,125.[18] In another settlement a jury drawn from Seward and Valdez was more generous in compensating the estate of E. A. Reed, railroad engineer. Reed died when his locomotive fell through a bridge that had been partially burned but not repaired. The award was $20,000.[19]

The railroad construction boom provided the company with more options in settling litigation. J. E. Dyer, operator of a pile driver, permanently crippled his leg in a construction train accident. He sued for damages, then desisted when the company gave him a small settlement and permitted him to run an unlicensed saloon and gambling place at the mouth of the Tiekel River. Unfortunately, Dyer succumbed to temptation. "He spent all his money from both sources," his lawyer said, "as rapidly as he could in drunkenness and riotous living." When his money was gone Dyer pleased everyone by "disappearing from Alaska," thus abating "a public nuisance."[20]

* Closing Down *

The Great Depression foreshadowed the end for Kennecott. Copper prices fell to five cents a pound in 1931. The company dropped its expensive leaching process and still lost $2 million that year. Further disaster occurred when a railroad bridge washed out in October 1932, causing the company to close the mines in 1933–1934. Reporting on Alaska's mineral industry in 1933, Philip S. Smith of the U.S. Geological Survey spelled out the obvious:

It must be remembered that the mines near Kennecott, which have contributed perhaps 90 percent of the Alaska copper, have been mining a unique deposit, not comparable with any other known deposit in the world, so that inevitably their mineral wealth is being depleted and there is no justification for expecting that their loss will be offset by new discoveries of equally marvelous lodes.[21]

Ore tram originating at the Bonanza Mine. Courtesy of the McCarthy-Kennicott Historical Museum, No. B7-17.

Kennecott's 1938 annual report stated: "The Alaska property was operated until the latter part of October when all ore of commercial value was exhausted and the property closed down. Equipment having any net salvage value was removed and shipped out before abandonment of railroad properties." The report went on to explain: "Production from this property has averaged only 525 tons copper per month since 1928 and therefore cessation of these operations will not affect earnings as this tonnage can easily be made up from other properties [outside of Alaska]."[22]

Overall, Kennecott mined a total of 4,626,000 tons of ore, averaging 13 percent copper. Smelting this ore produced 591,535 tons of copper and 9,000,000 ounces of silver. According to William Douglass, the company netted $100 million profit on the $200 to $300 million in ore sales. Among the great copper mines of the world, Kennecott ranked eleventh, but no other surpassed or equaled the high mineral content of its ore.[23] Kennecott's influence on Alaska's development cannot be measured by production statistics. Its importance in the territory's economy cannot be exaggerated. Kennecott's Alaska operation, which had been launched for placer gold extraction in several regions, was declining. Its large investments in the Wrangell-St. Elias region heralded a new era of corporate expansion and provided a much needed payroll for many years.

✳ The Kotsina-Kuskulana District ✳

The Kotsina-Kuskulana district lies in the west end of Chitina Valley on the southwest slope of the Wrangell Mountains. Though small in area, sixteen by twelve-and-a-half miles, it was considered for many years to be rich in potential for copper and possibly gold and silver as well. The region may be the best example in Alaska of disappointment

Men building a cable tower. Courtesy of the McCarthy-Kennicott Historical Museum, No. B3-21A.

following long-proclaimed expectations of wealth. Focus remained on the region's potential for so long because of its proximity to the Kennecott mines about twenty-five miles away and the resemblance of its mineral formations to those of the fabulously rich Kennecott group.

Government investigation of the district began with Oscar Rohn in 1899, followed by U.S. Geological Survey in 1900, 1902, 1907, 1912, 1916, 1919, and occasionally thereafter. The region's high mountains, separated by narrow valleys, made exploration difficult, hazardous, and expensive. The valley floors of the Kotsina and Kuskulana drop to levels of 2,000 to 2,500 feet and surrounding peaks rise from 5,000 to 7,395 feet. Most of the valleys which are tributary to the Kotsina and Kuskulana are hanging valleys, so-called because their mouths are above the level of the main valley floors and can be entered only after a steep climb of several hundred or a thousand feet.

Even after construction of the Copper River and Northwestern Railway, access to the district remained problematical. Prospectors still sledded in their provisions during winter. Mail and small items could be brought in from Strelna over summer trails via Rock and Strelna Creeks or by Roaring and Nugget Creeks. Miners wanted a wagon road down the Kotsina River to Chitina or some other point on the railroad but did not get it. Most of the claims still active in 1922, when Fred H. Moffit and J. B. Mertie Jr. of the U.S. Geological Survey investigated the district, bordered tributaries some distance from the Kotsina. Among these were the Cave, Peacock, Mountain Sheep, and Blue Bird claims on Copper Creek. Others on Amy, Rock, Lime, Roaring, and Peacock Creeks, the Sunrise Creek group, and the Silver Star group (considered valuable for silver rather than copper) were owned by Neil and Thomas Finnesand. Among the Kotsina River claims those on Elliott Creek, discussed later in this chapter, were "more widely known than any other copper-bearing locality in Chitina alley except Kennecott." Here, as elsewhere, miners had dug tunnels—some exceeding a thousand feet—searching for valuable copper ore.[24]

✳ North Midas Mine and Others ✳

In 1916 the North Midas Copper Company staked prospects on Berg Creek, a tributary of the Kuskulana River twelve miles from Strelna. Earlier claims here had expired for want of recent assessment work. Midas went to work on tunnels and soon was mining ore from two levels reached by separate adits. Midas shipped out a carload of gold ore in winter 1918 and that summer installed a mill, crusher, and cyanide plant. A Roebling cable tram 4,600 feet long, capable of transporting five tons an hour, connected the mine to the mill. Production in 1919 was only forty ounces of gold and 513 ounces of silver. The mill shut down in 1925.

Geneva Pacific Corporation became interested in the North Midas and other copper claims in the 1970s. These other claims included the Nelson Mine, one that Kennecott tried to develop in the 1930s, and the Binocular Prospect developed by pioneer prospector Martin Radovan. Radovan came to Alaska to work on the Copper River and Northwestern Railway and later mined placers on Dan Creek and a lode on Glacier Creek. His greatest feat was in staking a group of claims on Binocular Prospect near Glacier Creek. The existence of a large copper stain high on the face of a steep-walled recess in the mountains had intrigued prospectors for years. No one had been able to reach the stain, but many scanned it with binoculars—hence the name.

After several unsuccessful attempts had been made to reach the remote face, Kennecott Copper Corporation tried a new approach in 1929. The company brought in several expert mountain climbers to reach the outcrop, but at the end of summer they called it quits without succeeding. Meanwhile, Radovan climbed to a gulch just north of Binocular Prospect and put in a hazardous week cutting steps hundreds of feet along the face of the cliff until he reached a point two hundred feet below the Binocular stain. From this point he scaled the wall, using ropes and steel spikes driven into rock crevices. Radovan staked claims and did some work before giving up on the difficult site.

Geneva Pacific purchased the claims from Radovan before he died in 1975 at age ninety-two. The company hired a mountain climber to help workmen reach the site to build a helicopter landing pad, making further investigation easier. The prospect did not prove to hold the mineral riches that Radovan and the company had hoped. Title to the claims was donated to the National Park Service in 1985. The 250-acre donation included eighteen mining claims, six mill sites, and a number of buildings.[25]

Ore train and workers at a landing chute, deep within the Bonanza Mine. Courtesy of the McCarthy-Kennicott Historical Museum, No. B8-14A.

Ore tram and dog team near Bonanza Ridge. Courtesy of the McCarthy-Kennicott Historical Museum, No. 000366.

❋ Hubbard-Elliott ❋

Philip S. Smith of the U.S. Geological Survey correctly predicted in 1933 that no other rich copper lodes would be found in Alaska. Rumors have circulated for half a century that the syndicate simply switched to more accessible prospects outside Alaska, that plentiful copper still existed in the region. As recently as 1964 Charles G. Hubbard, then in his nineties, told a historian that the long-time head of Kennecott, Stephen Birch, was ruthless and unscrupulous and refused to develop claims Hubbard offered for sale. The record of the Hubbard-Elliott holdings, however, suggests that both Hubbard and his partner, Henry Elliott, profited from their copper claims. The prospectors had entered the Copper River country in 1897 but did not discover significant copper until 1901. They located on Elliott Creek, a Kotsina tributary, and found more prospects from 1902 to 1904. They expected to reap a fortune.

The Hubbard-Elliott Company attracted national attention. Publicity often helped miners find investors, and the partners were pleased by a full-page spread in the *Chicago Record-Herald*, including pictures and full endorsement of their estimates of potential.

"Fabulous Wealth Strike . . . Copper claims covering four miles of territory . . . the ore in sight, at present market prices, is $112,000,000, but it may reach a billion dollars or even more," headlined the story. The reporter described how Hubbard and Elliott crossed the Valdez Glacier in '97, suffered through the winter in a scurvy-ridden camp, and spent two fruitless years searching for gold before they stumbled on a mountain of "boronite [sic], black oxide, glance, gray and native copper . . . the richest large body of ore yet discovered." The partners confessed that marketing their ore, which would "run 50 to 70 percent copper" constituted "a cloud to this dazzling prospect of wealth: there are no means of transporting the ore to the coast for shipment to the mills." Talk of a railroad was in the air, the story said, and perhaps a line would be built within two years. Until then, the two miners would "work their claims and get ready for the hoped-for railroad."[26]

The partners asserted that "experts" had confirmed their high estimates of Elliott Creek ores, and over the years there were many "experts." One engineer traveled from Cedar

Rapids, Iowa, to Seattle and Valdez in 1904. He and a packhorse outfit left Valdez on July 27, following "the new railroad right of way," then the government trail through the "Lowe River Canyon [Keystone Canyon]," on a trail "narrowed down to only a few inches along the side of the mountain . . . on our left was a wall hundreds of feet, on our right, sheer precipices hundreds of feet." Out of Camp Wortman the trail deteriorated even more with mud and snowdrifts. One horse slid down two hundred feet on its side. At Beaver Dam Roadhouse, "run by two old maids from Boston," the travelers refreshed themselves, then pushed on to Ernestine on 30 July and Tonsina the next day. He made the twenty-five miles to the Copper River on 1 August, crossing on Doc Billum's ferry. He finally reached Elliott Creek four days later to enjoy bunks in the Hubbard-Elliott cabin and "first class grub."

Next morning, the engineer visited the Albert Johnson, Guthrie, Marie Antoinette, and Elizabeth claims. The diamond drill on the Elizabeth revealed "enough ore in sight to keep a railroad busy and of the finest quality." Another "expert" also showed up to confirm "the finest proposition he ever expected to see." The visiting engineer gathered samples from several mines, then relaxed to hunt, fish, and read when the weather was bad. Later in August, Stephen Birch appeared, looked at the ore samples, "and said they looked good." The cut on the Elizabeth had reached twenty-five feet. Early in September the engineer from Iowa started out to report to his employers—either Henry Champlin of Chicago or his uncle.[27]

In July 1907 Hubbard and Elliott were still boasting of their mines. Readers of the *Alaska Monthly Magazine* learned that they owned "the greatest and richest copper properties to be found anywhere in the world." It would be impossible to exaggerate the "size and richness" of their claims, according to a magazine writer who believed that "the real truth is stronger than any fiction of the ordinary mining country." The new company was completing a plant at a cost of $50,000 "and will undoubtedly be shipping ore within a few weeks."[28]

All the hype—whether truth or fiction—came to naught. The partners sold some stock but never did ship any ore, nor did anyone else. Stock sales supported mining ventures of the vigorous Hubbard for the next sixty years, but otherwise the Elliott-Hubbard Company affairs were only interesting because of litigation they inspired. Elliott's wife sued for divorce in 1907 and demanded a large share of the mine properties through a grub-staking agreement. Judge James Wickersham determined that she had not been her husband's backer on the expeditions that resulted in allegedly valuable claims. The Hubbards went to court in 1916, subsequent to a divorce, over his reneging on a mining property deed he had given her in 1906. The court refused to give the property back to him.[29]

The history of the Elliott Creek claims may be richer in incident (or better reported) than other copper prospects in the region, but the bottom line remained the same. It was far easier to announce "another Jumbo" than to find one.

⁂ Kennecott: "Octopus" or Benefactor? ⁂

In Alaska the syndicate, often called "the Guggs" because of its connection with the Guggenheim fortune, was either lauded for its development of resources or condemned for monopolistic practices and political corruption. James Wickersham, a friend to Birch and Jarvis until becoming congressional delegate in 1908, described the syndicate's:

attempt to control the great natural resources of Alaska in 1910 [which] destroyed the last Republican administration, split the Republican party into two factions, which destroyed each other in 1912, and gave the country eight years of President Wilson and his policies.

Wickersham was referring to the celebrated Ballinger-Pinchot controversy involving charges of fraud in the syndicate's interest in acquiring coal claims in Alaska and the subsequent withdrawal of coal lands to entry.[30] The Ballinger-Pinchot dispute loomed large as an issue affecting mining in the early years of the century. In essence it was a controversy over resource development and occasioned the nation's first widespread public debate over conservation.

In 1904 Congress permitted entry to Alaska coal lands under private survey (because public surveys were lacking) but restricted individual holdings to 160 acres. When Clarence Cunningham located a number of claims, allegations surfaced that the Morgan-Guggenheim syndicate was involved in a scheme to control all the territory's coal. President Theodore Roosevelt responded by withdrawing all coal lands from entry by executive order.

Gifford Pinchot, the nation's chief forester, pitted himself against Secretary of the Interior Richard Ballinger on the conservation issue. Ballinger, appointed secretary by President William H. Taft in 1909, had been commissioner of the General Land Office when an interior department investigator exposed an apparent Cunningham-syndicate relationship. Commissioner Ballinger ignored the allegations, which were pressed by Pinchot, an ardent conservationist, in 1909–1910. Taft fired Pinchot for suggesting that he was in cahoots with Ballinger in the syndicate's plot to control public lands. Eventually, Congress investigated the affair and exonerated Ballinger. Pinchot did not give up the battle. Roosevelt took up his cause as a campaign issue when he ran as a third party candidate in 1912 against Taft and Woodrow Wilson.

All the heat of the national controversy focused attention on Alaska mining and development and on the territory's aspirations for home rule. Many Alaskans believed that having effective representatives in Congress and their own elected legislature would smooth the way to economic development. Alaska did get a congressional delegate in 1906, and Wickersham successfully opposed Taft's plan for a military commissioner rule in 1909–1910. In 1914 the coal lands were opened for entry, but the great expectations for their value had faded. By 1914 the Panama Canal had opened to create lower coal freight rates from the East to the West Coast. Also, petroleum production began in California.[31]

The bitterness expressed toward the syndicate by its detractors during the controversy dismayed Dan Guggenheim. Others who had helped develop the frontier had been revered. Some Alaskans agreed that the syndicate deserved credit rather than censure. C. L. Andrews, formerly a long-time customs officer at Sitka, Skagway, and Eagle, praised the company in the *Alaska-Yukon Magazine*:

The men who are furnishing the capital for this road certainly have faith in Alaska. The United States bought the country for $7,200,000 and revolted at the price. She has put nothing into it since, beyond the revenue she has taken out; made no improvements of any moment worth mentioning; she has experimented in anomalous laws, and has prevented settlement of the accessible parts by withdrawing the coast in reservations; she has not even surveyed the land so a settler can get a farm without paying more for a survey than a pre-emption cost twenty years ago in the Western states. Yet here are men putting more than twice as much into developing the country as the United States paid for the whole,—for this road is estimated to cost $15,000,000 by the time it is completed.[32]

Decades later Archie W. Shiels, who had been a storekeeper for Michael Heney during railroad construction, quoted a speech Simon Guggenheim made in 1910 directed against conservationists who argued that Alaska's riches belonged to the people. Guggenheim noted that the wealth was useless until found and developed:

Men and capital must do the work, and it is risky for both. Both . . . are entitled to rewards commensurate with the risk, and if Alaska is to be developed at all, the interests of those two classes must be guarded as jealously as the interest of those who sit in comfort at home.

Children playing around a Maypole at Kennecott during the 1930s. Courtesy of the William C. Douglass Family.

Shiels's argument followed the same vein:

When Kennecott was worked out and they quit Alaska, they were accused of taking untold millions out of the country and in return leaving nothing but a hole in the ground. No credit was given them for the millions they had put into the country in the way of taxes, wages, purchase of supplies, not to mention the purchase and operation of the Alaska Steamship Company, and just let me say that Alaska never did have a better or more satisfactory marine service than that given them while the Alaska Steamship Company was being operated by the Syndicate, all the political critics to the contrary . . . they spent over fifty million dollars in Alaska—not such a bad hole in the ground at that.[33]

Writing in the *Engineering and Mining Journal,* L. W. Storm ridiculed the assertions of the syndicate's enemies that the company had monopolistic tendencies. He argued that the Guggenheims owned only a single group of mines in a vast district. Other powerful capitalistic interests, including those of Calumet and Hecla and James Phillips Jr. of Nevada Consolidated were in the field before the Guggenheims.

The idea that there is any effort on the part of the Morgan-Guggenheim syndicate to control this extensive copper belt, save inasmuch as their railway is the first to penetrate it, is the subject of mirth in every prospector's cabin and in every operator's camp throughout this vast district.[34]

Whatever miners and other Alaskans believed was not as easily summarized as Storm indicated. If many had not agreed with Wickersham's charges, he probably would not have won the biannual delegate elections from 1908 to 1914 when the controversy raged furiously. The syndicate might have fared better if it had not tried so hard to dominate

Alaska politics. Copper River and Northwestern Railway workers, many of whom were not eligible to vote, were encouraged to oppose Wickersham at Cordova in the 1908 election for congressional delegate. This upset Wickersham, who had already been annoyed by the syndicate's publication of earlier correspondence showing his interest in being retained as company counsel by the Guggenheims. Another batch of letters leaked by company officers revealed that Wickersham had not favored home rule for Alaska earlier, although he had made demands for a territorial legislature and other home-rule measures the thrust of his campaign.

After Wickersham gained office, conflict with the syndicate continued, particularly over control of political patronage. Wickersham opposed the influence of the syndicate at every turn. By the time Stephen Birch got around to asking Wickersham to name his price for dropping his unrelenting attacks on the syndicate, it was far too late. Wickersham had become the champion of the people against the powers of evil—and the evil was represented by the syndicate and its supporters. But for its blunders and corruption, the syndicate might have fared much better during the storm of the Ballinger-Pinchot controversy. Support for President Taft's plan for a military government for Alaska over more democratic institutions would have been less suspicious.[35]

Wickersham gained the ammunition he needed when H. J. Douglas (not to be confused with Kennecott Supt. William Douglass), recently fired as syndicate auditor, provided evidence of M. B. Morrisey's role during the first Hasey trial (see Chapter 9). Douglas identified John Carson as the "bag man" who saw to it that Morrisey received money from the company's "corruption fund." A Carson letter to syndicate director David Jarvis extolled the services of Morrisey, whose "acquaintances with many of the government's witnesses and control over them placed him in a position to be of the greatest service." Carson's letter intimated jury tampering. Records of the disbursements to Morrisey were too brief to be convincing evidence of bribery but, as Wickersham pointed out, Douglas did not have all the evidence that might exist.[36]

Wickersham knew how to draw press attention to the possible chicanery of the Guggenheims. The syndicate men cooperated, too. They blundered into providing him with a congressional forum for inquiry when they brought charges against U.S. Attorney John Boyce and U.S. Marshal Dan Sutherland. Boyce and Sutherland were dismissed because of alleged excessive zeal in prosecuting Juneau banker C. M. Summers for assault. Summers and his friend, Gov. Walter Clark, supported the syndicate. Clark convinced the attorney general that Boyce and Sutherland prosecuted Summers merely because he opposed Wickersham. Whatever the truth, the dispute over the firings and replacement of the officers with John Rustgard and Herbert Faulkner was aired when a Senate subcommittee met to consider the fitness of the new appointees. Wickersham and Sutherland argued that the dismissals followed the efforts of the officers to investigate Hasey jury bribery charges. This may not actually have been

A fire in the power plant and machine shop at Kennecott.
Courtesy of the William C. Douglass Family.

the case, but Wickersham missed no opportunity to strike out at his old enemies.[37]

The new officers were confirmed despite Wickersham's best efforts. The attorney general, however, could not resist Wickersham's demands for a thorough investigation of the Keystone Canyon trials, the election frauds at Cordova, and other questionable actions by the syndicate. Agents of the Justice Department went over the court records, interviewed a number of individuals, investigated the activities of suspects, and examined all the 1907–1908 telegraph communications of syndicate officers. Examiner S. McNamara reported the results of the investigation in February 1911. He concluded that "Morrisey is pre-eminently a scoundrel" and that "irregular methods" had been used by the Hasey defense. U.S. Attorney Elmer E. Todd of Seattle reviewed McNamara's report and agreed with his conclusions. "Improper methods" had been used by the defense, but the government did not have enough evidence to support a successful prosecution. Both men called for further investigations of possible bribery in the Cordova election matter and of possible Sherman Antitrust Act violations in collusive bidding for government contracts between the syndicate and a rival company.[38]

It was chicanery in a coal contract that eventually resulted in the prosecution of some syndicate officers. H. J. Douglas reported that the syndicate's David Jarvis had agreed with officers of another company on the price for coal to be offered for shipment to Forts Davis and Liscum in Alaska. Further investigation and much urging from Wickersham led to a federal prosecution of company officers at Tacoma, Washington.

Jarvis's involvement in corrupt practices of the syndicate pained many of his friends in Alaska and elsewhere. Jarvis had been admired by President Theodore Roosevelt, who considered him the embodiment of manly virtues—courage, decisiveness, intelligence, and integrity. Jarvis established himself as a national hero in 1898 when, as an officer in the U.S. Revenue Marine, he directed an overland reindeer drive to save whalers caught in the arctic ice. Later, as Alaska's collector of customs, Jarvis enhanced his reputation. Roosevelt offered his favorite Alaskan the position of territorial governor in 1906 and, when Jarvis declined, accepted his recommendation of Wilford B. Hoggatt. Jarvis chose the more lucrative job as a director for the Alaska syndicate.

Jarvis was not among those convicted in October 1912 because he took his own life in June 1911, shortly after indictments were issued. Jarvis, who has been treated with great sympathy by historians of the event, left a cryptic note: "Tired and worn out." The *New York Times* story on his suicide observed his boldness "beyond the realization of people who did not know Alaska—whether lobbying for legislation, seizing railroad right-of-ways by power of Winchester, fixing jurors, or playing corrupt politics."[39]

A fair assessment of the syndicate requires some editing of some of the stronger statements made by Wickersham and the glowing tributes recorded by syndicate fans. Many syndicate supporters like Margaret Harrais of Fairbanks were inclined to blame the government for policies that restricted the company's benefits to Alaska, including the failure to extend the Copper River and Northwestern Railway from Chitina to Fairbanks. Harrais believed that "poison gas artists" had given financier J. P. Morgan a bad name: "He was featured as an octopus who was fastening his tentacles on Alaska's resources to suck the life-blood out of us." Harrais believed in J. P. Morgan as quoted at her dinner table by her guest Stephen Birch while the Copper River and Northwestern Railway surveys were under way. According to Birch, Morgan had said:

When you go into that Tanana country, I want you to pay particular attention to the agricultural possibilities . . . If those pioneers want to stay there after the gold is mined out, I'll build a railroad in there for them. I don't care a damn what it costs me, or whether I get a cent of the investment back! I'd like to make it

*possible for them to remain. John D. Rockefeller has built churches and Andrew Carnegie libraries, as their
monuments—I am going to build a railroad to benefit those Alaska pioneers as my monument.*[40]

This story made Harrais "gasp for a moment," but she believed it. Morgan did not fulfill
his promise, but Harrais thought it was because the conservationists led by Gifford Pinchot
excoriated everyone who wished to develop Alaska, and their nastiness dissuaded Morgan.
Yet Morgan did make it possible for Birch to develop the copper mines, and "give employment to thousands of men at good wages, give the prospector a chance to earn a grubstake
and keep him in Alaska, and enriched the world by over $200,000,000 in new wealth." Harrais
believed that the syndicate chose to invest its Kennecott profits elsewhere because of the
ugly treatment received in Alaska.[41]

Historians have been divided in evaluating the syndicate. Jeannette P. Nichols believed
that the syndicate exploited Alaska through its control of shipping and political corruption.
Robert Stearn and Lone Janson expressed a more favorable view of the syndicate.[42] Melody
Webb offered a more balanced summary:

*The syndicate touched every facet of life—political and economic, national, and local. In part, Alaska's
small population invited this impact. The company's steamships carried nearly all supplies and passengers
between Alaska and Seattle. Its railroad was the longest and best constructed in the territory, with equitable
rates while operating at a loss each year. Its fisheries, canneries, and merchandise outlets supplied needs to
a developing territory. Its copper production stimulated other mineral development. And its large capital
investment brought economic opportunity to an isolated area. Most important, the syndicate was the parent
from which the giant Kennecott Copper Corporation grew, providing the foundation for the more adaptable
corporation. The syndicate, however, did involve itself in a brand of both national and local politics that at best
must be judged as "misconduct." Overall, its role in Alaska affairs seems more positive than negative.*[43]

✳ One Prospector's Story ✳

The emphasis on Kennecott's role should not overshadow the place of individuals in the
region's mineral development. Ocha Potter, a mining engineer, prospected in the country
from 1905 to 1913 and was responsible for discovering the Mother Lode. Working in
Houghton, Michigan, he was hired by investors to investigate an alleged "mountain of
copper" found by prospector H. H. Greer. The young man went out to Seattle early in 1905,
found some old sourdoughs to advise him on outfitting, and took passage on a small
steamer to Valdez. From Valdez Potter followed the Valdez Trail as far as the Tonsina River,
then headed down the Copper River to the Chitina River and upriver to the Lakina River. He
followed a big outfit with thirty sleds heading for Kennecott for part of the way.

After weeks of hard work, Potter and his two packers got their two-horse outfit to the
base of Mount Blackburn, where Greer had made his discovery. "I had been waiting impa-
tiently to see Greer's mountain of copper which was to enrich our backers, enable me to
complete my college education, provide me with professional work, and assure my financial
independence," Potter wrote. But it did not take long before the letdown:

*One look and my world collapsed. Although my experiences in Michigan copper mining had been limited,
I immediately recognized the deposit as consisting of a few inches of ore spread on the face of a "fault" in the
formation. I drilled three or four short holes by hand and charged them with the dynamite we had so
laboriously brought from Seattle nearly two thousand miles away, and when the smoke cleared after the
explosions, Greer's "mountain of copper" and all my rosy dreams had been blown into Kingdom Come.*[44]

Potter refrained from mentioning his conclusions to Greer and the packers. They were in
a remote country where a summer of prospecting had been planned, so Potter got busy look-

ing around the area. In nearby gulches they staked some gold claims, then as the snow retreated up the mountain, they followed the line. "We found several outcroppings of copper sulphide ore which we also staked and also later proved worthless." But the days were pleasant, and game was plentiful. "One day we counted 132 big horns and 14 mountain goats grazing peacefully within sight."

Despite the disappointment, Potter's company followed his recommendation for further prospecting of the Chitistone country in the 1906 season. He returned to Valdez in March and added prospector Tony Dimond to his party. By May the party reached its destination and built a log cabin on the Chitistone River a few miles from Skolai Pass. All summer they followed a "limestone-greenstone contact through

The company's hospital at Kennecott. Courtesy of the James McGavock Collection.

valleys and over mountains up the headwaters of rivers and small streams." They found nothing of commercial value, so they crossed the Skolai Pass to the White River country. Before winter they returned across the pass, then built a camp near where they wanted to sink shafts during the winter. Dimond returned to the coast with the horses, and the others drove shafts for several weeks. Later, Potter went out to the coast to contact his backers.

In April Potter and Dimond brought in supplies for a final season of prospecting. From their Chitistone base they headed up the Chitina. Near Chitina Glacier they made a temporary camp, then prospected up a narrow valley toward Mount St. Elias. Along the way they made an interesting discovery of a crudely made hand sled: "It had been left there by a party of three or four prospectors who had several years before made their way from Yakutat Bay on the coast over the ice fields and across the St. Elias range to the Chitina River where they had built a raft and finally found their way out to civilization." That anyone had been able to reach the interior from Yakutat was amazing to Potter. "I salute them for their courage and hardiness," he said, "although I have never learned their names, they were of the breed that extends frontiers and builds empires."

Potter doubted that he was going to extend the mining frontier, as they had again failed to find interesting prospects. They returned downriver to Kennecott, where they were refused permission to visit the mine. They made their way up McCarthy Creek to the headwaters, crossed a small glacier, and arrived at the Kennecott Mine late at night. "The mine crew was sleeping and there were no guards. I had brought candles and we climbed down the one small shaft and thoroughly inspected the deposit, with conscience untroubled by the graduate engineer's professional ethics."

Potter, like others before, expressed amazement at the richness of the ore:

Studying the faults in the formation I jumped at the conclusion, later proved to be correct, that the published geologists' reports on the Kennecott copper deposit had been wrong in their conclusion regarding its character. I decided that the ore body ran across the mountain range and not parallel to a limestone-greenstone contact as described in all the official literature on the subject. If I were right, then the Kennecott claims had not been properly staked and government mining regulations would limit their mining to their side lines only, a few hundred feet down.

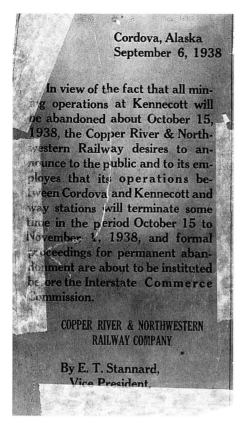

Cordova, Alaska
September 6, 1938

In view of the fact that all mining operations at Kennecott will be abandoned about October 15, 1938, the Copper River & Northwestern Railway desires to announce to the public and to its employes that its operations between Cordova and Kennecott and way stations will terminate some time in the period October 15 to November 1, 1938, and formal proceedings for permanent abandonment are about to be instituted before the Interstate Commerce Commission.

COPPER RIVER & NORTHWESTERN
RAILWAY COMPANY

By E. T. Stannard,
Vice President.

The announcement of Kennecott's closure in Cordova's newspaper. Courtesy of Valdez Museum.

To test his theory, Potter examined the top and McCarthy the side of the mountain and found good ore signs. He staked these two areas for "two or more miles along the Kennecott claims but at an angle of 90 from them in accordance with my ideas of the nature of the deposit, a perfectly legal but not too ethical procedure." Then Potter returned to Valdez to record his claims and to Michigan to report to his employers. He returned to his geology classes at the University of Michigan, continuing his studies while awaiting the decision of his company. It was an anxious time for him. The world's leading copper experts and the U.S. Geological Survey had published findings which he had contradicted. Why should anyone pay attention to a student? In January 1908 one of his backers summoned him to his office and asked him to plan another expedition to prove up on the most valuable claims.

Potter hired two experienced miners in Seattle, "highgraders" from the Tonopah fields who had left their Nevada jobs hurriedly after mine owners hired detectives to trace disappearances of high-grade ore. They reached Valdez in mid-February but were ninety days on the trial before reaching their camp site in May. Selecting twelve of the most promising claims, Potter drove a tunnel across them. The tunnel had no practical purpose except to meet the legal requirement that a certain amount of work be done each season. Potter believed that the ore would be discovered only at considerable depth, and he did not want to tackle that work until securing his claims.

Later that summer a government surveyor provided an official survey of the claims. Inspecting them would have required a two-hour climb, which Potter and his men did every day, but the government man preferred to take Potter's word on all relevant matters. Potter also followed the letter of the law to claim ground which eventually would be occupied by a mill and a town. Ground could be claimed only if gold were discovered and Potter could not find any, so he did a little salting to meet the needs of the government survey.

Potter started for the coast in August with his wife and young child. Getting out in summer presented greater problems than had the frozen trails of his entrance into the region. Mrs. Potter thought walking would be a lark until blisters crippled her. The party had to build a boat, risk the treacherous Nizina Canyon where a party had drowned the year before, and float down the tributaries to the Copper. On the Chitina they were surprised to see a steamboat, the first voyage of a boat that would ply the lower Copper for five years during railroad construction. Thanks to completed construction work, Potter could avoid the treacherous rapids above Childs and Miles Glaciers. A good trail had been cut along the banks of the river, so they abandoned their crude craft and boarded a construction boat which could take them to the rail head. They reached Cordova via the new railroad.

Six years passed before Potter again became involved in the Alaska copper claims. Nothing had been done on the claims save mandatory token work required by law, but the company's interest was aroused enough to send Potter and another mining expert out again in 1913 to examine the properties. The expert, who was employed by the Kennecott Corporation, was prepared to recommend a purchase of the claims if they were as Potter had described them. Unfortunately for Potter, the Kennecott expert was elderly and lazy. Much like the earlier government survey, he did not care to climb for two hours to examine the mines. But, unlike the government surveyor, he was unwilling to take Potter's word for anything. In fact, he was sure from his examination of fractional claims below what Potter had shown him, that the mountain claims lacked commercial value. Potter was so infuriated at the man that he stormed out of camp and started for the coast alone. Luckily, he ran into a U.S. Geological Survey party led by Alfred Brooks and was able to travel with them to Tonsina. On the voyage to Seattle he began to feel guilty about the $60,000 his company had spent supporting his recommendations:

The claims on which I had expended so much of my former employers' money and for which I had risked not merely my own life, but the lives of my wife and son and others, had been rejected as not worth examination by a mining expert employed by one of the world's great copper producing companies. I must have been dreaming dreams, seeing things that were only visions because of my inexperience when I staked those claims and recommended their development.

Back home in Houghton the disillusioned Potter advised his company to sell when a speculator offered to pay the company all it had invested plus 6 percent interest. The speculator quickly sold stock without any trouble and "in due time the Kennecott Copper Company bought a controlling interest." The Mother Lode property, as Potter reflected sadly, "has paid many millions of dollars in dividends, just how many millions I have never quite had the heart to learn."

✸ Conclusion ✸

The Kennecott story is of utmost importance to the history of the Wrangell-St. Elias region. Copper produced there made the region one of the most valuable in Alaska, and the company town operation, common elsewhere, had not yet taken hold in Alaska. As production figures indicate, the yield from Kennecott gave substantial economic life to the region for many years, and its payroll helped support several communities. Construction of the Copper River and Northwestern Railway affected the entire region and stimulated maritime transport and other commercial activities. What was perhaps most significant about Kennecott's influence on Alaska's economy was the timing of the development. Ore mining and shipping began at a time when mining activity had fallen off in most other sections of Alaska. Kennecott represented the bright side of the economic picture, and its success stimulated prospecting in the region and otherwise encouraged capital investment.

The involvement of the Kennecott Corporation in mining and transportation, particularly maritime transportation, gave it an impact on the territory's economy that evoked controversy. Divisive, too, were the company's excursions into the political process and its illicit efforts to increase profits. Nevertheless, the structures that remain at the mill, mines, and townsites are among the best preserved, most significant historic site in all the Alaska parks.

Billy James and Matilda Wales at their
claim on Little Eldorado Creek in the
Chisana district. Courtesy of the Alaska
State Library, Best Collection.

Chapter

＊ ＊ ＊

Chisana

The Wrangell-St. Elias region was the scene of Alaska's last major gold rush—on the Chisana River in 1913. Partners Billy James, N. Peter Nelson, and Fred Best were early investigators of mining potential in the White River country in 1912. Later, a local Upper Tanana Native known as Indian Joe claimed that he had led James to a gold-quartz lode and to placer gold that sparked the stampede. James denied that Joe had anything to do with the placer discovery and claimed that the Indian's information on quartz prospects did not result in any valuable deposits. Whatever the truth, James and his partners returned the following season for more prospecting on Bonanza Creek.

Andy Taylor, also prospecting in the area, returned with Nelson to Dawson for supplies, while James moved up to Little Eldorado. About 700 feet upstream, he panned about forty dollars' worth of gold in only a few minutes. This yield stirred James's expectations. He thought perhaps he had found another Klondike.

Billy James had been a hard-rock miner in California when the Klondike discovery drew him north in 1897. According to one story, his eagerness induced his sale of a valuable prospect for $4,000 per claim, which later produced millions. He panned his way down the Yukon and up into the Seward Peninsula without achieving any remarkable success. By 1908 he drifted into the White River country, grubstaking himself by trapping and hunting. Matilda Wales, James's long-time companion, must have been considered a hearty prospector in Dawson because she was chosen by Edward Erikson to locate claims. She staked No. 1 Chicken Creek for Erikson on June 30, 1913. Wales and other discoverers could not immediately protect their claims by recording them as a local recorder did not reach the remote district until July 22. This time lag encouraged claim-jumping litigation and some violence.[1]

Among the original discoverers, Fred Best was well known in the Fortymile country as the former co-owner with Frank Purdy of the Cassiar Roadhouse. Thanks to his diary and letters home we have an informative, personal record of the development. He had been doing casual labor on the Dawson waterfront when he got a chance to go prospecting in the White River country. He was a veteran Klondiker who had left Stoneham, Massachusetts, as a boy for a life at sea then switched to a quest for gold. As a prospector he had never struck it rich but had made a living for some years operating a roadhouse at Cassiar until he grew tired of it. Writing home to his parents in August 1912, Best expressed his enthusiasm about the chance to go prospecting once again:

My partners are N. P. Nelson and Billy James, both good men and old timers. Billy has been up there before and has some good prospects and picked Nels and me to go back with him. We may strike something good. I hope so anyway, but if we don't the trip will do me good and it is a country that is fast coming to the front. I think we stand a good chance of getting hold of something worthwhile. We have a fine outfit and a good boat and hope to have a successful trip. I have wanted to go up to that country for several years, but have never been footloose so I could do it.[2]

Stampeder on the trail to Chisana about 1913. Courtesy of the Tacoma Public Library.

A year of travel and prospecting passed before Best rejoiced in the fulfillment of every prospector's dream—the discovery of gold in paying quantities. On Number 3 above Bonanza he garnered 75 cents to $1.50 a pan. James and Nelson had made the discovery claims, and all the men worked in a frenzy to shovel in enough gravel to give them a big cleanup. Digging was relatively easy because, although the depth of the overburden varied, bedrock was shallow. Some of the diggings were only fourteen to sixteen inches down at some points, but on other claims it was necessary to dig through six to eight feet of overburden. Regardless of ground depth, plenty of work attended this kind of mining besides digging. Best had to go to Chavolda Creek to whipsaw lumber, for example, then pack it to his claims to make sluice boxes. Owners often hired laborers if a claim looked good, but even James, who had the richest claims, could not get enough help. He was willing to pay top wages but would not hire men without their own grub because food prices were high and shortages were a threat.

✳ Dawson Gets the News ✳

Unprepared for a winter's stay, Fred Best returned to Dawson in July. He enjoyed being the center of attention after making the trip from the head of the White River and down to Dawson by boat in seven days. His diary recorded his role as the bearer of glad tidings:

Thurs. July 17th—Everyone asking me about it and some quite excited as I am first from there and the only one who knows the facts.

Fri. July 18th—The reporter saw me today and a big piece in the papers tonight and all the town excited and getting ready to stampede.

Sat. July 19th—People going batty and all kinds of questions being put to me, by all kinds of people.[3]

Best did not exaggerate prospects discovered by James, Nelson, and himself. He was sure that a "good camp" would develop, but he would not offer any estimates of the claims' value. Best made it clear that several creeks had been staked from end to end, a fact quickly confirmed by Andy Taylor and Tommy Doyle. Other prospectors on the scene at Chisana included Dud McKinney, mayor of Forty Mile, and Mike James, Lem Gates, Carl Whitham, and Fred Wann. Due tribute was also paid to "Billy Johnson of the Cascade Laundry, who grubstaked James and Nelson."[4]

After folks in the Yukon and Alaska assimilated the news of a new gold strike they became keenly interested in the geography of the region. The Chisana country was one of those "near but far" areas. Looking at a map showed it to be about 260 miles from Dawson via the White River tributary of the Yukon and no more than ninety miles from Kennecott, the terminus of the Copper River and Northwestern Railway. But, of course, the veterans knew that distances were relative, and much depended on the season of travel. Nothing about the strike warranted a stampede, said Billy Johnson, who might just as well have saved his breath. Men were more willing to listen to the rumor that "the gravel carries pay from the grassroots down and that there was an abundance of water for sluicing."[5] One reason for the "grassroots down" rumor was in the speed of the fortunate discoverers in returning to Dawson with an impressive amount of gold. As the Fairbanks newspaper noted, they had been able to begin "shoveling in immediately after having made their locations."[6]

It had been a long time since Dawson had been the center of gold excitement, so the arrival of the Chisana men stirred great interest. One storekeeper displayed the nuggets Taylor and Doyle brought in and drew a gawking, excited crowd to his shop window. The lucky miners claimed that they had shoveled in their 200 ounces of gold in two days work on their claim.

❋ Boosting the Camp ❋

The talents of a mining camp's boosters directly affected its evolution. Boosters from other places often shared in the excitement of a new strike that affected local people. Anyone interested in rushing to a new strike sought out various sources of information, especially first-hand accounts. Newspapers carried quotes from miners themselves but could not always be taken at face value, as editors were often unblushing, indiscriminate promoters of their own town's interests. The boosterism of the people of Chitina and its newspaper, however, appears to have been based more on a submission to a general feeling that great prosperity lay ahead for Alaskans. "There is no doubt that it is the richest since the Klondike," exulted the *Chitina Leader*. Stampeders were arriving from every camp in the

Dog team leaving Chitina for Chisana about 1914. Courtesy of the Valdez Museum, P1986.99.3.

David's "Spruce Point" Roadhouse on the McCarthy-Chisana trail, 1915. Courtesy of the Alaska State Library, Stanley Collection, PCA 184-118.

interior, and mines on Dan and Chititu Creeks had been shutdown for want of men, said the paper. The towns of Blackburn and McCarthy were "practically deserted," and half of Chitina's population had left. The railroad had to put on a special car at Chitina to handle the outflow.[7]

Even Seattle felt the excitement. The *Leader* was delighted to report that President J. E. Chilberg of the Seattle Chamber of Commerce predicted an immediate "exodus" of a thousand people from Puget Sound. A report from Cordova indicated that modern technology might play a role in the stampede: "A movement is on foot to secure Captain Martin, the aviator who made the aeroplane flights at Fairbanks, July Fourth . . . and prevail upon him to go to McCarthy and run an aerial express for passengers . . . the distance is little over 100 miles, and it is believed that many of the stampeders would avail themselves of this means of travel."[8]

❋ Promoting Routes ❋

Chitina folks expected most stampeders to begin arriving soon after news of the big strike reached the Outside. The *Chitina Leader* followed events closely and was quick to note a sensational advance in transportation—the arrival of John Ronan and John Ferguson from Fairbanks by auto "in 45 hours running time." This suggested the feasibility of an efficient overland route in the future. "It demonstrates that with the expenditure of a reasonable sum of money" the Alaska Road Commission could convert the government road to a summer auto route. Somewhat prophetically, the *Leader* suggested that if Col. Wilds Richardson "were to succeed in building a boulevard in the interior country he might succeed in immortalizing his name." Richardson's name finally did grace what became the highway between Fairbanks and Valdez from which the Edgerton Highway links Chitina.[9]

Chitina residents lauded the Chisana strike as a world wonder, seeming to accept that the gold had lured away many of its own residents Chitina, of course, stood to profit from development of a large mining district, but only if everyone realized that the Copper River and Northwestern Railway route was the best approach to the gold field. According to the *Leader*, other towns had committed terrible acts to promote competing routes to Chisana. As an example of duplicity, the Chitina paper cited an extra edition of the Skagway newspaper which falsely described the drowning of sixteen men and fourteen horses on the Chitina route. Sponsors of this "viciously false rumor" were, of course, promoting travel via Skagway and Whitehorse.[10]

When Chitina got the news of the Chisana strike in early July, the *Leader* quickly reported that Cordova offered "the most feasible and short route" to the stampede. With the railroad it had the "logical route" for prospectors from every part of the Tanana and Yukon below Fairbanks and from Outside. Rushers from Fairbanks could travel light over the government trail to Chitina and take the train to McCarthy, outfit there, then take pack horses over the Skolai Pass to White River. "From there the crossing of a small divide, a little over 20 miles, places outfits on the Shushana river."[11] By contrast, from Dawson the route was 350 miles.

The *Chitina Leader*, deploring "the peculiar transportation conditions which forces American mining companies operating in American territory to buy their outfits in Canada to escape payment of entry," called for a Copper River and Northwestern Railway extension over Skolai Pass, "a feasible and comparatively inexpensive extension." The *Leader* complained that such an extension would have been built long before to reach reported copper deposits but for "the repressive attitude of the government in its Alaska railroad policy."

❋ Water Route ❋

A gold stampede was just the thing to stimulate a flagging economy. Community boosters preferred a nearby discovery, but distance did not always deter promoters. Thus, news of the Chisana strike in 1913 galvanized Fairbanks businessmen to advertise their advantages in Seattle and Alaska newspapers. Never mind that Fairbanks was 500 hard miles away from Chisana. The Fairbanksans argued that there was no better supply center nearer. Though a glance at the map might make such claims appear exaggerated, the argument had some merit. Dawson, much closer to

Chisana stampeders navigating the 'goat trail' above the Chitistone River. Courtesy of the Alaska State Library, Zacharias Collection, PCA 178-2.

(Above) Packing on the Skolai Creek trail in 1915. Courtesy of the Tacoma Public Library, Stanley Mason Collection

(Right) Horses hauling sleds across the Russell Glacier in 1915. Courtesy of the Tacoma Public Library, Stanley-Mason Collection.

(Facing page) A pack train crossing the Russell Glacier in Skolai Pass. Courtesy of the Rasmuson Library Archives, University of Alaska Fairbanks; Capps Collection, 83-149-1409N.

Chisana, had drawbacks as a jumping-off place. "Remember," the *Fairbanks Times* noted, "goods shipped by the Canadian route are subject to customs duty at boundary line."[12]

Fairbanks promoters called upon geography and sentiment to bolster their chances. The Tanana, they claimed, was the "natural highway" because the Chisana formed part of the Tanana River headwaters and, of course, Fairbanks lay on the Chena River a few miles from the Tanana. The Tanana route, they insisted, was the "all-American" way that avoided the upper Yukon and, therefore, Canadian territory. Miners should not be misled by the apparent logic of the White River route to Chisana, promoters argued: "The river at best is only navigable to the head of the Donjek, by boats such as those of the Sidestream Navigation Company, and that point is 105 miles from the scene of the strike . . . any kind of steamboats at most times of the year have all kinds of difficulty in navigating the White River."[13]

Part of the optimism in Fairbanks was founded upon the belief that the upper Tanana could be reached with ease. Everyone realized that even shallow-draft steamboats were useless. Poling boats, however, worked fine. W. H. Merrit, an upper Tanana miner, alleged that "it is possible to get within twelve miles of the diggings in a poling boat." Another trader, W. H. Newton from the Healy River on the upper Tanana, said that from Tanana Crossing to the Chisana "the water is so slack that the wind will blow a boat upstream." This good news was appended to Newton's warning that swift currents between Fairbanks and Tanana Crossing would inhibit travel: "The best way then would be to mush to Tanana Crossing, build a boat there, and pole to the near field."[14]

Logistical factors dominated individual planning and the economic development of all mining regions. Transportation to the Chisana was complicated by the fact that no reliable supply base was any closer than the points of origin of most stampeders (Dawson, Fairbanks, and the Copper River rail belt). Traders on the upper Tanana, like W. H. Merrit and W. H. Newton, were not prepared to supply a huge influx of miners. Merrit did try to seize the opportunity for his Nabesna Trading Company by establishing a new post farther up the Tanana. He loaded ten tons of provisions on *Dusty Diamond*, a shallow-draft steamboat of 101 tons that had been in service since '98. Even with a new post, however, he warned that supply costs would be high: "The camp for the present at least will be a dollar a pound camp."[15]

The *Dusty Diamond* voyage ended at Thirtymile house on the Tanana, where Merrit was forced to unload his cargo. He had hoped to reach the mouth of either the Nabesna or Chisana, but his boat could not buck the swift waters of the upper Tanana and suffered hull damage. Others tried with smaller boats, including *Martha Clow* (98 tons), *Reliance* (291 tons), *Sushana* (49 tons), and *Tetlin* (65 tons). Shippers expressed optimism about reaching the new diggings, but by early August water depth had dropped to the level that even small motor boats could not get above Salcha. The most notable success was the voyage of the Northern Navigation Company's *Reliance* to the mouth of the Nabesna. Miners aboard the vessel hiked or poled from that point and the Northern Navigation men laid out a townsite, but it was too far from the diggings to thrive as a supply center.[16]

When navigation halted in October, boats froze in at various points on the Tanana. Only *Tana*, which got within nine miles of the Nabesna mouth, and *Tetlin*, which got a short distance up the Nabesna, got within striking distance of Reliance City. The much-touted Tanana route flopped, though poling boat traffic remained steady through 1914. Promotion alone could not overcome geographic realities, and by late 1913 a more rational "all-American" route from McCarthy and the Copper River and Northwestern Railway had been established via Skolai Pass.

By August 16 stampeders already were returning to Chitina. They did not knock the Chisana strike but had been unable to stay long for want of provisions. Billy James, Carl

Whitham, and others were still making big cleanups, but the ground was already beginning to freeze.[17] The reports that reached other Alaska towns from the diggings in late August were not encouraging. "There is not a claim left in the diggings for the hundreds of stampeders who are now enroute from all directions," reported a Fairbanks newspaper. A number of men had just arrived at Dawson from Chisana with this news, which meant that the stampeders would have "to do some pioneering on their own account" from the new camp. The miners also had the latest news on the food situation:

There are no supplies for sale in the camp, although those in need of grub are offering several times Dawson prices. Packers from Donjek and McCarthy are getting $1 a pound for everything they land at the diggings. All of the meat consumed thus far has been supplied by the Indian hunters, but it is reported that there is some beef now enroute from Whitehorse by way of Kluane Lake.[18]

Orderly conditions prevailed at the camp, and squabbles were few. "Some claims have been jumped, but only in cases of blanketing. The legally staked claims have been unmolested."[19]

❈ Canadian Interests ❈

One of the early reporters on the Canadian route to the diggings was a Whitehorse physician, L. S. Sugden. In July 1913 he traveled the Kluane Trail and White River country with a movie camera. After going to McCarthy, then taking pictures of the trail from that place to the new gold camp, he supported the Canadian route as the most practical. His films would convince travelers "beyond any doubt," as he told friends, of the hazards of the McCarthy route. "No person, after seeing these pictures, will consider for a moment the taking of that route for there will be visual evidence of the absolute impassibility [sic] of either the Chitistone or Skolai trails during the winter season."[20] Travelers must avoid the "death traps" that these trails offered, he argued in public lectures in Whitehorse and Skagway sponsored by Whitehorse merchants. He had sharp words for the boosters of Cordova:

We saw the Hazelet party who were sent in by the Cordovians to stake a route over the Chisana and Nizina Glaciers, they failed to get through—the Cordovians are a wonderful bunch. Alive to the great benefit to be derived from a stampede, they subscribed $5,000 in twelve hours to send Mr. Hazelet in just to look up a trail. They have since subscribed a like amount as a publicity fund and are going to get the business in the right manner. They have had a taste of what stampede money is like, and it savors very much of milk and honey, and they want more.

A roadhouse on the Hazelet trail near the summit of the Nizina Glacier, 1914. Courtesy of the Tacoma Public Library, Stanley-Mason Collect.

In Cordova the doctor's sniping was discounted. The newspaper editor alleged that Sugden's chief interest was in getting funding for a trip outside to publicize the Canadian route. The doctor may honestly believe that the later method [Skagway-Whitehorse] of reaching the Chisana is the more practical, and if so we have no argument with

Famed freighter Sidney "Too Much" Johnson leaving Bonanza City for McCarthy, 1915. Courtesy of the Alaska State Library, Stanley Collection, PCA 184-79.

him. But from his published interviews we are constrained to believe that the principal object is to absorb a publicity fund that he seeks to have raised.[21]

Sugden called the Cordova editor a liar: "I am not putting over anything on anybody," he said. "I can back up any statement I have made." Skagway and Whitehorse merchants believed in the doctor and raised $500 to send him to Seattle. Once in Seattle, Sugden wired for more money to spread the good word and received another $335. It is unclear how much influence the doctor's promotion had on the movement of stampeders. Some did use the Skagway route, but most prospectors entered from Cordova and McCarthy because it was the more convenient route. Sugden apparently came to realize this himself or had other reasons later for endorsing trail improvements on the Skolai Pass route out of McCarthy.[22]

The Canadian government showed its support for the Chisana prospects by launching a new mail service. Officials hoped that Dawson could serve as a supply center even if the diggings were across the border in Alaska. Mounties would carry mail from Dawson to the border and transfer to U.S. carriers there.[23] Other Canadian interests rose to the potential opportunity of the Chisana, particularly the White Pass and Yukon Railway. Early in October the superintendent of the steamer division announced that construction of a small passenger and freight steamer for Kluane Lake had begun. It would provide service from Silver to the foot of the lake, a distance of forty miles, from mid-October until navigation became impossible, usually by December. Stampeders using the Canadian Yukon route could benefit from the new service. Nor had the railroad company neglected the overland portion of the route. A large crew was working on the trail between Whitehorse and Kluane. When workers completed upgrading the first half of the trail, they would move to the end of Kluane Lake and improve the trail to the White River and Chisana that lay within Canada.

The Miner's Home Bar in Chisana City, early 1914. Courtesy of the Alaska State Library,
Zacharias Collection, PCA 178-97

"It is a certainty now," the company affirmed:

> . . . that when the freeze-up comes the trail to the interior will be in excellent shape for its entire length. Road
> houses, with good accommodations, are already scattered at short intervals along the trail as far as the Kluane
> lake and in a short time the trail beyond will be equally well supplied with accommodations for beast and man.[24]

People in Seattle followed news of the Chisana strike closely. New gold discoveries in
Alaska always profited the Puget Sound city. When Billy James visited Seattle in October,
newsmen hurried to interview him at the Frye Hotel. He described a piece of bedrock, "six
feet square, jutting from the Little Eldorado creek," that proved to him that he had found a
rich deposit. His affirmation of such wealth cheered Seattle people.[25]

✳ Conflicting Reports ✳

In early September reports surfaced of starvation at Chisana. One source of this unpleasant
rumor was said to be Bert Johnson, a Fairbanks freighter who carried goods to the camp in
August, returning in early September. A newspaper quoted him as saying that "there is
absolutely no grub in the Chisana and no means of getting any at this time . . . men are in a
starving condition, and some are known to have perished from hunger and exposure . . . it is
an insane move to try to get to the diggings now, owing to the deep snow and lack of supplies." Wait for the snow before making the trip, he advised prospective stampeders, and go
in from Gulkana, "the only way to go, winter or summer."[26]

By mid-September disappointed stampeders began arriving back in Fairbanks. Most had
stayed only long enough to find that all the creeks had been staked before starting back to
civilization. Some evaluated the prospects even before they reached Chisana. Jack Bigelow
and Frank Lawson, "two of the most widely known mining men of Alaska," turned back on
the trail after "they learned sufficient of the true conditions." Other men encountered along

the way described the fully staked streams and other particulars in a convincing way, making them "certain that there was nothing there to interest them."[27] The Fairbanks men reported no signs of starvation at Chisana. "Hungry Mike" Goonan doubted there would be any grub shortage, "and if there should be any cases, it will be the fault of the sufferers themselves, as game and birds are so abundant that the stampeders could almost kill them with a stone."[28]

As with any stampede, hardship and danger stalked the unwary and inexperienced. One stampeder was brought to Dawson from the upper White River, "where he was found wandering in a dazed and half-starved condition." Other arrivals at Dawson from the diggings reported that numbers of stampeders were missing, "and it is feared that they are lost." Apparently men wandered from the main trails to hunt game, "and afterwards were unable to retrace their steps to their outfits."[29]

As usual, early camp mail delivery was uncertain. Some mail came via Dawson and some by way of Cordova and McCarthy with willing packers. Long delays in delivery were common. Miners regularly petitioned the post office for service. The post office contracted for semi-monthly service from McCarthy but changed the name of the town from Johnson City to Chisana.

In September Ned McGuire of Fairbanks made a strike in town just fifty yards from the post office and store. The eleven-foot prospect hole yielded five to twenty cents a pan of coarse gold. Amidst the excitement of this discovery were cries of fraud. Many miners believed that McGuire or someone else had salted the claim. Their suspicions were further aroused when McGuire filled up his prospect hole and announced that he would not attempt any more work until spring. W. R. Healy of Chitina was willing to believe because he claimed to be the original locator of the ground McGuire had worked, and he intended to do assessment work. As the controversy raged, opportunistic fellows staked all the ground in town, then sat back to await future developments. The town lot prospect eventually proved to be a fake, so the town was saved.

The Shushanna Cafe in Chisana City, 1914. Courtesy of the Alaska State Library. Zacharias Collection, PCA 178-90.

❋ The First Winter ❋

Residents passed the first winter debating the likelihood of future prosperity. Uncertainty dogged early efforts until long-range prospects were confirmed or hopes dashed. Optimistic forecasts freely flowed from miners and townspeople, almost as if talking could make it so. As Grace Bostwick observed in her reports to a Seattle newspaper, the "several hundred able bodied, serious-minded men . . . believe in the future of the country or they would not stay so far outside the comforts of civilization at the heavy expense of mere existence alone."[30]

Bostwick estimated that some eight thousand to ten thousand people had passed through the diggings since the discovery of the year before, but most left immediately after a quick look around. Probably only a tenth of the arrivals remained long enough to stake claims. Far fewer still did any work on their claims. The number of female residents was among the closely regarded signs of a camp's progress. As respectable women took up residence, it was seen as a sign that the place would show some permanence. Chisana was doing all right on this score by spring 1914 with twenty-three women, although four of them lived in the summer settlement at the mouth of Bonanza Creek and two were on the White River. Grace Bostwick reported that "'at homes' and receptions are occasionally a feature of social life." Even more promising was the evidence that women "have brought in clothing with them, so many are garbed much like their sisters outside, instead of in the rough, pioneer clothing of a few weeks ago." With such gains as these it is no wonder that "men mostly shave now, where formerly they were rough and bearded." The town's two bath tubs were kept busy.[31]

R. J. Fisher wrote to a friend in Juneau, reporting 350 cabins, two restaurants, two barber shops, one drugstore, one Red Cross nurse, one jail, and seven petitions out for saloon licenses, "but it is no trick to get all the booze you want." Fisher observed that the price of food had declined from an average figure of a dollar a pound to half that amount as many of the fall arrivals stayed only long enough to sell their excess supplies before decamping for other places. At the Thanksgiving Day dance one hundred men and eight women had a wonderful time: "It was not amiss to see many of the men dancing together."[32]

The wild side of mining communities—gambling, drinking sprees, show girls, and other diversions of the demi-monde—was absent from Chisana's culture. Fred Best kept a diary and recorded all his visits to town from his claims over the 1913–1914 winter. His habits were sedate. He enjoyed chatting with friends and a good meal at a restaurant or someone's home, then he waited a while for mail before returning to camp. It was all pretty dull.[33]

Bonanza City about 1914. Courtesy of the Alaska State Library, Stanley Collection, PCA 184-74.

The Gambling House in Chisana City. Courtesy of the Alaska State Library, Zacharias Collection, PCA 178-99.

In February 1914 Chisana folks argued that their community had more log cabins than Circle, Fairbanks, or Dawson and deserved to be called "the largest log cabin town in the world." Four hundred cabins was one estimate, including seven general stores, a saloon, two restaurants, a clothing store, and "roadhouses galore." Among the 500 to 600 residents, twenty-five women graced the place.[34] Best reported that there were no children in camp, "and I have not seen a white baby since I was in Dawson last July."[35]

✳ The 1914 Mining Season ✳

Best let most of his ground on lays to other miners in the spring of 1914, which freed him of much worry and also gave him the chance to make good money hauling material for others. He had a fine horse, and the camp was bustling. "I expect there will be a good deal of money come out of this camp this summer," he wrote home, "and I hope to have a good piece of it myself if all turns out well."[36] It would be June before they would see much gold, but everyone was enjoying the sunshine, although guarding their eyes against the bright reflection from the snow by wearing snow glasses. "We get tanned as dark as the Indians."[37] The camp had survived the winter without any food shortage, but Best planned a hunt to replenish his meat cache. Food prices were expected to remain high over the summer "unless more comes in over the sled trails. It is expensive to pack anything in here on horses in the summer—much harder than over the snow in the winter."[38]

111

A hunting trip in the Chisana district about 1914. The couple on left is Mr. and Mrs. Fletcher Hamshaw.
Courtesy of the Tacoma Public Library, Stanley-Mason Collection.

Miners not only faced difficulties at Chisana related to its remoteness but a water shortage as well. The 1914 season was particularly dry, and water was essential to all placer mining operations regardless of their scale or particular technology. A miner had to calculate his chances of making a profit accordingly. How far and by what means would water have to be transported? How much effort or money would be required for sluice boxes, dikes, pipes, and ditches? As a mining entrepreneur Best calculated the costs of his operation closely:

With the high prices, it takes a good piece of ground to stand paying men $6 a day with board—another $3.50 a day in addition, and make some money. If the ground has good pay dirt he can take money out pretty fast. On No. 1 Eldorado, four men took out $800 a day last summer and about $500 a day all the time they worked, but that was very rich, easy diggings. I don't expect to do anything like that, but do hope to do well and have a good pile of change by next fall if all goes well.[39]

Best's ground, including what he planned to mine himself and what he let on lays, was relatively easy to work because of shallow bedrock. Later he would hire men to shovel the dirt into sluice boxes. "Men come to me for jobs about every day, but I will not hire any until later on and I don't know how many I shall need yet. I shall wait until everything is ready, then I may put on quite a bunch and shovel in all I can while the season lasts." Best's ground on No. 3 Bonanza Creek did not compare with No. 1 Eldorado, where "four men took out $800 a day last summer," but he had hopes for profits in 1914 despite the high wages needed for miners and high transportation costs.[40]

Miners had no trouble figuring out when the season ended in 1914. Creeks rose several feet in a few hours in mid-August, wiping out the unwary along the creeks who lost flumes, dams, and sluice boxes. Others, whose claims were not along the creek, continued their cleanup. Best made a few thousand dollars, though he hired forty men in July and August and paid $400 daily in wages. Bonanza Creek had been good to him and he could exult: "I am on the paystreak at last! And I hope it will keep up."[41]

Reports on the district's long-range prospects remained conflicting through the summer of 1914. Harold H. Waller, a young U.S. mineral surveyor, who was a university undergraduate, predicted that the season's production would be $400,000—". . . a good little camp. . . . It is not a poor man's camp, nor is it a rich man's camp," Waller said. "It's simply a sporting proposition. The ground is 'spotted,' and what looks like a rich find often peters out when worked a short while." Waller, then better known in Seattle as a star oarsman of the University of Washington rowing crew, assured newsmen that the camp "is far from being a fizzle," as some had reported. Charles Range on Skookum Creek would take out $40,000, and Carl Whitham on No. 2 Little Eldorado "ought to clean up $20,000." He did not think that Fletcher Hamshaw and the others who bought out Billy James's discovery claim would fare well—perhaps their gain would be only one-fifth of the $500,000 they had expected to get.[42]

Waller played an interesting role in Chisana. He had been in the country before the 1913 stampede and had hired Fred Best, not yet a rich miner, to hunt meat for him. The Skolai Mining Company had hired Waller to investigate its copper lode claims, some of which were only twenty miles from Chisana. He received his instructions from Horatio E. Morgan, company manager. As the district's first recorder, Morgan's professional conduct had outraged miners as well as stockholders, most of whom lived in Akron, Ohio. Whether Morgan was a crook or merely incompetent is unclear, but the sterling performance of Anthony Dimond in straightening out the recording books on his arrival at Chisana endeared him to all miners.

The Skolai Mining Company's letterhead proclaimed "she's a wonder," in reference to its lode claims, but this boast was never fulfilled. Copper prospects did not prove as valuable as expected, and Morgan's huge expenditures for development were not warranted. The company secretary told Waller that he was baffled by Morgan's expenditure of more than $50,000 in the three-and-a-half seasons: "I couldn't for the life of me find where even the half was spent on our properties, making good allowance for provisioning." Waller, who provided plans for tunnels and other surveys, was among the company's creditors when it went broke some years later.[43]

(Left) Mr. and Mrs. Fletcher Hamshaw at camp near the mouth of Little Eldorado Creek about 1914. Courtesy of the Tacoma Public Library, Stanley-Mason Collection.

(Right) Mr. and Mrs. Fletcher Hamshaw at their home, presumably on Bonanza Creek. Such elaborately decorated walls were considered fashionable at the time. Courtesy of the Tacoma Public Library, Stanley-Mason Collection

A *Fourth-of-July foot race at Hamshaw's camp, July 1914. Courtesy of the Tacoma Public Library, Stanley-Mason Collection.*

⁕ U.S. Commissioner Anthony J. Dimond ⁕

Tony Dimond's appointment as U.S. commissioner was warmly applauded in the district. Most considered his predecessor corrupt, and Dimond was known to be fair and honest. "He is courageous and has a mind and will of his own," said the *Leader*. "There will be no juggling with records, no over charges and no connivance with big interests to the detriment of the hardy son of toil."[44] Dimond hesitated, then, fortunately for his later political career, agreed to accept the appointment. Taking the post was a gamble because a commissioner depended on filing fees for his remuneration. "If the camp is good," Dimond told a friend, "I will make a lot of money, if it's a failure, I'll lose a thousand dollars, which it will cost me to get in there."[45]

Dimond trekked into the Chisana from Valdez with Frank Hoffman, the new appointee for deputy marshal. Arriving in November, Dimond was appalled at the state of recording records, the food scarcity in camp, and the paucity of gold. "If they could find as much pay as we can find on Young Creek," he wrote Joseph Murray, "they would go wild." By spring, as disappointed miners drifted away, Dimond realized that his gamble would not pay off. His fees were not enough to support him, and in July he returned to Valdez to join Thomas Donohue's law firm.[46]

⁕ Trail Improvements ⁕

George C. Hazelet returned to Cordova in October after blazing a trail across the Nizina and Chisana Glaciers. His route served as a foot path or sled road winter and summer. The route was short and practical with no grades exceeding 10 to 12 percent. He had staked the Nizina Glacier trail sixteen miles to the summit, and work was under way staking the descent and Chisana Glacier. Relief stations had been built on both sides of the summit,

114

and roadhouses sprang up at several locations. Within thirty days Hazelet expected travelers would find "all the comforts of home" in existence from McCarthy to the Chisana diggings.[47]

Hazelet's initial promises for the trail were fulfilled. In late November his party, using horses and double-enders, returned to McCarthy over "the splendid trail" of seventy-eight miles. Skagway folks doubted its existence. "Mr. Hazelet . . . was probably laboring under strong mental stress, produced no doubt by a sight of gold in the Chisana," observed the Skagway newspaper. The *Chitina Leader* scolded doubters, and citizens of Cordova and the Copper River country were enjoined to "spread the facts."[48] Unfortunately, funds raised by subscription had not met all the costs, and a bank note of $2,100 was outstanding in 1915.[49] Great improvements in the trail were announced in November 1913 with the Alaska Road Commission's decision to build a bridge over the Nizina River during winter. Work had begun the previous year, but materials were delayed and construction was postponed. The bridge, 525 feet long with two spans of 150 feet each, would rise seven miles from McCarthy.[50]

✳ Litigation ✳

New discoveries always brought disputes over priority of claim locations, claim boundaries, claim jumping, and conflicting interests of various parties. The grubstake tradition certainly benefited poor prospectors who needed backing for their endeavors, but it was a major source of litigation. Courts often had to determine whether a prospector had an obligation to backers. Billy James and his partners were sued within a couple of months of their discovery by hoteliers Hugh Brady and Henry Dubois of Dawson, who gained an injunction restraining further mining on the discovery claims. The pair relied on a grubstake agreement allegedly made in 1909 which gave them partnership rights in the Chisana claims.

Miners followed litigation over mining claims closely. In the 1914 term of district court, sixteen major cases filled the calendar. Of these, twelve concerned the power-of-attorney issue raised when locations were established before the arrival of Recorder H. E. Morgan. Facts varied, but the basic question—whether claim jumpers could take advantage of the inability of locators to file in a new district—was decided against the claim jumpers.[51]

The landmark case, which also determined the rights of parties in other related suits, was *Sutherland v. Purdy.* Other cases, like *Cloninger v. Findlanson,* relied on the Sutherland decision as precedent. The Cloninger case

Hamshaw's mining camp on Bonanza Creek at the mouth of Little Eldorado. Courtesy of the United States Geological Survey, Capps Collection, Photo 603.

115

Miners working near the head of an unidentified creek in the Chisana district. Courtesy of the Tacoma Public Library, Stanley-Mason Collection.

displayed the opportunism of claim jumpers. Archie Cloninger, a waiter in a Chitina hotel, heard that locations made by Chisana's original locators were invalid because the power of attorney had not been properly recorded. He rushed to the new district in July 1913, reached Bear Creek on August 1, examined the monument and corner stakes left by Taylor on No. 1, then checked the recording book kept by Harold H. Waller. Since there was no recording of a power of attorney held by Taylor for A. H. Findlanson, Cloninger returned to Bear Creek, staked, and began work. Soon he and his partner, Ed Maddox, made an open cut forty feet long, three feet wide, and four and a half feet deep. On August 15 Taylor ordered him off the claim, and subsequently Cloninger sued for possession. At the trial Findlanson's attorney asserted that Cloninger was not a true miner but an unscrupulous fortune hunter who, rather than prospecting, had headed straight for honestly made locations to seize the benefit of a technicality. Cloninger would only admit that "I found what I was looking for," and jurors probably agreed with Findlanson's attorney. The decision in Findlanson's favor, however, turned on a stipulation between parties that the result would be governed by the circuit court of appeal's decision in *Sutherland v. Purdy.*[52]

Dan Sutherland, like Tony Dimond, was a well-known miner at the time of the Chisana stampede. In 1898 he had been with Jack Dalton and others at Pleasant Camp, British Columbia, for the Porcupine strike. A year later Sutherland got involved in a criminal prosecution, charged with assault with a deadly weapon for throwing rocks down on a group on miners. Sutherland and his friends considered the others claim jumpers, but the prosecutor did not present enough evidence to convict him of assault.

Sutherland was also involved in important civil litigation at Chisana. Frank Purdy, who ran the Cassiar Roadhouse with Fred Best, took exception to Dan Sutherland's staking of a

116

fraction on Big Eldorado Creek. Purdy worked the fraction despite Sutherland's location, and Sutherland sued for possession. For most miners litigation involved an expensive disruption of work. Sutherland left the White River in December 1913 for the trial in Cordova. At the end of March the case had not yet been heard, and Purdy petitioned for a postponement. Sutherland complained about the time for prospecting he had already lost by leaving the Chisana district and the prospect of further losses if he were forced to remain in town:

A poor man is dependent upon his labor as are his witnesses. All are waiting. They need to get off for summer work . . . and could be ruined by ten days delay. They would be unable to do annual assessment on their claims.

Practical problems were involved. The winter trail over Nizina Glacier between McCarthy and Chisana would start thawing in early April, and after mid-April it would be dangerous to travel. Men would have to exit via Skolai Pass, utilizing either the path down Skolai Creek or the so-called "goat trail" down the Chitistone River. Considered extremely dangerous, both routes included a twelve-mile crossing of the Russell Glacier.

Sutherland's protests forestalled Purdy's delaying tactic, but the trial result was not favorable. A jury chaired by famed photographer E. A. Hegg ruled against him in April 1914. Eventually, Sutherland prevailed after an appeal, but it was January 1919 before another jury declared in his favor.[53] Sutherland did not grow rich in mining, but he did make friends, including Judge James Wickersham who became congressional delegate in 1908. In later Wickersham political campaigns, Sutherland acted as his campaign manager and became his successor as delegate in the 1920s. Sutherland and Wickersham were Republicans and lost their influence when the Democrats came to power in 1932. Wickersham had gotten back into political harness, replacing Sutherland in 1930, but was badly beaten by Tony Dimond in the Franklin D. Roosevelt triumph two years later.

Miners checking sluice at Hamshaw's Camp on Bonanza No. 6. Courtesy of the Tacoma Public Library, Stanley-Mason Collection.

Mining on Glacier Creek near Chisana about 1914. Note use of the sluice fork to catch large stones. Courtesy of the Tacoma Public Library, Stanley-Mason Collection.

❋ Chisana's Development ❋

The big question about any new camp was its permanence. Would the camp develop as a town or quickly fade away as it appeared that the placers offered no sustained yield? Everyone concerned watched for signs, and no sign was more suggestive than major investments in properties. Thus, when Frank Manley, John J. "Jack" Price, and E. J. Ives paid a reported half million dollars for the thirteen discovery claims owned by Billy James and his partners—Matilda Wales, William A. Johnson, and N. Peter Nelson—the future looked bright. The James group had cleaned up $35,000 in 1913, and experienced mining men had enough confidence in the long-range potential of their claims to buy them for big money (although undoubtedly less than the half million reported).[54]

The Chisana decline was obvious by summer 1914, but those who remained continued to demand better services. It was more difficult at a camp where the boom had collapsed swiftly because people tended to dismiss the place. In fact, the Chisana boom had been well out of proportion to the region's wealth, yet it had been productive for a time. The working miners there did not want to be abandoned by government, particularly by the Alaska Road Commission. Trail work was always a priority need, and the Chisana miners petitioned for improvements every season.

Bad trails made hard work harder and high costs higher. One weary miner described the conditions in 1915 graphically: "You load your horse up with a hundred or so of grub and lead him into the mire. He flounders around until he is all in and you then remove his pack and cut poles which are placed under his body and head." Then you try again over "a ten mile wavering road of muck."[55] But mining went on as some 150 men, most of them on Bonanza Creek, extracted gold "with satisfactory results." Yields were not as high as expected, but the main problem was lack of water.[56]

Other activities in 1914 included the resignation of U.S. Commissioner Dimond and the sale by Manley, Price, and Ives of their option to purchase the discovery of James and his partners. Though the option price paid by Manley, Price, and Ives had been $40,000, that paid by their purchaser, Fletcher T. Hamshaw, was not made public. Price could not help bragging though, claiming that his gain on the transaction had been $50,000. Obviously, Dimond, Manley, Price, and Ives saw the future more clearly than did Hamshaw, one of the many victims of mining speculation.[57]

All the anxiety over transport routes among rival businessmen proved to be pointless after a couple of production seasons. The new diggings played out rather quickly after 1915. The peak yield in 1914 was $250,000; in 1915 the gold valued $160,000; and by 1916 the take was only $40,000. Of the Chisana development as that of any other placer district, the life of the camp can be traced in gold production statistics. The records kept on Chisana were excellent and even extended to the numbers of working mines in each season and the numbers of miners on the job:

Table 3
Chisana Mining District—Yearly Production 1913–1942

Year	No. of Mines	No. of employees	Total production
1913	not recorded	not recorded	$40,000.00
1914	22	325	250,000.00
1915	17	110	160,000.00
1916	12	40	40,000.00
1917	11	44	40,000.00
1918	[8]	[14]	15,000.00
1919	[10]	[24]	27,000.00
1920	8	8	20,000.00
1921	6	16	23,000.00
1922	9	25	29,000.00
1923	9	22	23,000.00
1924	8	[20]	23,400.00
1925	6	[18]	24,000.00
1926	5	[15]	18,000.00
1927	[5]	[15]	15,000.00
1928	5	12	16,000.00
1929	5	12	7,000.00
1930	6	12	5,800.00
1931	[6]	12	3,000.00
1932	[6]	[12]	7,000.00
1933	[7]	20	16,000.00
1934	7	20	16,300.00
1935	10	[24]	21,000.00
1936	8	20	37,500.00
1937	[8]	20	30,000.00
1938	9	20	29,000.00
1939	[8]	20	20,000.00
1940	[8]	20	14,000.00
1941	[8]	[20]	14,000.00
1942	[4]	[8]	8,000.00
TOTAL			**992,000.00**

* bracketed figures are estimates.

CABINS ALONG CHISANA TRAILS

DOCUMENTATION OF THE CHISANA TRAILS AND THE SOLO MOUNTAIN SHELTER CABIN WHICH ARE WITHIN WRANGELL–ST ELIAS NATIONAL PARK AND PRESERVE WAS UNDERTAKEN BY THE HISTORIC AMERICAN BUILDINGS SURVEY (HABS), A DIVISION OF THE NATIONAL PARK SERVICE. THE PROJECT WAS EXECUTED UNDER THE GENERAL DIRECTION OF ROBERT J. KAPSCH, CHIEF OF HABS/HAER, AND JOHN COOK, ALASKA REGIONAL DIRECTOR, NATIONAL PARK SERVICE. RECORDING WAS CARRIED OUT DURING THE SUMMER OF 1982 BY ROBERT SPUDE, PROJECT DIRECTOR, STEVEN PETERSON, HISTORICAL ARCHITECT, JOHN LOWE III, PHOTOGRAPHER, AND MICHAEL LAPPEN AND DANIEL TAYLOR, HISTORIANS, WITH THE SUPPORT OF THE WRANGELL–ST ELIAS NATIONAL PARK AND PRESERVE STAFF.

CHISANA TRAILS.

FROM 1913 THROUGH 1915, THE CHISANA REGION BETWEEN THE WRANGELL AND NUTZOLIN MOUNTAINS DREW MINERS FROM ALASKA AND CANADA IN SEARCH OF GOLD. BEGINNING AT MCCARTHY, PROSPECTORS FOLLOWED TWO TRAILS, THE GOAT TRAIL THROUGH CHITISTONE GORGE, AND THE WINTER TRAIL FLAGGED BY GEORGE HAZELET ACROSS THE NIZINA AND CHISANA GLACIERS.

INNKEEPERS OPERATED ROADHOUSES (R.H.) AND THE ALASKA ROAD COMMISSION BUILT SHELTER CABINS (S.C.) FOR THE USE OF TRAVELERS. SOLO MOUNTAIN SHELTER CABIN, FIFTEEN MILES SOUTH OF CHISANA, IS ONE OF A STRING OF CABINS ALONG THE 78 MILE SUMMER TRAIL. THE ROUTES WERE LITTLE USED AFTER THE ADVENT OF AIRPLANE TRAVEL IN THE 1930'S.

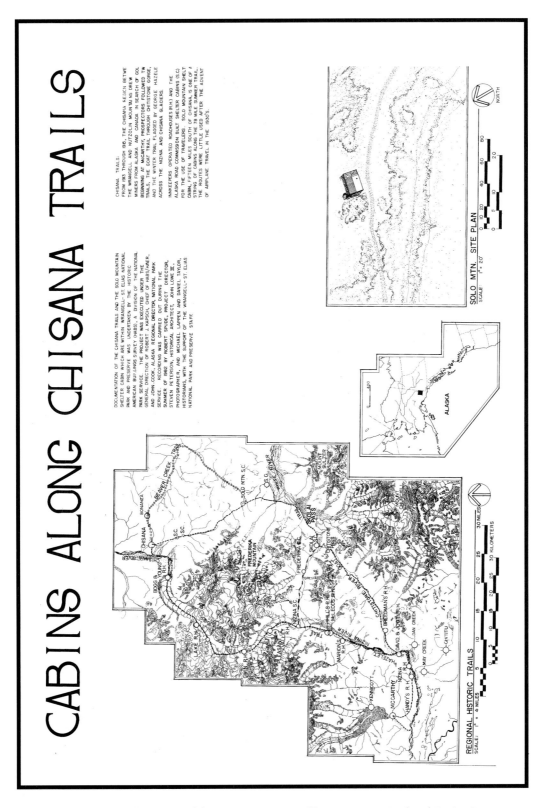

Cabins Along Chisana Trails. Courtesy of the Historic American Buildings Survey, National Park Service, Steven Peterson, 1982.

Storm over Mt. Sanford. National Park
Service photo by M.W. Williams, 1993.

Chapter

*   *   *

Finding the Boundary

On a map the boundary between Canada and Alaska looks irrationally drawn. The line along the 141st Meridian runs north to south for much of the distance, then wavers at the southern end short of the Pacific Ocean. From this point near Mount St. Elias the line straggles southeast across the mountains, enclosing a long appendage that reaches as far south as Dixon Entrance and bars open access to the interior. International diplomacy figured prominently in the fixing of the boundary. Negotiations between Russia and Great Britain early in the nineteenth century and subsequently between the United States and Britain had momentous effects on the interests of Canada. The diplomatic history concerning the border location has no relevance to this study, but the practical surveying work does. The international border includes a section of the Wrangell-St. Elias National Park and Preserve boundary, established only with great difficulty. Diplomatic negotiations over the boundary before the survey can be tersely summarized. Trade rivalry between the Hudson's Bay Company and the Russian American Company led to negotiation of a boundary between Canada and Alaska in 1825. For want of surveys or even basic exploration of some regions, borders were described in general terms for the narrow coastal strip of southeastern Alaska south of sixty degrees north latitude. The nations agreed that Russia would hold the territory from the crest of the mountains to the sea as long as this point fell no farther inland than thirty nautical miles. Once vaguely settled, the entire matter of the border died down until after the Alaska purchase and, more particularly, the Cassiar gold rush.

Though the need for a survey was obvious, pressure declined after the Cassiar rush in the sparsely settled territory. President Ulysses S. Grant recommended a boundary commission in 1872 and President Grover Cleveland asked for a preliminary survey in 1885, but Congress neglected to provide funding. For a time thereafter neither Canada nor the United States vigorously pursued final resolution. Finally, a government study commission advanced the argument that would interpret the 1825 agreement in a way advantageous to U.S. interests. Canadians argued that the line should be drawn to leave some coastal inlets, including Skagway and Dyea, within Canada. Without such a line there could be no entry into the Yukon Territory interior from the coast except through American territory. The Klondike stampede made fixing the boundary a matter of urgency. A joint high commission was appointed, and negotiations began in 1899. Eventually, the Americans prevailed, and the entire southeastern coastal strip was determined to be part of Alaska.

✳ Surveying the 141st Meridian ✳

Finding a boundary line for non-coastal regions proved to be nearly as difficult as negotiating for it. In 1905 the parties agreed upon the 141st Meridian as the boundary except for the Alaska Panhandle. Negotiators for Great Britain and the United States agreed to fix the meridian at a single point, using the telegraphic method of location, and project the line north to the Arctic Ocean and south to the flank of Mount St. Elias. Surveyors knew before they reached the field that some means might have to be found to fix the line across higher sections in the Mount St. Elias region that might prove impossible to reach. Later surveyors of the southern end of the line detoured westward to make their triangulations, following the drainage which culminated in the Chitina River. This necessary diversion allowed them to establish the mean distances, elevations, and geodetic positions to maintain integrity of the line.

O. H. Tittman, chief of the U.S. survey party, hired Thomas Riggs Jr. to join the group under Clyde Baldwin. Riggs, a Princeton graduate in engineering who had been in the timber business in Washington state before joining the Klondike gold rush, had worked on the survey from 1903 to 1905 and had an independent mind. Riggs argued that surveyors should be permitted to accomplish more than locating a line. Why not do triangulation work and map the country accurately as they passed through? Tittman agreed with Riggs's argument, and Riggs signed on as assistant surveyor. He was on his way to Yakutat via San Francisco when the great earthquake struck the city by the bay. Riggs was greeted by an old friend at Skagway, Harriet Pullen, a hotel keeper-hostess of the old gold rush town. He took the train to Whitehorse and a barge to Dawson, meeting other friends en route, including Frank Slaven, a miner who in earlier years had entertained stampeders with his boxing prowess. Riggs admired Slaven's philosophy of life: Nothing hurts except the fear of being hurt, so conquer such fears, including that of dying, which he also believed did not hurt. Though he had been absent from Dawson for six years, Riggs found plenty of old friends still around to talk with before taking a steamer downriver to Boundary—the point fixed for the 141st Meridian line.[1]

The surveyors gathered at Boundary in June 1907, provisioned and equipped for a season's work. Forty-eight pack horses purchased in Yakima, Washington, provided transportation. A Canadian, A. J. Barbazon, and the American leader, Clyde Baldwin, divided the men into small parties for specific tasks, including projection, reconnaissance, triangulation, topography, vista and stadia, and monument building. A friendly rivalry prevailed. The men had not been involved in the boundary controversy and had no reason for hostility. Every American party had an attaché from the Canadian force and vice versa. Riggs and other Americans in the small party he headed poked fun at the Canadian attaché, F. H. L. Lambert, because he was a tenderfoot, a recent graduate engineer who had resolved to take the good life with him to the field. Lambert's portable rubber bathtub drew immediate ridicule, and George Bird was unkind enough to nail it to a tree, claiming self-defense: *"The god damned thing had me scared and I wasn't going to let it get loose and stampede my horses."*[2]

The remoteness of the country made survey work difficult. Only two places on the meridian— where the Yukon and Porcupine Rivers crossed—offered access by water transport. Elsewhere, parties depended on pack horse transport over hill, tundra, and swamp. Progress seldom exceeded two miles an hour during the six hours daily that animals could be worked. Men had to travel light, each carrying a twenty-pound load of personal gear and bedding. Mosquitoes and gnats made travel in summer merely irritating, but as parties stretched the season to work on into the autumn, it was neither comfortable nor safe. As Riggs noted:

When ice is thick enough to just break through with the weight of man, when the wolves howl around the camp, when in the morning huge fires must be built to thaw out tents and pack-rigging, while packers freeze their fingers tying packs on the dejected and shivering ponies.[3]

The surveying season generally lasted about 100 days and, with so much ground to cover, the men worked seven days a week. "Sundays do not especially exist as a day of rest," Riggs said, "unless it is storming too hard to even move camp." Breakfast was delayed until 7 a.m. on Sunday and the Fourth of July rather than taken as usual at 6 a.m., and work ended for the day at 5 p.m., rather than 6 p.m. or later.[4]

Thomas Riggs summarized his boundary survey experiences for the general public in several articles. He took considerable pride in five years of work, making "the straightest of the world's surveyed lines." Despite the time and effort involved, the survey left no imposing monument, no lasting structure:

The actual visible results of the work consist of a vista 20 feet wide cut through all timber, monuments set at intervisible points not more than four miles apart, and a detailed map of a strip of country extending for two miles on each side of the boundary.

Prominent river crossings and main points of travel were marked by five-foot aluminum-bronze sectional shafts, each weighing 300 pounds and set in a ton of concrete. At less important points three-foot aluminum-bronze cones were set in 1,500 pounds of concrete. The line extended 600 miles from near Mount St. Elias to the Arctic Ocean. Completion in 1912 encouraged miners of the Wrangell-St. Elias region because it suggested possible extension of the Copper River and Northwestern Railway beyond Kennecott. Riggs noted that an extension to the Skolai Pass would reduce transportation costs and stimulate development. Miners had to pay thirty-five cents to a dollar a pound for freight brought to Canyon City on the White River from Whitehorse.

Riggs, practical and hard working on the job, could indulge in a bit of romance when the task had been completed. Then he could reflect on the "true spirit of man" as manifested by efforts performed under severe conditions and the test faced by the tenderfoot which "shows whether he is worthy of the life of a surveyor or whether his adventures in life should be limited to the selling of pink and blue ribbons." He saw values in the endeavor beyond the survey itself, one related to:

. . . an unexplainable fascination about the North. The very hardships lend a paradoxical charm. The vast solitudes, uninhabited and lonely, have an irresistible call. The surveyor dreads the day when he shall have thrown his last diamond hitch, broken his last camp, and from the deck of a homeward-bound steamer, have watched a free life fade away in the mist with the distant hills.[5]

The 1909 season turned out to be a busy one for survey crews in the Wrangell-St. Elias region. They started from Canyon City on the White River in late May, laid a base line that crossed the boundary, and measured on the south bank of White River. Triangulation was extended southward to the northern slopes of Mt. Natazhat, then northward to connect with the previous season's triangulation. Then "a scheme was laid out and observed from the boundary up the valley of the White to Skolai Pass, where connection was made with several United States Geological Survey stations."[6] Riggs, a careful reporter of his official activities, also included comments on peripheral matters in his diaries. One incident concerned his meeting a German and his Irish wife, Dawson residents who showed up at the surveyors' camp in the White River area in acute need of help. Both looked more than sixty years old, yet they dared travel this hard country seeking gold. Riggs wondered at their unlikely dreams and poor preparation for the trail. The surveyors fed the couple, helped them clean up and rest a bit, then sent a packer with them as a guide to the Skolai Pass. Later, when Riggs reached Valdez at the end of the season, he inquired about the travelers. No one in

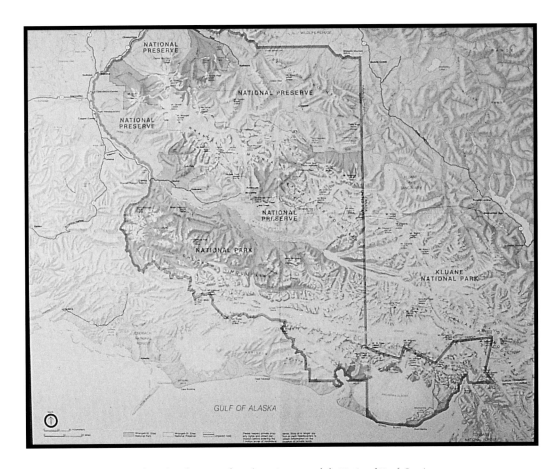

Wrangell-St. Elias National Park and Preserve boundary. Courtesy of the National Park Service.

town had seen them. "Perhaps," Riggs reflected gloomily, "a thousand years from now their bodies will roll out of the boot of the Russell Glacier."[7]

As an old Klondiker, Riggs retained interest in mineral discovery and of prospectors known to him. He observed a steep hill south of White River, near Kletsan Creek, where much native copper showed. "Jack Dalton had hunted all over the hills but had never found it," he recalled. But Dalton had obtained quite a number of large copper nuggets from placer operations some years previously, and one of the largest nuggets found came from this country. Stories about Jack Dalton were always exchanged among the old-timers in Alaska. Dalton was a legendary figure, a man of importance in Wrangell-St. Elias regional history as well as other sections of Alaska.[8] Riggs sometimes recorded natural phenomenon, such as a splendid display of the aurora: "I will never forget my last night out from Lake Kluane," he wrote in 1909:

It was clear, cold, and still. The Northern Lights started as a low white arch across the horizon. They grew brighter and brighter, turned to color. Soon the entire heavens were carved with the most grotesque whirls and eddies of all the colors of the spectrum, suddenly appearing and suddenly disappearing. I have never seen anything like this.[9]

Foul weather in August 1909 defeated some high country projects that Riggs had planned. Surveyors failed to occupy topographic camera stations on Natazhat and some high adjacent peaks. In connection with this effort a party crossed the range at the head

126

of Holmes Creek, twelve miles west of the boundary, and tried to climb Natazhat from the south. The climbers never reached the summit but did acquire considerable useful information on the country south of the range. The official report of the trip highlighted its difficulties when the men faced winter conditions in August:

The trail led over the divide on glare ice, where steps had to be cut for nearly half a mile, then down a long ridge of loose scoria and out onto a badly broken fork of the Klutlan Glacier. It began to snow, but we had to go on, as it would have been impossible to re-cross the divide in the storm, and reached camp at 8:30, worn out and chilled to the bone, and found the tent down and everything wet or frozen. We shoveled away the snow for a small space with snowshoes, put up the tent as best we could and crawled into our scanty bedding. During the night it snowed 25 inches, and continued snowing the greater part of the day. Even with the coal oil-lamp burning full blast and three men in the little seven by seven tent, the thermometer registered only 32.[10]

The 1912 season loomed large in the Wrangell-St. Elias region. Surveyors wanted to locate a line across the glaciers and vast ice and snowfields between Mounts Natazhat and St. Elias. Owing to the great elevation of the Natazhat ridge, where it is crossed by the border, and the ruggedness of the country that had defeated the climbing attempt in 1909, it seemed impossible to project a line south by the standard methods. The surveyors decided to go round the ridge and carry on a scheme of triangulation from the western end of the White River system of 1909 across Skolai Pass, south, and up the valley of the Chitina to the line. An America party undertook the work, which involved exploration, as the upper Chitina region was virtually unknown. From Cordova the party traveled by rail to McCarthy, then on to Skolai Pass at the head of White River, hauling their supplies on horse-drawn sleds. Despite persistent bad weather in the high country, they managed to recover the four stations established in 1909 and complete the triangulation across Skolai Pass and down Skolai Creek. In late July the surveyors joined another party that had worked up the Chitina towards the line. The Chitina party had accomplished considerable plane-table topography in the Chitina and Anderson Glaciers. The combined party then measured a base in the Nizina Valley before returning to Cordova in September. The season's work had been fruitful, and the Nizina River elevations at Monument 126 were connected with two bench marks made earlier by the U.S. Geological Survey based on railway levels carried up from Cordova—"the mean discrepancy being 1.6 meters."[11] The survey team felt good about the season and noted that they had overcome major obstacles:

One section lived for some time on two sheep and some ptarmigan which they were able to shoot, and a six-year old sack of flour which they had fortunately discovered cached in a tree. One man fell over a bluff, and, though unhurt, decided to leave the survey, as did another who fell into a crevasse and escaped unin-jured. A horse that fell over a cliff was killed, and there were many close calls for the men climbing the steep bluffs of the snow-covered mountains. Then in the fall, snowslides having incapacitated the railway, the parties had to walk for sixty miles and descended the Copper River for eighty-five miles in overloaded small boats.[12]

Thomas Riggs Jr. and Asa C. Baldwin were the U.S. chiefs of survey parties for the 1913 season, while J. D. Craig led the effort for Canada. Many of the assistants and packers were veterans of previous seasons, including Fred Lambert, the Canadian who brought his portable bathtub during his first season. Excitement about the Chisana gold strike dominated other events in the region that season. The surveyors were accustomed to little contact with travelers or inhabitants along much of the line, and the stampede constituted "an annoyance." Stampeder traffic from Dawson flowed over the survey trail from the glacier, and many gold seekers paused at the surveyor's camp. Their sociability often went unappreciated, as the boundary reporter noted:

As usual, about seventy-five per cent of the stampeders were very inadequately equipped for a trip of this description, and as they seemed to consider a government survey party a sort of general supply depot, it became the duty of the survey to provide meals for them, to sell them what provisions could be spared, and even to provide clothing and shoes, in addition to furnishing minute directions as to how to get to the diggings.

Riggs and other survey leaders also feared defections of their people in the excitement over gold. They recalled colorful Klondike stories about sailors deserting their ships at Skagway to join the stampede, but, happily, the packers and cooks of the survey stood fast.[13] Surveyors encountered other stampeders in September after they completed the numbering and inspection of monuments in the region. Traveling from White River over Skolai Pass, they met stampeders on the route from Cordova. "The same lack of preparedness was evidenced here by the throngs on the trail," complained a survey reporter: "Ill-equipped, without any idea of outdoor life, and treating their poor animals outrageously, they found the mountainous trail trying and dangerous, and the quiet, steady advance of the survey pack-train, with its well-broken animals, was a source of wonder and admiration to them, for they were ignorant of the fact that most of the survey horses were 'old timers' at that sort of work."[14]

Other parties of the 1913 season worked in the country between Anderson Glacier and Mount St. Elias. Season goals included completion of topography as far as St. Elias; location of points and line projection across the valleys at the head of the Chitina; location of Mount St. Elias by triangulation; and the ascent of St. Elias. The men left McCarthy in March, freighting their supplies to the Chitina Glacier by horse sled. From that point supplies were transferred to pack horses, then dogsleds, and, where animals could not travel, by backpack. Making an early start was a good idea, but temperatures of forty below and deep snow hindered progress. It was late April before the parties reached their starting points.

A Canadian party succeeded in reaching the summit of Mount Natazhat that season, and the Americans were particularly keen to climb Mount St. Elias. The surveyors knew all about previous climbs and the valuable scientific work of Israel C. Russell in the early 1890s, but their chief mission was to determine the mountain's relationship to the boundary. Controversy over its location had been sharp since 1874, when William H. Dall had placed it slightly west of the 141st Meridian. In 1892 a U.S. Coast and Geodetic Survey expedition under J. E. McGrath made an extensive trigonometric survey in the vicinity of Yakutat Bay to determine latitude of the summit at 60° 17′ 35″; longitude of 140° 45′ 32″; and elevation of 18,024 feet. Thus, the mountain became recognized as one of the boundary peaks. The Duke of Abruzzi was first to reach the summit in 1897, but the "land of desolation" north of St. Elias described by Russell was still unexplored.

The surveyors recognized that this "land of desolation" borders the 141st Meridian south from Mount Natazhat to strike the St. Elias Range west of the summit. They calculated that the boundary should be drawn from Mount St. Elias to the 141st Meridian parallel to the coast. Asa C. Baldwin led a party charged with determining the line from that marking the coastal strip to the meridian. Five Americans and two Canadians set out with two man-hauled Yukon sleds, traveling as light as possible. They traversed the Chitina and Logan glaciers to reach the base of the great mountain on June 22, traveling mostly by night to take advantage of a harder snow surface. After deciding against the northeastern route used by Russell and Abruzzi, because it would require more sledding and crossing of a second divide en route, they settled on trying the western approach. From their base camp at 7,500 feet, the mountain towered another 10,500 feet above them. As they examined the face of the mountain, they spotted distant avalanches seeming to creep down the sides of the mountain and heard dull roars from their passage:

At 19,500 feet, Mt. Logan is the tallest mountain in Canada and the largest mountain massif in the world. Its sheer relief surpasses Himalayan proportions.

As the moving mass gained in proportions and speed, it swept everything before it, and reaching a precipice, would shoot out in a stream like foaming water and disappear in the depths below. Long afterwards, clouds of snow-dust hung in the air and the dull rumbling continued.[15]

Climbing from the west seemed impossible, but they pushed on. They reached the top of the divide to behold the same scene that had been described so graphically by Russell. Baldwin was also impressed by the sight and by their first view of Mount St. Elias. "It came into view late one evening just as the sun was setting," he wrote. Although thirty miles away, "it seemed close enough to touch, and its height was so exaggerated that I despaired of ever reaching those blue shadows. It towered in the sky so calmly, so coldly, so majestically that it seemed of another world." The intervening land did not appear to offer an easy progress:

It was a wide valley through which ran a mighty river whose course we could trace seeping in graceful curves to the southwest as far as the eye could see. The river and its many side streams were not rivers of limpid water but were frozen and congealed into a solid mass over which lay a deep accumulation of snow. There was not a black object to be seen anywhere except a few sharp peaks that projected their heads above the flood of white. It was a stretch of primitive chaos. This was the land Russell saw from the shoulder of St. Elias and was the land that was to occupy our attention for several days to come.[16]

By June 28 the climbers had progressed to 13,500 feet, where they set up camp. From this point they made a final dash and reached 16,000 feet before a severe snowstorm forced them to give up. Even had they reached the summit, weather conditions would have pre-

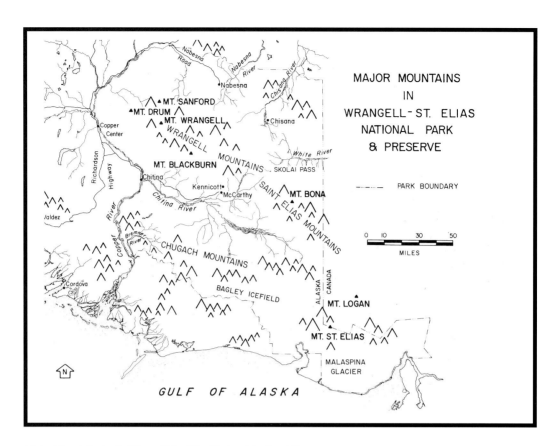

Major Mountains in the Wrangell-St. Elias National Park and Preserve

vented accurate observations. They descended the mountain much quicker than they had
climbed, hurrying past hazards to reach food stores at the base camp. Not until they had
packed up the base camp and moved to the camp on the Logan Glacier, involving a four-day
trek, could the men again enjoy some comforts. "That evening," Baldwin wrote:

> . . . *we camped in the willows and for the first time in thirty days looked upon green things and flowers and built a real fire and once more heard the birds sing, whose song was perhaps no sweeter music to our ears than the gurgle of the big, black bean-pot.*[17]

Despite the failure to reach the summit, the trip provided the data needed for their
measurements. By coincidence, their highest camp was later determined to be only 128.2
meters west of the 141st Meridian. The commissioners decided that the point of intersection
with the Alaska coastal strip boundary should be on the meridian at the latitude of their
camp, which was also a camera station. Thus was the difficult boundary connection
determined. Completion, or near completion, of the survey was a newsworthy event, as
was the effort to climb Mount St. Elias. In September 1913 the *Seattle Post-Intelligencer* reported that "the running of the world's longest straight line boundary . . . has been practically
completed." A reporter, who interviewed D. J. Fraser of the Canadian survey party as he
passed through Seattle en route to Ottawa, recorded the survey highlights. "The great line,
running as straight as the crow flies, from Mount St. Elias directly north over moving glaciers
and some of the world's highest peaks, extends to the edge of the Arctic Ocean, dotted every

three miles with a permanent stone monument." The project had cost almost $1 million because surveyors "had to cling to the arrow-line course of the survey, no matter where it led them." Transport and logistical considerations involved were comparable to those faced by polar explorers. Fraser pointed out that in the hundred-mile section between Mounts Natazhat and St. Elias sites for only three monuments could be found.[18]

* Survey Personnel *

Participants in the survey included some articulate writers who described their work in such popular journals as *National Geographic*. Thomas Riggs Jr. was one who had an interesting and varied career in Alaska. He wrote about his participation in the Klondike gold rush, but his post-survey career was distinguished by his appointment as Alaska's governor in 1918, following his service on the Alaska Engineering Commission from 1914 to 1917. Riggs left Alaska in 1921 after his term expired to establish a New York office as a consulting engineer. The boundary involved him again from 1935 until his death in 1945, as he was appointed U.S. Commissioner of the International Boundary Commission in Washington, D.C. [19]

Asa C. Baldwin was another distinguished engineer and author. He earned an undergraduate degree in engineering at Case University. In 1909 he was appointed as civil engineer with the U.S. Coast and Geodetic Survey and initially served aboard the survey's cutter *Surveyor* in marine surveys around Kodiak and the Aleutians. After his service with the Boundary Survey from 1910 to 1913 and another year as consultant to the Boundary Commission, he established himself as a consulting engineer in Valdez. Baldwin advised the Kennecott Copper Corporation, was field engineer for the Copper River and Northwestern Railway, and served with the U.S. Army Engineers in France during World War I. Baldwin maintained offices in Valdez and Seattle for some years, working as a mine promoter. During 1926 and 1927 he made two transcontinental tours lecturing about Alaska. Mining speculation made him a millionaire, then wiped him out in the Great Depression, and he turned to farming in New Rochelle, New York, and elsewhere. "Things were getting blue in 1935," he noted, when an old friend from Alaska, Emil Hunya, offered an appointment with the International Boundary Commission at $8,000 a year. The appointment allowed time for other consulting. From 1936 through 1940 he was president of the Yellow Band Mines located in the Bremner Range within the Wrangell-St. Elias region. The pioneer surveyor and distinguished engineer died in 1942.[20]

* Conclusion *

The boundary survey represents a significant event in Wrangell-St. Elias history. International negotiation and field cooperation developed then is still active today among Canadian and U.S. officials. The work added immeasurably to geographic and scientific knowledge of the region, as close attention was given to glaciers and other prominent physical features. Field crews studied the notes of their predecessors and offered their own observations and conclusions for those who followed.

Early mountaineers from the Israel C. Russell Expedition (1890 or 91) resting on their approach to Mt. St. Elias. Courtesy of the Rasmuson Library Archives, University of Alaska Fairbanks; Hamlin Collection, 728-47N.

Chapter

❊　❊　❊

The Mountaineer Explorers

The first eighteenth-century maritime explorers observed with awe the towering peaks of the St. Elias Range but contented themselves with marking their positions on charts and naming a few of the most prominent. Not until late in the nineteenth century did mountaineers become interested in the St. Elias mountains. The pioneer mountaineers included scientists who sought to contribute to knowledge and adventurers motivated by the strenuous challenge of climbing.

❊ Mount St. Elias ❊

Mount St. Elias holds the distinction as one point of the original discovery by Vitus Bering. For a long time conflicting estimates of the great mountain's height and its location in regard to national boundaries challenged geographers. Neither Bering nor Capt. James Cook made estimates, and the French navigator La Perouse made a very modest guess of 12,672 feet in 1786; Malaspina did better in 1791 with an estimate of 17,851. Russian hydrographic charts maintained this elevation until 1847 when the Russian scholar Tebenkof reduced the estimate to 16,938 feet. The British calculation was even lower, as its admiralty charts in the 1870s recorded a mere 14,970 feet. In 1874 the U.S. Coast and Geodetic Survey insisted on a lofty elevation of 19,500 feet, give or take five hundred. In the 1880s British climbers reduced it to 18,500 feet, and in 1890 topographer Mark Kerr lowered it to 15,350. Israel C. Russell and the U.S. Coast and Geodetic Survey reached an agreement in the early 1890s of 18,100, give or take a hundred feet. There the controversy rested until accurate surveys finally were accomplished. St. Elias is somewhat unusual among the world's mountains in that early observers underestimated the true elevation of 18,008 feet. The first guesses at the height of most mountains usually are too high. The broad base of the mountain made it appear less lofty to early explorers.

Longitude and latitude were equally vexing to geographers of the same period. Estimates of latitude ranged from 60° 15′ 00″ N to 60° 22′ 36″ N. Longitude varied from 140° 10′ 00″ W to 141° 00′ 12″ W. The precise location was a matter of more import than the mountain's elevation as this determined whether it was within Canadian or American borders. Actual longitude is 140° 55′ 30″ W and latitude is 60° 17′ 40″ N. The mountain is sixty-seven miles northwest of Yakutat and on the boundary line.

Though Bering usually is given credit for naming the mountain, better evidence indicates that it was not named until some years after its discovery. Eighteenth-century cartographers began using the name, taken from Cape St. Elias, and thus it was established.[1]

❋ First Climb ❋

The *New York Times* sponsored the first climb of St. Elias in 1886 with an expedition under Lt. Frederick Schwatka. Newspapers often sponsored exploration in those days, as it guaranteed them an exclusive story and plaudits for contributing to science. Schwatka had gained a reputation as a northern explorer through his voyage from the sources to the mouth of the Yukon River in 1883. The middle and lower river had been well charted, but he provided the first accurate chart of the headwaters and upper river.

Schwatka, who headed a U.S. Army expedition, annoyed the Canadians by providing names for prominent features within Canada, but he did good work. He was a lively writer of periodical articles, and his book, *Along Alaska's Great River*, published in 1885, stimulated interest in Alaska. Schwatka was not an expert mountaineer, but he had the help of the experienced Lt. H. W. Seton-Karr of the British Army. He was also assisted by a scientist, Prof. William Libbey Jr., as well as packers and Indians. One of his white packers, Jack Dalton, later became famous for his own northern exploits.

The party disembarked from U.S.S. *Pinta*, commanded by naval Capt. N. E. Nichols, on July 17, 1886 at Icy Bay. Schwatka pushed inland sixteen miles due north into the St. Elias foothills. He discovered and named the Jones River and the Agassiz and Guyot Glaciers. By July 25 he reached the foot of St. Elias after moving along glaciers for the last fifteen miles of the trek:

All around us was a wild scene of alpine and arctic desolation, and on a scale that nearly overpowered the senses. Mr. Seton-Karr said that the Alps seemed like toy representations of the colossal chain ahead of us, all white with snow, steel blue with glacial ice, or black with frowning flanks of igneous rock. Cumulus clouds threw over the snow shadows like gigantic fields of retreating black.[2]

From the base of the mountain Schwatka planned an attack up Tyndall Glacier by three lightly equipped men. He hoped that forty hours of almost continuous ascent would bring them to the summit. He soon learned that the climb would not be easy as his first view of the glacier had indicated:

At a long distance they looked easy enough of ascent, but nearer inspection revealed an ice cascade, that bane of alpine climbers, on every one. The perpendicular descent of the smallest was probably hundreds of feet, and being at an inclination of not less than from sixty to seventy five degrees they were simply impassable.

He thought they might be able to climb rock ridges protruding from the ice and reach snow and ice courses at about ten thousand feet, but his goal was too optimistic:

As we advanced the crevasses became wider and wider, and at some points we walked as if on the comb of a roof. As the traverse crevasses became wider the snow bridges became scarcer, having tumbled into the abyss below, and at last we reached a point where no man could go unless furnished with wings.

The men devoted the afternoon to attempting an alternative route but were again thwarted by crevasses. Schwatka had to give up at 7,300 feet, but tried to put the best face on his failure: "Nine-tenths [of the climb] was above the snow level, and which is believed to be the highest climb above the snow limit ever made—a result well worth the expedition."[3] Schwatka got the Indians of his party to convey them by canoe to Yakutat, where they waited a month before *Pinta* picked them up. During that time he had frequent glimpses of the distant peak he had hoped to conquer, but the weather always closed in again after a short time. The sightings confirmed his conclusions: "The lack of continuous fine weather, an absolute necessity in an alpine attempt over unknown paths, was the most formidable obstacle in conquering this king of the continent."[4]

❋ Topham Expedition ❋

In 1888 Harold W. and Edwin Topham, George Broke, and William Williams attempted yet another assault on the summit. The party disembarked at Icy Bay on July 13, following the route used by Schwatka to the mountain base. The Topham brothers and Broke were British; Williams was an American. Williams wrote an entertaining account of the expedition, which put Schwatka's efforts into somewhat clearer perspective:

The [Schwatka] party succeeded in getting very near the foot of the mountain, a distance of about forty-five miles from the sea, but owing to the unfavorable state of the weather, combined with other causes, all attempts . . . were abandoned. . . . Only nine or ten days were spent away from the beach.[5]

The party did not command enough political clout to get transport on *Pinta* from Sitka and had to rely on the charter of a local sealing vessel. They left Sitka on July 3 and reached Yakutat a week later on *Alpha*. The Yakutat Indians had few opportunities to work as packers for whites crossing the pass to the Yukon River headwaters, but they knew that their services were valuable. Topham had to negotiate hard to beat down the asking price of the two men he needed from three to two dollars a day. Once Topham's party completed preparations, Indian canoes conveyed the group to Icy Bay in ten hours.

Topham was better equipped than Schwatka had been for a major climbing expedition. Provisions included 1,400 pounds of bacon, ham, beans, flour, smoked salmon, dried apples, tea, and coffee—enough for forty days. They estimated that the trek would take only twenty-eight days of actual travel away from their base camp on the beach. They started out on July 16, walking through patches of strawberries and glacial streams and then ascending the Agassiz Glacier. From there they had a choice of two routes to the summit, and they chose the one Schwatka had not tried. Williams marveled that the Indian packers preferred wearing their moccasins on the difficult crossing of moraines, ice, and snow, despite having been given boots, which they wished to have intact for later wearing. "The average Indian is a competent being," Williams noted with some arrogance:

. . . though it takes some time to discover his good points. He is quick at grasping ideas, and is especially good at imitating what others have done . . . he deals with the white man at arm's length. He is exceedingly distrustful, nor does he cease to be so until he has become thoroughly convinced of the honest intentions of the stranger.[6]

The party was forced to abandon its attempt to reach the eastern end of the Chaix Hills. They retraced their steps to the hills, then started northeast as Schwatka had done, passing Lake Castani (Caetani), named by Schwatka, along their way. They moved up Tyndall Glacier, past the base of the mountain, onto St. Elias itself, rejoicing that they had already achieved a record by getting beyond Schwatka's highest ascent and onto the mountain. Then Topham and Williams pushed on, roped together, cutting ice steps as they climbed. They reached a crater at 11,400 feet but found it impossible to go on. Beyond the crater rose a 1,500-foot-high mound, which could be climbed by cutting ice steps, but the task could not be accomplished without camping overnight. They needed packers for this, experienced mountaineers, but none were available. "Even then success would not be certain," Williams noted, "unless another year should find these same slopes covered with firm snow rather than ice."[7] Williams had to find joy in the scenery rather than the attainment of his goal:

The day was cloudless; the whole scene was one that baffles description; It surpassed in grandeur though not in picturesqueness the very best that the Alps can offer. Roughly speaking, the eye encountered for miles nothing but snow and ice. I had never before realized the vastness of the Alaskan glaciers, though during the past fortnight we had spent many a weary hour in crossing immense moraines, one of the glaciers we looked down upon was not less than sixty miles long, while another attained a breadth of twenty-five or thirty miles.[8]

The party reached its shore camp on August 7, and started immediately for Yakutat. After four days at Yakutat Williams went south to Sitka on *Active*, a small trading schooner loaded with miners. Those remaining behind had a harder time until one of them hired an Indian crew for a weeklong canoe trip to Sitka and sent a schooner back for the rest of the party from there. A gale at sea struck and damaged the schooner, which had to put back to Yakutat for repairs. It was September 17 before the climbers reached Sitka.

Williams expected other climbers to continue the challenge. It comforted him to state that the next expedition would have the advantage of following a marked course to 11,400 feet. They would be able to get that far within six days of leaving Icy Bay, while his party had needed sixteen days "owing to the absence of all definite information concerning the mountain proper."[9] He did not insist that the best climbing route had been determined:

It is not at all unlikely that the true way to the summit is to be found on the northern side, where fewer rocks and better snow would probably be encountered; how to reach the northern side of the mountain is a problem yet to be solved. But whether successful in reaching the top or not, no party composed of men who enjoy walking and climbing amidst the finest of alpine scenery will ever regret having spent the summer in making the attempt to ascend Mt. St. Elias.[10]

✻ First National Geographic Expedition ✻

In 1890 the National Geographic Society sponsored a major St. Elias expedition under Israel C. Russell, a geologist who would become the leading authority on the region. Russell planned to avoid the south or ocean side ascent, "where the sandstone slopes are almost perpendicular," for a climb of the eastern face from the head of Yakutat Bay. Paying heed to the laments of earlier climbers, he recruited packers in Seattle, "seven stalwart woodsman," to avoid a dependence on Indians. Mark Kerr was the expedition's geographer whose concerns included fixing the elevation of the mountain.[11]

On June 24 the expedition reached Sitka on *Queen*, skippered by Capt. James Carroll, then sailed off for Yakutat on *Pinta*. At Port Mulgrave, Russell noted an Indian village on the southeastern end of Khantaak Island and another on the mainland a couple of miles to the east. The mainland village boasted a store maintained by Sitka merchants and the Moravian mission of the Rev. Karl J. Hendrickson, a son of Sweden, whose assistant was also a Swede. The native population was about fifty, and their appearance impressed Russell:

The Yakutat Indians are of fine physique, have well-built houses of their own design and workmanship, and live by hunting and fishing. They are 'canoe Indians,' and spend a large part of their time on the water in quest of salmon, seals, and sea otters.

From the sale of sea otter and other skins and hand-woven baskets to merchants at Sitka, the Yakutats gained enough cash to give them a definite air of prosperity.[12]

Russell had a good eye for scenery and a facile pen for description. He noted the icebergs jammed against the shore by high winds:

Many of the larger bergs, stranded in thirty to forty feet of water, stood like rocks against which the heavy

Members of the 1912 Dora Keen expedition cross a steep section on Mount Blackburn. The Kennicott Glacier is in the upper portion of the photo. Courtesy of the University of Washington Library, Dora Keen Collection, 16694.

swells broke in splendid sheets of foam. The shattered waves, dashing high in the air, often quite obscured the icy ramparts that sought to hold them back. The icebergs are of pure, glittering white or of turquoise blue, with every intervening tint and shade that a painter could fancy; those of deepest color had recently been turned over, or had been repeatedly swept by the breaking waves.

During a severe storm he described the scene:

The hoarse roar of the tempest, mingled with the grinding and crashing of thousands of tons of ice, rendered sleep impossible. The raging waters, the black, stormy heavens, the strange moving shapes on the shore, like vessels in distress, now faintly visible in the uncertain light, and now buried in foaming brine, made a strangely fascinating picture.

In contrast, Russell described the happier scene soon after landing:

The veil of mist vanished from the mountains, revealing for the first time to our eager eyes a scene of surpassing beauty. The days of sunshine in a land of mist and rain are so lovely, the air is of such wonderful transparency, and the warmth is so welcome, that even the most stoical cannot resist their inspiration.[13]

Russell's romanticism dominates his descriptive writing. He was a scientist trained to record natural phenomena, yet his prose conveys an appreciation of the ethereal beauty of the scenery. As he stood at the base of the magnificent mountain range, seeing the snow-clad peaks beyond, he expressed great serenity:

The waters of the bay flashed brightly in the warm sunshine and broke into foam where kissed by the breeze. Scattered over the broad shining plain were thousands of icebergs, seemingly a countless fleet of fairy boats with hulls of crystal and fantastic sails of blue and white. When the summer days fade into the long northern twilight marvelous mirage effects are added to the beauty of the softly lighted, far-reaching view. Floating bergs miles away become of huge proportions and assume strange, deceptive shapes; at times appearing like fountains gushing from the sea, but most often simulating magnificent cities with towers, battlements, and minarets of unknown architecture.[14]

The party traveled to the head of Dalton River and Glacier (later renamed for Turner), then ascended slowly. "Crevasses were wide and deep, cutting the ice in fantastic shapes," Kerr reported. For three weeks their passage over the rough moraine averaged only two miles a day because they had to make several trips to bring up their provisions and equipment. It was tough work: "The rocks tore our shoe leather and cut our feet, and human endurance was exerted to the utmost to force our way over this rough and icy glacier." They moved from the Dalton Glacier moraine, to the Lucia Glacier, which Kerr named for his mother, to Hayden Glacier. By July 25 they had reached an elevation of 2,500 feet and made camp on the glacier. "All around was a snowy expanse broken by curious shapes," Kerr wrote, "with nothing living except a raven, which suddenly and hoarsely croaked above my head. I felt like offering the bird an apology for being there."[15] As they climbed, they skirted crevasses that threatened to block them from their goal. As menacing as crevasses were to climbers, they fascinated scientists. Kerr liked to lie on the lip of wide ones and peer within:

As I looked into the depths of the crevasse, I grew bewildered in endeavoring to discover its age, and pictured to myself the time when almost the whole world was an ice-field, grinding and twisting out forms so familiar to us at places where now one could scarcely believe the ice had ever formed.

Other discoveries suggested conditions of the long distant past: "I discovered a hill of fossil mussel-shells, and also ferns and flowers, embedded in the rock, evidences of a great ocean once rolling over these rock masses."[16] Fog impeded their passage, and occasionally avalanches of ice thundered down nearby slopes. Kerr let his imagination roam as he looked over the immense ice fields split by huge crevasses. They were such a jumble of shapes, yet a pattern emerged:

I could see a picture where the white-robed choristers and surpliced priests passed in endless file, while the huge black masses of shaley rock of the higher peaks stood out like the spires of a mighty cathedral, the lower slopes, the pipes of an immense organ, to which picture the thunder of the avalanche supplied the deep diapason.[17]

The climbers finally reached a pass that cut off further ascent. In fog and rain and threatened by avalanches, they retreated to Blossom Island where their base camp had been established at 1,400 feet, just inland of Malaspina Glacier. For several days they made a reconnaissance of the area, then set out on August 2 up the Marvine Glacier (named by Russell for Archibald Marvine, an American geologist). After two days they reached Pinnacle Pass at 4,200 feet. Extending northward out of sight lay the largest glacier they had yet encountered, and they named it after William Seward, the U.S. secretary of state who championed the purchase of Alaska. The glacier flowed into the Malaspina Glacier, which covered the entire side of Yakutat Bay. At this point Kerr made measurements of St. Elias's height, finding that it had been vastly exaggerated at 19,500 feet. Actually, it was only 15,350! Beyond the Seward Glacier they could see an imposing peak and named it after William E. Logan, the former director of the Geological Survey of Canada.

While waiting for the return of two packers who had gone down to bring back provisions, Kerr had ample time to observe the Seward Glacier. It seemed always to be moving, changing in one way or another as ice avalanches broke free. He was amused to recall the concern of mountaineers in the Swiss Alps over anyone even speaking in a normal voice while crossing a glacier for fear of starting an avalanche: "If such a mountaineer were suddenly transported to the great Seward Glacier and felt the glacier tremble and listened to the constantly falling avalanches from the crags of Elias and Cook, I imagine he would throw away his alpenstock and flee in dismay."[18]

On 18 August they started up again, crossing Dome Pass to the Agassiz Glacier, which had been discovered by Seton-Karr and Schwatka but not traversed by them. They worked upwards, cutting steps and using ropes when necessary, reaching five thousand feet by August 22. Now they were ready to tackle the march to the summit, which looked to be about five miles away. Fierce snowstorms drove them back. When the weather improved, Kerr tried again, but a fall and heavy rain discouraged him. Gloomily, the men decided that the storm had defeated their six-week effort. If it had held off a day, "the scalp of St. Elias would have been in our belt and we could have finished the trip with great rejoicing." They had reached 9,500 feet and made valuable scientific observations, so the season had been productive.[19]

Kerr was rather proud of his finding that St. Elias was much lower than had been estimated earlier—yet he underestimated it by some 3,000 feet. Other findings of the expedition were more significant, as in laying to rest the earlier conjecture that the mountains were not ancient volcanoes:

. . . but are composed of stratified sedimentary beds which have been broken up by profound fractures and heaved up as great mountain blocks. The huge pyramid presented by St. Elias when seen from Yakutat Bay is not a volcanic cone . . . but is the end of a roof-like ridge.[20]

❋ Second National Geographic Expedition ❋

Russell returned to the mountain in 1891 with another small expedition funded by the National Geographic Society. He sailed from Port Townsend on the Revenue steamer *Bear*, commanded by the famed Michael Healy, and reached Yakutat on 4 June. Healy's second officer, Lt. D. H. Jarvis, later to be the Alaska executive of the Kennecott Copper Corporation, helped the party land at Icy Bay. Unfortunately, three boats capsized in the heavy surf and six men drowned, including Will Moore of the Russell party. The party followed the route of the previous year but profited from previous experience to make better time. They pushed up the Agassiz and Newton Glaciers, and Russell was pleased to reach the crest of the divide that allowed him to view the country to the north. He anticipated that he would see country something like that viewed earlier from the Chilkoot Pass at the head of Lynn Canal, a comparatively low, wooded country with lakes, rivers, and, perhaps, signs of human habitation. What he saw was very different:

What did meet my eager gaze was a vast snow covered region, limitless in its expanse, through which hundreds, and perhaps thousands, of barren, angular mountain peaks projected. There was not a stream, not a lake, and not a trace of vegetation of any kind in sight. A more desolate or a more utterly lifeless land one never beheld.

What lay on the other side of St. Elias had interested Seton-Karr, who had tried to ascend the mountain with Schwatka in 1886. In 1890 he traveled into the interior by way of the Chilkoot Pass and tried to approach the mountain from the interior side.[21] From the ridge which provided him such a panoramic view, Russell started for the summit. As the climbers cut steps for their ascent, they were keenly aware of the "sheer descent of from 5,000 to 6,000 feet below us all the time. The breaking away of a foothold, or the loss of an alpenstock, might at any time have precipitated us down those fearful cliffs, where not even the crevasses would have stopped us before reaching the bottom of the amphitheater in which our tent was placed, fully a mile in vertical descent below."

They pressed on over a long afternoon to reach an outcrop of rock at 14,500 feet. "The great snow-slope continued to tower above us," Russell said, "and we saw with deep regret that we had not the strength to reach the summit and return to our camp, already 6,500 feet below us." Going down was easier than coming up but not without travails. For one stretch their ice steps had been obliterated by an avalanche, so one climber, secured by a rope, went ahead to cut new steps.[22]

A snowstorm canceled plans to make a fresh start the next day, July 25. They started up again a couple of days later but were discouraged by avalanches:

Only a roar like thunder, and the trembling of the glacier on which we stood, told that many tons of ice and snow were involved in the catastrophe. The rushing monster, starting a mile above, came directly towards us until it poured down upon the border of the slope we were ascending; then, changing its course, it thundered on until it reached the floor of the amphitheater far below. The cloud of spray rolled on down the valley, and hung in the air long after the roar of the avalanche had ceased.

Under these circumstances Russell concluded that it would be foolish to push on that day. They cached their packs and retreated to camp. For several days storms kept them from moving, then heavy fog rolled in. All their blankets and clothes were wet from melting snow, and another ascent seemed impossible. On August 1 they started back for Icy Bay. They eventually reached their old camp on the south side of the Chaix Hills, then crossed the extreme western end of Malaspina Glacier, "just at its junction with another vast plateau of ice stretching westward. Where these two ice-fields join there is a depression which marks the subglacial course of the Yahtse River."[23]

Once back at Icy Bay, Russell got to work measuring the elevation of the mountain and restored the great reduction Mark Kerr had made. Russell measured a base line about three miles long on the beach, "and from its extremities obtained the angles necessary to determine the height of Mount St. Elias and neighboring peaks. These measurements were repeated many times in order to obtain an accuracy as great as was possible with the method employed. The height of Mount St. Elias, thus obtained, is 18,100 feet." As Russell allowed for a deviance of one hundred feet either way, his measurement proved to be close to the official elevation of 18,008 feet established later. Russell also fixed the latitude at 60° 17' 51" N and the longitude at 140° 55' 30" W. This location was important because, as Russell believed, after studying the conventions made between Russia and Great Britain regarding the boundary:

. . . the mountain peak is a mile and a half south of the boundary, and therefore in U.S. territory . . . The mountain is thus practically at the intersection of the boundary of southeastern Alaska at the 141st Meridian and is one of the corner monuments of our national boundary.[24]

✽ Victory on Mount St. Elias ✽

An Italian expedition led by His Royal Highness Prince Luigi Amedeo Di Savoia, Duke of Abruzzi, conquered St. Elias on July 31, 1897. An account of the expedition by Filippo de Filippi credited expert Italian alpine guides for its success. The expedition also had the help of Indian packers for the first stages, along with a contingent of Americans recruited in Seattle and led by E. S. Ingraham. The Italians had the resources to make the trek in fifty-six days and attained the record. Abruzzi was an adventurer, a mountaineer, and did not pretend to have any concern with scientific investigation beyond approximately confirming Russell's calculation of the summit elevation. For background information Filippi relied on the publications of Russell, whose contributions were rewarded with a place name.

Numerous illustrations and a readable, detailed narrative enhance the official account of the expedition. C. L. Andrews, one of the American packers, also documented the trip in his unpublished diary. Andrews, born in 1862 and raised in Oregon, had been deputy county auditor in Seattle until his party lost an election in 1896. He joined the Abruzzi expedition as an opportunity to see Alaska and was to spend most of his life in the north as U.S. Customs official in Sitka, Skagway, and Eagle and on the Seward Peninsula and in the Arctic in the School and Reindeer Service. Aside from all his other accomplishments, particularly his advocacy for the Eskimo, Andrews was a good writer and historian. He got along well with the Italians but was not awed: "The prince behaves very much like an ordinary mortal when he is on a glacier," he noted. Andrews liked the prince more as he spent more time with him: "The prince is a gem for a scion of royalty, who has been well raised in every sense of the word—none of the aristocratic snobbishness about him."[25]

Though the first successful ascent of Mount St. Elias marked a special point in mountaineering history, it did not end interest in climbing the mountain. From time to time since the Abruzzi climb other parties have tried the mountain with varying degrees of success. But for its remoteness and the high cost involved in reaching the great mountain, climbing it would probably attract almost as many parties as does Mount McKinley. Another reason why climbing St. Elias is not more popular is because of the presence of so many other peaks in the region, some of which have not yet been climbed.

✽ Mount Wrangell ✽
Ahtna name: K'elt'aeni ("the one who controls the weather") when erupting:
Uk'eledi ("the one with smoke on it").

To Robert Dunn, who first saw 14,163-foot Mount Wrangell in 1902, the mountain typified, "more than any other mountain in Alaska, all that is remote and fabulous in the North." He believed that the Serebrennikov massacre of 1848 had kept whites away from the region

Robert Dunn nearing the summit of Mt. Wrangell in 1909. *Courtesy of the* Rasmuson Library Archives, *University of* Alaska Fairbanks; Capps Collection, *83-149-906.*

until Allen's visit demonstrated that the Ahtna were friendly. He reported that two Copper River Indians started up the mountain in 1907 and never returned. He thought that Mount Wrangell should have been challenged by mountaineers before Mount McKinley and Mount St. Elias for scientific reasons, "for on Wrangell alone, outside the antarctic continent, can you study the relation of an active cone to a great ice-cap."[26]

Dunn traveled over the Valdez Trail in July 1909 to satisfy his ambition to climb Wrangell, meeting a friend at the Tonsina River and heading east to the mountain. The mountain towered over "the burned and mean spruce forest" extending from its base, "surely the whitest, widest dome-shaped pile on earth." Local Native people called it "the one with smoke on it," but it had not belched forth any mud or lava during the ten years or so it had been observed by miners, despite that its crater was often aglow and productive of steam and ash. While crossing the Copper River on Doc Billum's ferry, the climbers were warned that they might die on the mountain. Dunn believed that Doc Billum, a handsome local Indian shaman who wore a top hat at all times, maintained his ascendancy over other Indians as a medicine man by foretelling disaster.[27]

The travelers did not fear Billum's prediction but did worry about the weather after deciding on the Cheshnina Glacier route. For days rain and snow obscured the mountain and kept them in their camp at 4,000 feet. When the view cleared they started up, laboring hard to reach 10,000 feet and an overnight rest. They got little sleep because of the cold but in the morning started up under clear skies and reached the summit with great joy: "I crack-led over the last snow and leaped upon the ash, in that damp and tarnishing breath of the

earth's bowels, with a mingled thrill of victory and apprehension that was glorious." Within the ridge he saw a brimming bowl of snow and ice, a huge basin or plain "two, three miles across . . . 13,000 feet and more above the sea . . . the world knows no desert like it."[28]

Because of its status as an active volcano and the comparatively intensive scientific study that has been conducted on Wrangell, we have many good descriptions of it. None, however, is more evocative of the peculiar lofty volcanic world than those recorded by Dunn:

The cone was all an oval of blackness. A great cavity was blazoned there, yawing upward to its tip. Streaked and crumbling cliffs wavered behind the concealing steam. In the momentary stillness of the air the shreds of vapor thinned and hovered and drooped along the rims. Then they arose at the center hairlike spires, as from a simmering vat. . . . The active crater that, and not very lively today. The core of fire upon this continent, inscrutable behind these snows— so near and easy to scale.[29]

Upon reaching the summit Dunn felt weary and dazed and for a dizzy moment peering into the crater he imagined he saw something strange at the bottom—"a thin ribbon, a tremulous blur . . . transparent, woven of many threads, like some gelatinous sea growth. . . . Was this a spirit crater, and Wrangell but the figment of a mountain!" Dunn stumbled back down to his base camp and recovered his senses as he descended. He had seen wonderful things, including a panoramic view of near and distant peaks and the valley floor—but, perhaps, not the "spirit of Wrangell."[30]

❋ Mount Blackburn ❋

Dora Keen is credited with the first climb of 16,390-foot Mount Blackburn, called K'als'i Tl'aadi ("the one at cold waters") by the local Ahtna people. A Bryn Mawr College graduate born in 1871, she had climbed in the Alps and elsewhere before coming to Alaska in 1911 to attempt Mount Blackburn. She failed on her 1911 attempt but returned the next year with a party assisted by John E. Barrett and his dog team and six other men, including George Handy, whom she married a couple of years later. She had no experience to speak of in expedition planning but had to do it all herself and knew its importance for any success. "That I was only five feet tall would matter very little. Success would depend rather upon judgment, endurance, courage, and organization."[31]

Keen's route was over the Kennicott Glacier and involved hoisting a ton of provisions up the glacier wall, then six days travel to cover thirty-one miles and rise 3,500 feet in elevation, reaching the foot of the mountain on April 26. Keen chose the steep Barrett Glacier, named the season before for her travel companion, for the start of the 11,000-foot ascent to the summit. Because of the danger of avalanches, after reaching a point they named Crevice Camp they altered plans to prepare for a quick, lightly equipped dash up. On April 30 they moved up without ropes, although for 3,000 feet the slope angle was sixty degrees. "Each took his own gait, the men's a top speed with rests, mine the slow but steady plodding of the Alps. . . . Our chief concern was due to the fearful ice masses which stood out to the right and left, always just one overhead in our zigzag trail." On the next stage they benefited from Handy's ingenuity, a rope and small anchor which allowed them to haul themselves over ridges without the labor of cutting steps in the ice. At 12,400 feet Keen figured that a final spurt of five to seven hours would get them to the top, but soft snow prevented an immediate start.[32] While waiting for cooler temperatures they were hit by a snowstorm that immobilized them for three days and depleted their food rations. On May 3 they had to retreat down the slope 3,500 feet to their camp for food. There three party members left to return to civilization, while the others prepared to start up again after the storm abated. It was May before the weather allowed them to begin their climb. The way was perilous. While camping at 11,000 feet a rushing avalanche narrowly missed sweeping them away:

Twice the deep rolling of falling ice made me sit up with a start just as a great mass went sweeping by. They were the most awe-inspiring sight I have ever seen, so wonderful, so thrilling to watch, that I wished I did not need to sleep. They passed so close that it was if the American Falls at Niagara were suddenly overwhelming us.[33]

It was May 19 when Keen and Handy reached the summit in an icy gale. All the other party members had given up along the arduous way, but they had proved tough enough to fight to the top. They took only a little time to rejoice in their achievement, then started down, taking three days to reach base camp and another two going down the Kennicott Glacier. According to Keen, their success and that of recent attempts on Mount McKinley:

. . . have proved that the secret of success lies in going early and using dogs. Our 1911 expedition had been the first to use dogs on a mountain and the one here recounted was the first to succeed without using Swiss guides, the first to live in snow caves, the first to make a prolonged night ascent, the first to succeed on an avalanche-swept southeast side, and the only Alaska ascent in which a woman has taken part—to the credit of men be it said. We succeeded because one man cared to succeed.[34]

More recent mapping of the peaks indicate that the southeast summit Keen reached was only 16,286 feet, and another peak one and a half miles to the northwest, first climbed in 1958, was 16,390 feet.[35]

❋ Mount Logan ❋

Mount Logan, at 19,850 feet the second highest peak in North America, lies within the Canadian portion of the St. Elias Range. Its first ascent in 1925 was from McCarthy and the Chitina River Valley and Glacier. The Canadian party of climbers was guided by Andy Taylor, one of the Chisana gold discoverers and the most knowledgeable man on the Wrangell-St. Elias region. A. H. McCarthy and Taylor made a reconnaissance journey in 1924 to determine the best route and prepare the way for the following year's effort. Starting from McCarthy they traveled by pack train to the foot of the Chitina Glacier, then backpacked fifty miles to the King Glacier, at the foot of the mountain. This trip confirmed the efficiency of the route and the necessity of winter freighting to lay down advance caches of supplies.

It was May 12, 1925, when the party set out from McCarthy, using six days to get to the end of the pack-train trail. Storms delayed their progress, but they managed to reach the summit where they paused for twenty-five minutes to celebrate their success before starting down. Heavy snowfall impeded progress and they might have lost their way but for their foresight in planting willow branches every one hundred feet to mark the trail. When they eventually reached terra firma, they had passed forty-four days on snow and ice, and were pleased to enjoy "the ecstasy of being once more amid green shrubbery."[36]

John E. Barrett, Dora Keen, and George Handy ascending Mount Blackburn with dogs, 1912. Courtesy of the University of Washington Libraries, Dora Keen Collection, 16696.

✳ Mount Bona ✳

Mount Bona, named by the Duke of Abruzzi for his racing yacht, was climbed in July 1930 by Allen Carpe (the greatest American mountaineer of his day, Carpe later died on Mt. McKinley), Andy Taylor, and Terris Moore. They started from McCarthy in mid-June for the Skolai Pass. As it was too early to follow the shorter summer trail up the Chitistone River to the Chitistone Pass, thence into the head basin of the Skolai Valley, they followed the winter trail up the Nizina, ascending Skolai Creek. By June 20 they got their pack animals several miles up Russell Glacier to establish a base camp. From this point they packed fifty pounds each over several days to reach their high camp at 10,300 feet, waited for favorable weather, then successfully raced to the 16,421-foot summit on July 2. Descending, the party started back for McCarthy across the Skolai Basin and the Chitistone Pass. The Chitistone dropped into a narrow canyon, "while the trail mounts high across steep-cut banks to avoid the cliffs. This passage is called the 'goat trail' and is truly an adventurous place, the mountain-side

Camp of an early Mt. Logan Expedition. Courtesy of the William C. Douglass Family.

being in places so steep that it is hard to believe that a horse could stick on it."

What impressed the climbers about this route was their knowledge, gathered from Andy Taylor, that some years before it had been "the principal pack route to the once flourishing Chisana district and the White River country!"[37]

❋ Mount Sanford ❋

Mount Sanford was first climbed by that intrepid pair of scholar-adventurers, Bradford Washburn and Terris Moore in July 1938. Called H*wiindi K'elt'aeni* ("upriver of the one who controls the weather") by the local Ahtna people, the mountain is remarkable for its unique shape, presenting precipitous cliffs from the edge of its summit to the south and east but showing a rounded cone on the north down to the 10,000-foot level. From this level the descent is sharp, but glacier tongues appear to offer an opportunity for climbers. Moore believed that Sanford remained unclimbed for so long because it was considered too easy. More than once he had heard it said that one could probably drive a dog team to the summit, but he doubted that the climb would be as easy as it appeared.

Moore, his wife Katherine, Washburn, and their packers used dogs to haul much of their gear, reaching the 10,000-foot level on July 18. The dogs were of great help in the packing, although someone had to go ahead on snowshoes and break trail for them. From the 10,000-foot level they seemed to have a clear route to the summit 6,000 feet above them and more than five miles distant over an immense snow plateau which sloped gradually upwards to a cone at 13,000 feet, then rather sharply up to the summit. They started up at night and reached 12,500 feet before abandoning their sledge. After some delay because of storms, Bradford and Terris prepared to dash to the summit from 14,500 feet. On July 21 they reached the 16,237-foot top to find a flat surface about one hundred feet square. The descent was one of great pleasure, skiing down 6,000 feet on powder snow.[38]

✳ Other Important Summits ✳

Intrepid mountaineers eventually reached most other major summits in Wrangell-St. Elias National Park and Preserve: A party led by pioneer Himalayan climber Noel Odell completed the first ascent of 15,700-foot Mt. Vancouver in 1949; 14,950-foot Mount Hubbard was climbed in 1951 by a team sponsored by the Arctic Institute of North America and led by Robert Bates; a party led by Peter Schoening and Victor Josendal first ascended 14,070-foot Mt. Augusta in July 1952; Mt. Cook (13,760 feet) was climbed in 1953 by a group of Seattle mountaineers led by Richard McGowan; and Heinrich Harrer, Keith Hart, and George Schaller conquered Mt. Drum (12,010 feet) in 1954.

✳ Conclusion ✳

Given the numbers and towering heights of many of the peaks within the Wrangell-St. Elias region, it is no wonder that the mountaineering literature is extensive. Only a small part of it has been cited here (see bibliography). In addition to books there are numerous articles and short notices of climbs on various mountains in mountaineering literature like the *American Alpine Journal* and the *Alpine Journal.* Mountaineers formed an interesting part of Wrangell-St. Elias region history. Many of them were prominent scientists who made significant contributions to knowledge. Among the modern climbers several names crop up repeatedly, including prospector and master guide, Andy Taylor; Terris Moore; and Bradford Washburn—all of whom would be distinguished choices as names for mountain peaks. Today climbers are still pursuing their recreation each season, challenged to achieve some distinctive record. They have a particular sense of the region and a consciousness of those who have gone before them.

Horse sleds leaving Wortam's Roadhouse on
the Valdez Trail. Courtesy of the Museum of
History and Industry, Seattle, Washington.

Chapter

❄ ❄ ❄

Transportation Routes

From the acquisition of Alaska by the United States in 1867, newcomers to the North usually arrived by sea. American traders and prospectors, like their Russian predecessors, made their early penetrations of the interior by way of the Yukon River. In moving away from the rivers they followed local trails used by Natives. Gradually, prospectors carved out crude trails where the need existed, but the development of major constructed trails did not commence until the gold-rush-era influx of population. The utilization of Native trails and development of mining trails within the Wrangell-St. Elias region is considered later in this chapter, after discussion of the government trail and the railroad. The first major trail affecting the Wrangell-St. Elias region was built following the explorations of U.S. Army Capt. William R. Abercrombie during the Klondike gold rush. Formally the route was called the trans-Alaska Military Road, but it was better known as the Valdez Trail.

❄ Abercrombie's Second Expedition ❄

With the 1897–1898 gold rush Capt. William Abercrombie, whose effort to ascend the Copper River in 1884 had failed, returned to explore the region. Frank C. Schrader of the U.S. Geological Survey attached his party to Abercrombie's expedition in 1898 and reached the present site of Copper Center before returning downriver. Abercrombie returned in 1899, and Schrader and the other U.S. Geological Survey men were to return in 1900 to investigate the great copper deposits of the country. Their observations in 1898 provided excellent descriptions of the gold rush setting. Abercrombie asked Schrader and one of his officers to investigate the Valdez Glacier trail after miners, aware of the difficulties in ascending the Copper River, requested information about the alternative route to the interior. Late in April the two men started up the glacier but were stopped for five days by a blizzard that dumped eight to twelve feet of snow on the glacier. When the snow turned to rain on May 2, the men trudged on to the summit where they saw "the size and trend of the Valdez Glacier, the character of the country in which it lies, the altitude of the summit and surrounding mountains, and the nature of the country at the head of the Klutena River on the inland side of the divide."[1]

The glacier trail was difficult. Nevertheless, it became the main route to the interior for want of a better entry. Much was made of its dangers, but as with Chilkoot Pass (gateway to the Klondike), its travails for travelers multiplied in direct proportion to the number of trips needed to move provisions inland. Though the trail itself was not innocent of terrors, much of its reputation derived from difficult conditions once stampeders arrived in the interior. Unlike Chilkoot travelers, those first crossing the Valdez Glacier had no established community nearby for support such as Dyea.

⁎ Valdez Trail ⁎

On the afternoon of June 16, 1899, the U.S. Army started building the first trail from the coast to the interior. The construction party headed by Captain Abercrombie followed the Lowe River to Keystone Canyon sixteen miles away before camping for three days to allow the soldiers to clear a passage through the narrow canyon to Dutch Flats. Reporting on the work, Quartermaster Clerk John F. Rice saw beyond the difficulty of pushing through this rugged bottleneck: "In the matter of picaresque scenery the Keystone Canyon is one of the finest in Alaska."[2] The party crossed the flats, traversed Thompson Pass, and reached the Tiekel River, where they met several prospectors "with pack trains en route to the Chettyna country." Following the valley to the northeast they crossed the south fork of the Tiekel River, then followed the north fork until reaching Stewart Creek, one of its major tributaries. From this high divide, the soldiers had a remarkable view of the country. Rice was impressed:

The moss covered mountain towers hundreds of feet above one on either side, while the perspective, as the eye sweeps the valley, is enchanting. . . . After several miles of travel we passed what was known at one time as Tiekel City, it having been destroyed by fire some few years before our arrival. Here we crossed another divide without much difficulty and proceeded to the headwater of Quartz Creek, which we followed down until we reached Belcaro, situated at the junction of Bear Creek.

There they encountered a party of fifty miners, "who were long on prospects and short on gold." The miners believed that mining could only be made to pay in the country when hydraulic machinery could be brought in.[3]

Ed S. Orr's stage leaving Valdez for Fairbanks about 1907. Courtesy of the Rasmuson Library Archives, University of Alaska Fairbanks; Whalen Collection, 75-84-290; Hunt photo C3210

Horse sleds approaching the summit of Thompson Pass. Courtesy of the Museum of History and Industry, Seattle, Washington.

From Quartz Creek the soldiers crossed another divide to Tonsina Lake, forded the Tonsina River, and eventually followed Grayling Creek "until we reached Glacier City, a town located on the Klutena River, about 85 miles from Port Valdez." In 1897–1898 Glacier City had been well populated with gold stampeders. Now the only resident was a soldier who guarded military stores placed there and operated a ferry across the Klutina. Some twenty-five miles farther on was Copper Center, where a handful of prospectors remained from the earlier peak population of 600. About thirty Indians had a camp for fishing. Two soldiers guarded another military cache here, so Rice replenished his supplies. The survey was on schedule: They had completed 110 miles in fourteen days.[4] The soldiers crossed the Copper River at this point and, guided by Indians, got onto the Millard Trail. This gold rush trail was well marked and easy to follow. As Rice reached the Sanford River he discerned some economic prospects: "The valley has the appearance of an excellent one for agricultural purposes. The terrain is rolling and free of brush and trees." After crossing the Sanford River the soldiers lost track of the overgrown Millard Trail. They went on along the foothills of Mounts Sanford and Drum until they saw the mouth of the Slana River in the distance, then crossed the valley and the Copper River, and on July 8 reached the Slana about eight miles above its mouth. Here they built a raft to cross the river, followed the heavily timbered west bank and then a ridge until they could see Mentasta Lake. On an old Indian trail they eventually reached the Mentasta Village, which was unoccupied. Rice noticed that the lake:

. . . is a very pretty body of water and the scenery above it is rugged and impressive. Above its waters tower the mighty spurs of the Alaska range. The fishing and hunting in this region is not surpassed in any other portion of Alaska.

The soldiers met twenty prospectors and three Tetlin Indians. The Indians said that "all but two of the Mentasta Indians had died the previous winter and that the two survivors had joined the Ketchumstock tribe." The Tetlin Indians felt none too secure in the unfamiliar

Winter travel was always difficult. One novel answer was to equip your horse with snowshoes. Courtesy of the McCarthy-Kennicott Historical Museum, no. B7-32.

country and were heavily armed as they looked for a favorable fishing ground. On July 12 the soldiers passed through the Mentasta Pass into the Alaska Range, reaching the Tanana two days later. On July 28, their fortieth day on the trail, they arrived at Eagle, about 425 miles from their starting point.[5]

Returning along the same route the soldiers ran into a caribou herd between the Slana and Sanford Rivers but were not successful in hunting. They reached Copper Center on September 2 and compared notes with Addison Powell, the surveyor attached to their expedition, who had been running a line from Copper Center to Mentasta Lake. Powell was not only a competent surveyor, but he was a fine writer and as fetching a raconteur as ever waded an Alaska stream.

Powell told many stories of that season's work in his wonderful narrative, *Trailing and Camping in Alaska*, including a thrilling chase for 150 yards by a grizzly he had wounded. To escape, Powell dived over an embankment into heavy brush, where he waited for other members of his party to shoot the bear. After a long time, hearing neither rifle nor bear, he crawled out for a look. The bear had wandered off. When asked why he had not shot, his companion only laughed, saying, "Hang it all, it wasn't my bear-fight!"[6] Rice reported on an equally startling incident just a day after meeting Powell at Copper Center. He was standing on a stump making observations, when:

I was violently precipitated to the ground by a sudden seismic disturbance. The trees swayed to and fro as if a hurricane was raging. In the midst of the convulsion of nature there was borne to our ears sounds resembling the discharge of heavy artillery. Some 15 miles distant we could see Mount Wrangell emitting smoke and lava. The scene was one of terror, as we expected every minute to see the earth open.[7]

En route to the coast from Copper Center the trail-blazing survey party met the construction crew headed by Captain Abercrombie at the Tiekel River. Going down to Valdez from that point was easy marching for the survey party because of Abercrombie's labors in pack-trail construction. As Rice noted, Abercrombie had finished the most difficult part of the trail, as it did not hit mountains again until reaching the Alaska Range. It would not be hard, he reported, to transform the trail into "a wagon or a railroad bed."[8]

❋ Trail Construction ❋

Despite the frustrations and hardships suffered by '98 stampeders, conditions looked very bright for the region in 1899. The new town of Valdez was thriving as a transportation and service center to the Copper River country, gold had been discovered on the Chistochina district, the Nikolai copper claim on the Chitina River was located, and Abercrombie began construction of the Trans-Alaskan Military Road from Valdez to Eagle. The start of the army's trail was not as immediately beneficial to miners as the construction that year of the White Pass and Yukon Railway to Lake Bennett was to travelers to Skagway, but it was meaningful. By choosing the route the government was not indicating faith in the southcentral region's mineral prospects. The route simply seemed a better choice, considering all distances involved, than one from Cook Inlet—the other major possibility for an "all-American" route to the interior. But the trail certainly helped prospectors who remained in the region. Copper Center and other points along the trail developed, and Valdez became one of the leading towns of the territory. Notwithstanding the trail's advantages, transportation costs remained high to the districts off the trail, and conditions did not improve until the Copper River and Northwestern Railway was constructed.

The army established a base for trail construction and a permanent garrison in April 1899. Captain Abercrombie chose a place near Valdez Glacier that he had used for a camp the previous year. A better site, not subject to the overflow of streams from the glacier, later was chosen and barracks were constructed. The reservation, three miles from the head of Valdez Bay on the south shore, served the army's needs for many years.

Trail construction proceeded vigorously during the 1900 season. An army transport landed at Valdez in April with Company G, Seventh Infantry, under Capt. J. B. Jackson, fifty-three civilians employed by the Quartermaster Department, and construction materials.

Hauling the disassembled steamboat Chitina *over the Chugach Range through Marshall Pass. Courtesy of the Anchorage Museum of History and Art, B62.1A.133; Hunt photo E 390.*

153

Since the town had no wharf, the lumber was floated ashore from the ship. Soldiers involved in trail construction seemed proud of their progress. Joseph Kerr, engineer officer, wrote folks at home about his work on "the trail that we are engineering across the country to Eagle City." He was proud to argue that "it will prove to be one of the most difficult pieces of engineering work undertaken." The mountains were obstacles as were "numerous ice glaciers ranging from 100 to 400 feet in height and 5 to 50 miles long." He reported on streams abounding in fish: "During the salmon season you can kick them out with your feet in the small streams," and the land:

The vegetation is very poor. The scenery is something magnificent that I could not describe it and do it justice. An ice glacier is something magnificent to look at, especially from the mountain tops, and see the sun dancing from one berg to another.

Kerr considered the mineral prospects excellent:

Alaska will in time prove to be one of the best mineral producing countries in the world. Copper and iron is in abundance. You can almost see the iron rust sticking out through the hills as the miners say.[9]

❋ Upgrade to Wagon Road ❋

In 1904 Congress appropriated $25,000 for an army survey to estimate construction costs for a wagon road. J. M. Clapp, who was reassigned from his job of supervising the construction of the Lake Washington Ship Canal in Seattle, took charge. Parties worked from both ends of the trail, with each having some twenty-five men with horses. Clapp finished in August and estimated the cost at $3,500 per mile. He started into Keystone Canyon and found "the winter trail by way of the creek bottom was impassable," and attempts to use portions of the summer trail caused great fatigue to horses floundering in snowbanks. The

The steamboat Nizina *in the Copper River's Wood Canyon. Courtesy of the Anchorage Museum of History and Art, B64.1.137.*

154

Steamboat fleet on the Copper River including the Chitina, Nizina, *and* Tonsina. *Courtesy of the Anchorage Museum of History and Art, B64.1.143*

men had to wade the cold, glacial streams, "four in number, soon after leaving Valdez," before reaching a scarcely passable trail: "The trail was wet and muddy most of the distance, and on the sixth day out everybody walked 18 miles to Tonsena." Further on the trail was worse. Clapp reported that "the animals mired in places, requiring assistance to extricate them. . . . Fully 50 per cent of the distance was exceedingly bad."[10]

Clapp was impressed by the Copper River valley:

This immense tract of country extends north and south fully 100 miles and east and west over 100 miles. The divide between this valley and the valley of the Shushitna is hardly noticeable, and the two valleys make up an immense area of flat land. . . . The fall of the river is rapid, being five-tenths foot to the hundred at Copper Center. The current is swift and the channel which winds from bank to bank splits up into minor channels, giving the river a wide and shallow appearance under normal conditions.

Clapp did not find the river fordable below the mouth of the Chistochina River. At the mouth of the Sanford River it was 250 feet wide and twelve feet deep. The river did not seem navigable above Copper Center or below the mouth of the Tasnuna River.[11] After gold strikes at Fairbanks in 1902-1903, the army diverted the trail's route from Eagle on the Yukon to Fairbanks on the Tanana River. Travelers bound for Eagle left the main path at Gakona, traveling over a trail that later became the Tok Cutoff highway.

❋ Trail Adventures ❋

Lynn Smith, a Rampart trader, started for Valdez in March 1904 by dogsled. Stopping in Fairbanks, which had not yet experienced its gold rush boom, Smith arranged to travel down the trail with mail carrier Joe Bennett. The trail out of Fairbanks was not marked, "nothing to follow—just three feet of snow. Got into our snowshoes—onto the gee pole

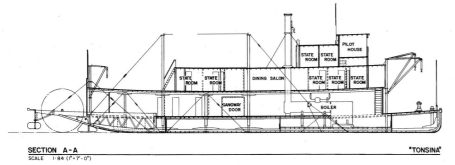

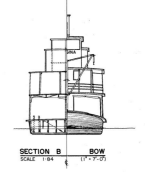

SECTION A-A "TONSINA" SECTION B BOW
SCALE 1·84 (1" = 7'-0") SCALE 1·84 (1" = 7'-0")
SOURCE: INTERNATIONAL MARINE ENGINEERING, NOVEMBER 1910, PUBLISHED DRAWINGS OF THE "TONSINA."

COPPER RIVER STEAMBOATS

BETWEEN 1907 AND 1911 THE COPPER RIVER AND NORTH-WESTERN RAILWAY OPERATED A FLEET OF STEAMBOATS ON THE COPPER AND CHITINA RIVERS IN SUPPORT OF RAILROAD CONSTRUCTION AND MINING OPERATIONS AT KENNICOTT. CAPTAIN GEORGE HILL SUPERVISED THE DESIGN AND CONSTRUCTION OF THE STEAMBOATS, BUILT FIRST BY PORTLAND THEN PUGET SOUND SHIPYARDS. THE BOATS WERE PATTERNED AFTER COLUMBIA RIVER STERNWHEELERS, THEY WERE DESIGNED FOR THE SHALLOW WATERS, SHIFTING CHANNELS AND SWIFT CURRENTS OF THE GLACIER FED RIVERS, THEY WERE KNOCKED DOWN AND CRATED TO ALASKA FOR REASSEMBLY, AND THEY OPERATED IN CONJUNCTION WITH A TRAMROAD AROUND THE NON-NAVIGABLE ABERCROMBIE RAPIDS.

IN 1909 THE MORAN SHIPYARDS OF SEATTLE BUILT THE 120 FOOT TONSINA AND THE 80 FOOT GULKANA AND CRATED THEM NORTH IN TIME FOR THE COPPER RIVER BREAK-UP THAT SUMMER. THEY PROVED THE RAILROAD'S WORKHORSES, THE GULKANA SHUTTLING FREIGHT ACROSS MILES LAKE AND THE TONSINA HAULING CONSTRUCTION MATERIALS BETWEEN RAPIDS LANDING AND CHITINA. AN ATTEMPT TO OPERATE THE UPRIVER FLEET AS A PASSENGER AND FREIGHT LINE PROVED UNFEASIBLE BECAUSE OF THE SHORT THREE MONTH SEASON. FOLLOWING THE COMPLETION OF THE RAILROAD IN 1911, THE STEAMBOATS WERE DISMANTLED. LUMBER AND PARTS WERE REUSED IN BUILDINGS IN CHITINA. THE WRECK OF THE GULKANA, DISMANTLED AT MILES LAKE, ALONE REMAINS — ITS DERELICT

HULL COLLAPSED AND ITS MACHINERY SCATTERED ALONG THE LAKE SHORE.

DOCUMENTATION OF THE STEAMBOAT GULKANA WAS UNDERTAKEN BY THE HISTORIC AMERICAN ENGINEERING RECORD (HAER) A DIVISION OF THE NATIONAL PARK SERVICE. THE PROJECT WAS EXECUTED UNDER THE GENERAL DIRECTION OF ROBERT J. KAPSCH, CHIEF OF HABS/HAER, AND ROGER J. CONTOR, ALASKA REGIONAL DIRECTOR, NPS. RECORDING WAS CARRIED OUT DURING THE SUMMER OF 1984 BY LESLIE STARR HART, PROJECT DIRECTOR, ROBERT L. SPUDE, HISTORIAN, AND DAVID C. ANDERSON, HISTORICAL ARCHITECT.

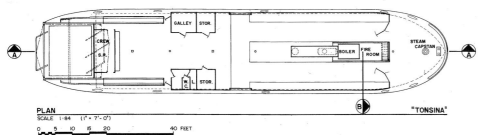

PLAN "TONSINA"
SCALE 1·84 (1" = 7'-0")

COPPER RIVER DRAINAGE
SCALE 1:1 600 000

Copper River Steamboats, plan of the Tonsina. *Courtesy of the Historic American Buildings Survey, National Park Service, David C. Anderson, 1984.*

[a pole extending from the sled that is used in guiding it] and gee poled the next 22 days." At the Little Salcha River another foot of snow fell overnight, so they lightened their sled loads and tied their sleds together and combined their dog teams, making a team about 50 feet long.[12]

On they went, steadily but very slowly. "Bennett ahead breaking trail and I on the gee pole on snowshoes with the two lines between my legs. It was slow hard work and making 2 miles an hour." Once beyond the Big Delta River they ran into the rabbit country—"rabbits by the millions and here we had our first rabbit tea." The camping routine was the same every evening:

Just before dark we would look for timber on the bank. . . . The first thing was to chain the dogs up to trees; next, to cut down a tree, getting two logs, tramp down the snow and start the campfire, get the dog bucket, fill with snow and place on campfire, putting in rice and sow belly. Then tramp down the snow and cut spruce bows and lay them down on the snow about a foot high for our sleeping bags. Then, something for ourselves. We would try to pick out some nice clean snow and fill the teapot and place it on the fire. After a few minutes look and see how much water we had and add a[n] inch of rabbit on top. Repeat this, skinning off the rabbit each time, then putting in the tea.[13]

It was exhausting travel. One night, after reaching a roadhouse, Smith offered Bennett $100 to cover the mail carrier's fine of $2 an hour for late mail, hoping to buy a day of respite from the trail. Bennett assured him that a night's sleep would fix him up, and off they went the next morning as usual. Once over the divide, conditions got a little easier. They ran into Harry Karstens, a mail carrier heading north, and marked his trail with Crackerjack boxes as they pushed south. "That morning we passed six dog teams headed for Fairbanks," Smith said, "and they told us they had struck rich pay on Cleary Creek and Gilmore Creek since we had left and for us to go back. All the gold in the world would not have induced me to return."[14]

Then they met another mail carrier who directed them to the Gakona roadhouse. Smith sent his dogs back to Fairbanks with other travelers and "made Copper Center on the ice." From there he rode a horse-drawn, double-ended sled. "Finally after 41 days of heart breaking work reached Valdez," Smith's ship was in port and he steamed south for his sister's wedding.[15]

A year later, in February 1905, Judge James Wickersham took the trail north from Valdez to hold a term of court in Fairbanks. He traveled with Bob Coles, "an active young Valdez prospector," and a six-dog team. As usual, the snow was deep in the Valdez flats and the Lowe River Valley. Snowslides were a danger in Keystone Canyon, but they got through safely to rest at the Wortman roadhouse at the foot of Thompson Pass. Skies cleared the next day, and the trail was well marked. By noon they reached the summit of Thompson Pass, then followed the trail on to the Beaverdam roadhouse and sleep. The next day they reached the Ernestine roadhouse. "At all the roadhouses along the trail we met many men and dog-teams transporting mining supplies into the Copper River country and to Fairbanks."[16]

Wickersham pushed on the next day for Copper Center. Along the way it began snowing, and darkness fell before they reached the Copper River bluffs. Pushing on in the dark the sled hit a pole lying across the trail and overturned, throwing Wickersham over the handlebars. "The force of the overturned sled dragged Bob and the dogs backwards down the hill until the sled was stopped by logs and brush. Our supplies were scattered when the sled turned over and over."[17]

With some effort they regained the trail and continued on to the Copper Center roadhouse for a much needed rest. Aside from bruises and scratches, Wickersham also had suffered a

Building the Copper River Railroad, 1909. Courtesy of the Anchorage Museum of History and Art, B64.1.156.

Building the CR&NWRR through Wood Canyon, August 1910. Courtesy of the Alaska State Library, Hegg Collection, PCA 124-66.

sprained ankle. The pair decided on a day's layover. "On the following day we enjoyed a fine hard-snow trail up the center of the river past the little valleys of the Klutena, Tazlina, and Gulkana and into the Copper from the wide flat in the west." At the mouth of the Gakona they stayed at "a good road-house." Moving on they encountered some difficulty: *The ice on the Gakona was covered with overflow which extended half a mile or more to the Copper where it disappeared beneath the ice. We were compelled to wade this cold water until we reached the road-house where we were informed that the Gakona flat valley up which our trail lay was covered with water.*[18]

On February 27 Wickersham reached the Chippewa roadhouse on the Gakona River. Meals cost two dollars and a place to spread one's blanket for the night cost one dollar. The next day Wickersham waded the icy river overflow all the way up the valley, crossing over the watershed between the Gakona and the Gulkana by afternoon. From the ridge:

. . . we had a glorious view of the high mountain summits of Drum, Sanford, and the Wrangell volcano standing far south of our position. Masses of heavy black smoke poured out of the great round crater on the Wrangell tableland, and rolled before the strong north wind across the mountain ice plain, without rising from its surface.[19]

In comparing the travel narratives of Smith and Wickersham, it is noticeable that trail conditions had improved over the year between them. But the great difference was due to the acceleration of traffic because of the development of the Fairbanks gold field. As Fairbanks continued to grow over the years, it was clear that the Valdez Trail would remain the primary route to the interior.

❋ Valdez Trail's Significance ❋

The army's work in first exploring the Copper River Valley, then building a trail and a wagon road through it to the Yukon was of great importance in the development of the region and of Alaska generally. Observations of the region's Natives made by Lieutenant Allen and other pre-gold-rush explorers provided information of a culture that changed swiftly when prospectors flocked into the country. Boosters of the region predicted that the Copper River country would gain and hold a large permanent population because of its mineral resources and transportation advantages. As it turned out, they were too optimistic. Mining developed only in a few locations, and when it declined most of the communities faded away. The railroad had a limited influence while it lasted. The other major road link, the Edgerton Highway, provided access from Chitina to the Richardson Highway (the old Valdez Trail).

❋ Policing the Trails ❋

The U.S. marshals and their deputies had all the authority needed to run down law violators on any trail or road, but finding culprits was not always easy. One incident that occurred in a remote region illustrates this point. Prohibition came to Alaska in 1917 with the passage of the Alaska Bone Dry Law. Surprisingly, the law was strict, even mere sanctioning of the possession of potable alcohol was illegal, and it was often strictly enforced. William D. Coppernoll, U.S. commissioner at McCarthy, invaded the mountain

Railroad tunnel construction at Mile 134, May 1910. Courtesy of the Alaska State Library, Hegg Collection, PCA 124-8.

The temporary railroad bridge across the Copper River. Courtesy of the Cordova Historical Society, 88-38-15, Hunt photo C4281.

vastness of the Wrangell-St. Elias region to catch a gang who were reportedly bringing in a dogsled load of liquor from Dawson over the White River-Chisana route. He dispatched Harry Cloes, a game warden, and Jack Hayes, a former policeman, to intercept smugglers Harry Boyden, Bill Berry, and Dan Campbell near the Nizina Glacier. Upon reaching the Nizina Glacier, Cloes left Hayes to watch for the smugglers while he, assisted by two mail carriers, circled the area to make sure that his culprits did not escape his trap. Unfortunately for Cloes and his companions, they were caught by a storm on the Rohn Glacier. As Coppernoll reported to the governor:

They were obliged to abandon one sled, robes, and turn one dog team loose, for the dogs became so weak that they could not drag the sled through the deep snow. Then they got lost, travelling in a circle for some time, and finally they had to make camp in the snow with but one robe for three days. They were in this predicament for three days and were without food for two days, and had to eat snow to quench their thirst. It is a wonder they did not perish.[20]

Finally, Cloes made it back to where he had stationed Hayes and learned that the smugglers had emerged from Skolai Pass and continued on into McCarthy. For some reason, as Hayes searched their sled, they admitted that they had been forewarned of the trap and had cached their whiskey in Skolai Pass. As Coppernoll reported, "Cloes went into Skolai Pass to try to locate this cache but the snow had fallen so deep that he could find no tracks." He did find where the smugglers had abandoned part of their gear and found signs that the smugglers had violated game regulations by killing mountain sheep to feed their dogs. Even worse, they had destroyed a shelter house on the trail, using the lumber to build a toboggan.[21]

Perhaps the whiskey cache is still in Skolai Pass. Cloes never did find the fifty to

seventy-five gallons of liquor, then worth $7,500 to $10,000 at McCarthy prices. His failure disappointed him and the commissioner, whose fruitless expedition had taken forty-one days and came near to causing the deaths of three men. We must assume that Coppernoll lost his zeal for enforcement of prohibition in the wilds of the Wrangell-St. Elias region.

❊ Richardson Highway and Alaska Road Commission ❊

Since 1919 the Valdez Trail has been known as the Richardson Highway, named for the first president of the Alaska Road Commission, Wilds P. Richardson. Richardson was a well-known pioneer, respected for his road work and as one of the two army officers assigned to the Yukon basin during the 1897–1898 gold rush to report on conditions and keep order. By 1929 the highway included 371 miles of gravel-surfaced wagon and auto road. It had two principal branches—the Edgerton Cutoff (from mile 92.4 at Willow Creek running thirty-nine miles to Chitina on mile 131 of the Copper River and Northwestern Railway); and the Chistochina Road, then under construction from mile 128 at Gulkana. The 1929 report of the Alaska Road Commission included statistics showing just how important the Richardson Highway had been in its construction and maintenance plans. The original trail had been considered finished in 1907, but it was upgraded to a wagon road by 1913. After World War I a major effort began to improve it to automobile quality. Steep grades were eliminated, narrow stretches widened, bridges and culverts rebuilt, soft spots drained and regraveled, and other essential work was completed by 1929. Fund allocations showed that in twenty-five years, 43 percent of the road commission's total budget of $14,400,000, or $6,158,000, had been dedicated to the Richardson. Of this amount $2,842,000 went to new construction and $3,316,000 to maintenance.[22]

Kuskulana Bridge. Courtesy of the National Archives, 126-AR-4C-13

The Alaska Road Commission helped fill a part of the gap in transportation following shutdown of the Copper River and Northwestern Railway by maintaining sixty miles of track that was used as a tramway between Chitina and McCarthy. The road commission played a role in communications as well. In 1926, when the U.S. Army Signal Corps abandoned its telegraph line along the Richardson after conversion to radio signals, the Alaska Road Commission took over the Fairbanks-Valdez line. The next year it constructed a thirty-nine-mile branch line to Chitina, and from 1931 to 1934 added 106 miles to tie Nabesna into the system when the Nabesna Road was under construction. Phones were available at all roadhouses on the highway, and a switchboard at Copper Center connected to Nabesna, Chitina, and Valdez. Phone users in Fairbanks talked to Valdez through a relay station at Rapids Roadhouse.[23]

Major road construction came to the region as World War II approached. In 1941 work began on both ends of the Glenn Highway, named after U.S. Army Capt. Edwin F. Glenn, who explored the Copper and Susitna River regions in 1898–1899. This new highway covered 189 miles between Anchorage and the Richardson Highway and made the Wrangell-St. Elias region much more accessible to major population centers. The town of Glennallen was established as a construction camp, and the Alaska Road Commission marked the movement from rail to road centers by transferring its shops from Chitina to Glennallen. The commission constructed its own electric generating plant and in 1943 provided power to commission employees who built homes there. By 1951 all but sixteen miles of the Glenn Highway near Sheep Mountain had hard surface.[24]

❋ The Copper River and Northwestern Railway ❋

The story of Alaska's first long-distance railroad is an epic one. Its builders confronted nature in a dramatic fashion to ram through the iron trail from the coast to the rich copper mines of the interior. Dramatic too were the conditions under which the route was chosen and the violent struggle between competing interests. The Guggenheim and Morgan interests realized that they had acquired one of the world's most valuable mineral deposits. They also knew that their holdings were worthless without construction of an enormously expensive railroad.

Engineers examined four different routes for a railroad into the upper Copper River. Two from Valdez would use either Thompson Pass or Marshall Pass into tributaries of the Copper, but both involved steep grades. Two more direct routes up the lower Copper started in Cordova and Katalla. The Cordova route did not appeal initially because it entailed bridging of the Copper River between two active glaciers and laying track over the Baird Glacier moraine. Katalla's route looked promising, particularly as it, like the Cordova route, would also give access to the Bering River coal fields—assumed to be a resource wealth of immense potential. Katalla's location on an unprotected ocean shore, however, contrasted with the deepwater harbor advantages of both Valdez and Cordova.

Businessmen dependent upon the views of engineers and the syndicate did not get the best advice from its hirelings. Initially, construction started from Valdez under George Hazelet. Subsequently, company officers concluded that the Copper River route made much more sense, and engineer M. K. Rodgers urged a move to Katalla. Rodgers was certain that he could construct a breakwater to shelter ships and a wharf sturdy enough to withstand the storms regularly sweeping across the coast. The company accepted his proposal, and the two structures were constructed at a cost of one million dollars. A fierce storm in 1907 destroyed both. The syndicate quickly abandoned the Katalla route.

Michael J. Heney showed better judgment than the syndicate people. Heney, famed for his construction of the White Pass and Yukon Railway from Skagway, started railroad construction from Orca Inlet (later Cordova) in 1906. Heney expected to sell out to the syndicate when it realized the error of its ways and concluded that his route was the only feasible one. Heney was right, of course, and in 1907, after he had pushed the grade work to Alaganik, the syndicate bought him out and hired him as grade contractor. Heney, one of the few Alaska folk heroes, showed his usual drive and organizational genius working for the syndicate, but died before the work was completed.

The rejection of the Valdez route by the syndicate encouraged the ambitions of promoter Henry D. Reynolds. Reynolds's place in mining history would be notable even without reference to the railroad rivalry. He was a wily operator of mining, transportation, and other commercial ventures whose ethical sense was perhaps overcome by his magnificent visions. Reynolds first appeared on Prince William Sound in 1901, and by 1907 his Reynolds Alaska Development Company had mineral production going on in the sound region and on Latouche Island. The syndicate's desertion of Valdez as a rail terminal inspired Reynolds to venture into the railroad field. Money flowed in from Valdez residents who believed that their future prosperity would be determined by a railroad. Investors were encouraged by Gov. John Brady's enthusiastic support of Reynolds's schemes. Brady, an honest, well-respected man, soon regretted his association with Reynolds, as the apparent conflict of interest caused his dismissal from office. His boss, the secretary of the interior, was aghast that the territory's chief executive would identify himself with commercial promotion.

Reynolds raised $200,000 for the Alaska Home Railroad in Valdez and arranged to hire work-
ers in Seattle. He also sought additional funding in Seattle and throughout the Northeast,
where he sponsored a weekly newspaper to promote company interests. He was no piker, as
the purchase of the Alaska Coast Company a shipping firm, revealed. One thing folks
enjoyed about the zealous promoter was his refusal to be intimidated by the syndicate.
In fact, he deliberately antagonized his great rival by sending a ship to Katalla to woo 300
railroad workers away from the syndicate.

In moving too far too fast with inadequate financing, Reynolds's railroad venture verged
on collapse. He tried desperately to get Tacoma capitalists to bail him out but failed. In
forfeiting his $100,000 option for purchase of the Alaska Coast Company, he lost the $47,500
already invested. Worse yet, he could not meet railroad construction payrolls. His Valdez
bank closed and Reynolds left Alaska. His efforts to raise money in the East were
unsuccessful, and he resigned his chairman position in January 1908. In April he was
indicted for mail fraud on charges of misrepresentations to attract investors. Charges were
dropped after he was adjudged insane.[25]

❋ Keystone Canyon Affair ❋

Before Reynolds's fall, he contributed to an instance of corporate violence that marred
the achievement of the Copper River and Northwestern Railway's construction. The
confrontation in September 1907 between Reynolds's Alaska Home Railroad and the
syndicate was perhaps inevitable given the high stakes and the intemperate individuals
involved. The Alaska Home Railroad had graded several miles out of Valdez with the
enthusiastic support of Valdez folks unwilling to face the death of their hopes for a railroad.
At Keystone Canyon, a narrow defile leading to Thompson Pass along the old Valdez-Eagle
road, the Home Railroad crew was confronted by a rock barricade placed by Copper River
and Northwestern Railway workers. The Home Railroad was on the verge of bankruptcy, and
its officers resented the interference of the well-funded syndicate road. Since the syndicate
had abandoned its Keystone Canyon grade, its defense of it seemed surly—and provocative.
Of course, the Copper River and Northwestern had the legal right to defend its grade, but
this did not extend to a right to shoot trespassers. George Hazelet, a feisty veteran of mining
and other commercial activities, was the man in charge of syndicate operations in the
region. He tried to intimidate the trespassers by getting U.S. Marshal George Perry to issue
temporary deputy commissions to two syndicate employees, Edward C. Hasey and Duncan
Dickson. Hazelet armed the two men and advised them to "be patient, take it cool, but I
look to you boys to protect my rights."[26] Marshal Perry anticipated but could not hold off
violence. He wired Valdez Deputy Marshal James Lathrop on September 16: "See that
Dickson and Hasey don't exceed authority and get us into trouble." Lathrop responded on
September 19:

I am satisfied Hasey has overstepped his authority. Hazelet is not trying to hold canyon but only his grade.
I advise you wire Hasey and Dickson to be careful and don't involve this office. Also wire Hazelet to same
effect. I look for no trouble over there of any nature. It is simple bluff.[27]

On September 25 the Home Railroad men, armed with tools and clubs, marched in a
menacing manner onto or near the syndicate's grade. Hasey, sheltered behind the rock
barricade with a rifle, shot three of them. Fred Rhinehart later died of his wounds. As most
Alaskans denounced Hasey's violent behavior, court officers swiftly convened a grand jury.
Gov. Wilford Hoggatt hurried to Valdez to investigate the affair. His sympathy for the

syndicate was obvious, but U.S. Attorney Nathan V. Harlan refused the governor's demands for indictments against the Home Railroad men. The grand jury indicted Hasey for murder and assault but, on the advice of Harlan and his deputy prosecutors—W. T. Scott and L. V. Ray—they did not indict Hazelet. At the time, they did not have evidence of Hazelet's instruction to Hasey to "protect my rights."

Hasey's case was transferred to Juneau to avoid the partisanship in Valdez. To forestall chicanery, the Justice Department, which did not have its own detectives at the time, sent Secret Service Agent E. P. McAdams to assist the prosecutors. Reporting in February 1908, McAdams found the atmosphere "terrible," and warned that the jury "will be subject to influences." Alaskans, who traditionally identified New York City and Washington, D.C., as the centers of corruption, would have been amazed at McAdams's opinion of their integrity: "It would take a Constitutional amendment to purify Alaska," he reported to his chief.[28]

Part of the unrest in Juneau grew out of the dismissal of Harlan at the governor's instigation. Within a month of the shooting, Hoggatt had opened his attack on Harlan, blaming him and Scott for failing to prevent the violence and refusing to indict the Home Railroad workers for inciting riot. Hoggatt charged that both men were private counsels to the Home Railroad contractor and that Harlan was a conspicuous drunk. Harlan considered himself a victim of the syndicate for his vigorous prosecution and rallied friends to protest Hoggatt's charges. Harlan was not a martyr of the Keystone Canyon shootout because some

Completing the roadbed for the Copper River & Northwestern Railway at Kennecott, winter 1911. Courtesy of the Washington State Historical Society.

The "million dollar" railroad bridge across the Copper River at the Miles Glacier. Courtesy of the Museum of History and Industry, Seattle, No. 18929; Hegg photo 560.

of Hoggatt's charges, notably those concerning his drinking, were confirmed by others.[29]

President Theodore Roosevelt always kept a close watch on Alaska events, and he responded decisively to Hoggatt's charges: "It seems to me Harlan and his sort should be removed at once and steps taken to provide men who will prosecute leaders on both sides in the recent troubles in Alaska, as Hoggatt recommends." Soon after the president heard from the attorney general of Hoggatt's interference in the case and reacted with anger: "It seems well-nigh impossible to be sure that we have got a decent man in Alaska."[30] As the government attorneys John Boyce, William Barnhill, and W. T. Scott prepared to try Hasey for murder in Juneau, they were well aware that the attorney general and the president were watching. "With an honest jury we can't keep from winning," McAdams assured John Wilkie, chief of the Secret Service.[31]

Hasey's defenders—Thomas Lyons of Juneau, John Carson of Tacoma, and Fred Brown and John Ostrander of Valdez—conferred often with Jarvis, Birch, Hazelet, and the syndicate's law firm of Bogle and Spooner in Seattle. Ostrander, the defense team leader, derided Scott and Boyce as "a pair of old grannies," and complained of Judge Royal Gunnison's slow pace. The presence of McAdams, "a bad actor," and "so-called detective" did not awe him: "I think we will be able to show him up." Ostrander planned to use M. B. Morrisey, a Home Railroad worker, as a defense witness, although he had been subpoenaed earlier by the government. Morrisey seemed eager to testify that some of the Home Railroad men had been armed, so the prosecutor had no use for his testimony. "Morrisey is acting on the square," Ostrander believed. The true role of Morrisey later taxed investigators of the trial. It was not his testimony, which had corroboration by other defense witnesses, that aroused suspicion, but his open-handed entertainment of and loans to other defense witnesses. Morrisey spent money provided by the syndicate and drew a salary from it during the trial and afterwards until he departed for parts unknown.[32]

The trial began in April 1908. Ostrander's confidence was not diminished by the sudden illness and death of Assistant U.S. Attorney Scott, or even the hostility of Judge Gunnison, "the most ignorant fool that ever sat on this or any bench." After several weeks of trial, jurors found that Hasey's apprehension of bodily harm from the Home Railroad gang justified his shooting and acquitted him of second-degree murder charges. The government persisted, trying Hasey for assault with intent to kill in February 1909. This time jurors decided that Hasey's gunplay had been unnecessary and unreasonable and found him guilty. Judge Gunnison sentenced him to eighteen months in the prison at McNeil Island, Washington. Initially, Hasey's attorneys prepared to appeal, then dropped it when syndicate officers encouraged Hasey to serve his time in return for receiving his full pay and other benefits. According to rumor the syndicate followed this course because of Morrisey's persistent demands for money.[33]

With Hasey in jail and the Alaska Home Railroad bankrupt and disgraced because of questionable activities by its promoter, the syndicate's reputation improved. Construction of the Copper River and Northwestern Railway and other developments captured public attention. Michael J. Heney, "the Irish Prince," was the railroad contractor and a widely admired figure. The new railroad was a greater challenge than the White Pass and Yukon Railway he had helped build during the Klondike gold rush era because of its far greater length, wider gauge, and the formidable obstacles posed by huge glaciers. But the Copper River line was the key to Kennecott profits and also answered the longing of Alaskans for an "all-American" route to the interior. Syndicate officers often declared their intent to carry construction of the railroad all the way to the Yukon River to achieve a combined rail-river route that would aid territorial development. Whether the syndicate was ever genuinely interested in building beyond Kennecott is not clear, but when the line reached the copper mines in 1911, construction terminated.

✳ Railroad Construction ✳

Construction plans called for a single-track, standard-gauge railroad running 131 miles to Chitina from Cordova, then branching to extend sixty-five miles to the Kennecott mill. The route from Cordova was south and east across the outwash from the Sheridan Glacier to Alaganik, a western slough of the Copper River, then northeast to the main channel of the Copper River delta. The first bridge was constructed at mile 27. The line crossed the delta to mile 39, Katalla Junction, then turned north for ten miles to its main crossing of the Copper at mile 49, where it passed in front of the Miles and Childs Glaciers. Following the right limit of the Copper, it ran through Abercrombie Canyon, across the Baird Glacier moraine and the Aken Glacier outwash to the confluence of the Tasnuna and Tiekel Rivers. There the line

Lt. Frederick Mears's private train standing in the Chitina depot, September 1914. Courtesy of the Rasmuson Library Archives, University of Alaska Fairbanks; Mears Collection, 84-75-408N; Hunt photo J1909.

entered Wood Canyon and followed the Copper to Chitina.

Coastal hemlock was cut for rail ties, and seventy-pound steel was used for the Cordova-Chitina line. From Chitina sixty-pound steel was used for the rest of the route. Out of Chitina the line crossed the Copper and continued east on the north side of Chitina River. As with the steel weight, construction standards were reduced for the Chitina-Kennecott mill route. From Cordova the maximum gradient was 0.5 percent and the maximum curvature was ten degrees; from Chitina 2.5 percent grades and fourteen-degree curves were permitted. E. C. Hawkins, another veteran of the White Pass and Yukon Route railway project, was the chief engineer in charge of railroad construction.[34]

Bridge building, particularly that of the "million-dollar bridge" at mile 49, provided the most dramatic highlights of the 1907–1911 construction period. In the summer of 1909, Hawkins and A. C. O'Neil, superintendent of bridge construction, took on the formidable task of bridging the 1,500-foot channel at mile 49, where the Copper flowed between Miles and Childs Glaciers. The project was unique because of the glaciers' impact. A mile above the crossing, the three-mile front of Miles Glacier discharged a volley of icebergs from early spring through late autumn. The largest of these icy behemoths weighed thousands of tons and coursed downriver with a twelve-mile current. Somehow, the ice had to be diverted

while the bridge was constructed. Once in place the bridge had to be protected from the annual spring river breakup when ice frozen to depths of seven feet would be loosed to smash against any structures in its way to the sea.

Construction started with three giant piers sunk fifty to sixty feet to bedrock. The piers, with their greatest diameter at eighty-six feet, were solid concrete armored with steel rails to better withstand the impact of ice. Work was done after freeze-up to avoid ice movement. With the piers in place, work proceeded rapidly in April and May in a desperate race to complete the structure before the river's breakup. All the timber falsework necessary to construction rested on the river ice. A disaster was narrowly averted when, after a series of fierce storms, the river began to rise, lifting its seven-foot ice cover and the bridge falsework with it. All hands worked furiously to thaw and cut out ice from around the piles to prevent pressure on the falsework. Despite these efforts, the cantilever construction falsework of the third pier was driven fifteen inches out of line. Hawkins, through a herculean effort, managed to force the 450 feet of heavy piling and substructure back into line with tackle rigging. Bridge work was then pushed forward and all the work was completed two days before breakup.[35]

✳ Steamboats Assist Construction ✳

Construction support and transport of materials was aided by the service of a stern-wheeler river steamer, *Chitina*, which was assembled on the Copper River in 1907. The sternwheeler was 109.6 feet long with a twenty-three-foot beam drawing six inches of water unladen. It weighed 187 tons gross, 169 tons net. Its hold was four feet deep. After construction in Portland, Oregon, under supervision of an experienced Yukon steamboater, George Hill, she was broken down and shipped by steamship to Valdez. The largest section weighed four tons. Since Abercrombie Rapids blocked navigation from the river's mouth, the disassembled boat was packed in from Valdez in sections using sleds and horses, following the Valdez Trail through Keystone Canyon, then eastward over Marshall Pass and down the valley of the Tasnuna River. It was a tough job, and one that probably would have been impossible in any season except winter.

Train crossing the Gilahina Trestle. Courtesy of the Alaska State Library, Skinner Foundation, PCA 44-2-153.

The freight arrived in good order for assembly at the confluence of the Copper and Tasnuna Rivers in April. Two pioneers of the region—George Hazelet and A. J. Meals—supervised the transport. Meals kept ahead of the freight with a crew of fourteen men and twelve horses ploughing the trail. The boat was launched on July 1 with the daughter of Chief Goodlataw, a well-respected Ahtna leader, performing the christening. Onboard equipment included capstan, derrick, and spars, essential to loading and for getting the boat off sandbars.

Chitina (originally spelled *Chittyna*) made her maiden voyage on July 4, 1907. In summer 1908 construction got under way above Abercrombie Canyon. Rapids Landing, thirty-five miles upstream from the ocean, was the limit of downriver navigation. It was established as a base for *Chitina*, which made four trips up to Bonanza Landing, the nearest point to the mines that could be reached by water. Other trips were made to a big construction camp being built at the mouth of the Tiekel River.

Heavy snow often delayed trains between the coast and Chitina. Courtesy of the Cordova Historical Society, 77-62-2.

Another boat, *Tonsina*, was built in the summer of 1908 at Cordova. At 120 feet with a twenty-foot beam, this boat was a little larger than her sister ship. She drew fifteen inches of water and was powered by 300-horsepower oil-burning engines. She also had fourteen staterooms and a dining room. As with *Chitina*, it was necessary to carry the new boat above Abercrombie Rapids. By rail and wagon the sections reached Rapids Landing in the fall. The craft was launched in July 1909. A month later a similar boat, *Nizina*, began service, as well as the smaller *Gulkana*, built at the same time to be a ferry on the lake below Miles Glacier. She had limited freight capacity but could push a barge carrying two railroad cars.

The boats functioned well from 1909 through 1911 during the short navigation seasons carrying freight and provisions for the 4,000 railroad workers to the points closest to their camps. Archie W. Shiels was in charge of provisioning, and steamboat captains included George Hill, Charles S. Peabody, Henry Bailey, Al Medley, Charles Griswold, and others. All skippers were experienced steamboat men, and they needed all their skills to navigate on the windy river. Captains had some close calls but lost no boats. The need for the boats ended after September 8, 1910, when the *Nizina* carried a load to the bustling town of Chitina, a place that had not existed when railroad construction started. A few days later the rails reached Chitina and the boats were laid up just above the town, serving as bunkhouses until the Kuskulana Bridge was built.[36]

✳ Railroad Progress ✳

Much of the material and provisions had to be transported during the winter by horse-drawn, double-ended sleds until construction permitted operation of a supply train. Some idea of the vicissitudes of winter construction is highlighted by one incident—the "loss" of a work train under the snow for twenty-one days in 1909. The 160 men aboard the train had to wait out the storm before they started digging their way from beneath a mountain of snow.[37]

At the peak of the railroad construction, 6,000 men labored on the project. Excavation totaled 5,180,000 yards, more than half of which was solid rock. A full 15 percent of the

196-mile railroad was built on bridges or trestles with 129 bridges between Cordova and Chitina. Of these bridges, five were major steel structures totaling 4,000 feet. The railroad's construction cost was $23 million. Geologist Alfred H. Brooks did not exaggerate in calling the completion of the railroad "the most important advance made in the history of Alaska transportation since steamboat service was established on the Yukon."[38]

After Kennecott closed the mill, rail service was shut down November 11, 1938. For some years local residents, including storekeeper Otto A. Nelson of Chitina, adapted automobiles to the rails and freighted goods to McCarthy. During World War II the rails were removed, and autos began using the railbed as a road. In recent years the state department of transportation has maintained a good gravel road between Chitina and the Kennicott River that follows the railbed for most of its route. The great steel bridge over the Kuskulana is still in use.

❋ Other Trails and Roads ❋

Only a few trails and roads ever were established within the borders of the Wrangell-St. Elias National Park and Preserve. The major trail system was the route from McCarthy over Skolai Pass (with an alternate trail over Chitistone Pass) to Chisana, thence to Slana and over a northern branch to Mentasta and Tanana Crossing and a southern branch to Chistochina, Gakona, and the Valdez Trail.

Some of the Indian trails were improved to accommodate miners. U.S. Army explorer Oscar Rohn found the Indian passage, later called the Kuskulana Pass Trail, north of the Chitina River in 1899. He observed that it commenced at the Chitina's mouth and went east along the southern side of the mountains to the Kuskulana River, thence northward, following the river and crossing the foot of the glacier to the Kuskulana Pass, thence over the pass to reach the bend in the Lakina River. Rohn cut a new trail from Lakina River to the Kennicott Glacier, a distance of fifteen miles. The trail served the Kennecott mining development until the Copper River and Northwestern Railway was built. According to pioneer miner Neil Finnesand, it was used by miners going between Kennecott and the Kotsina mining area.

❋ Millard Trail ❋

In June 1898 prospector Benjamin F. Millard pioneered a route to the Tanana-Yukon waters from near today's Copper Center. Travelers crossed the Copper River, bearing northeast near the bases of Mounts Drum and Sanford. Eventually, travelers crossed the upper Copper River near the mouth of the Slana and made for Mentasta Pass, which brought them through the Alaska Range to the Tanana River.

❋ Nicolai or Hanagita River Trail ❋

This sixty-mile trail runs from Taral, following Taral Creek over the divide to Canyon Creek, over another divide to Hanagita River, thence into the Chakina River drainage, and across the Chitina River into the Nizina River area. Historically, the route had been used by Indians passing from their winter homes at Taral to their summer fishing and hunting areas. There are alternative branches: one is the Chitina River trail to the mouth of the Nizina river, the other is the Hanagita River trail to the Chakina River, crossing the Chitina near the junction with the Tana confluence.

The early miners of the Bremner district followed a trail north from McCarthy to the Chitina River cut through around 1907. Other miners hauled their supplies down the Tonsina River, crossed the Copper River at Taral, where a cable conveyance was in operation, then went on into the Bremner region. When the Copper River and Northwestern Railway was built in 1911, prospectors took the railroad to McCarthy and packed over the McCarthy-May Creek Trail. Turning southward, they crossed the Chitina River near the Tana River before proceeding into the Bremner area. The Alaska Road Commission (ARC) upgraded the McCarthy-May Creek Trail to Bremner in 1914, generally following the old Nicolai Trail. Later ARC built another trail from the railroad at Long Lake, crossing the Nizina River, thence down the Chakina River to the older trail. In 1935 the commission built a thirty-mile tractor road to Golconda Creek to serve the Bremner Mining Company and the Yellow Band Mining Company, but the shutdown of the railroad in 1938 ended all their trail maintenance in the region.

Floods destroyed the Copper River Bridge at Chitina in August 1932. Courtesy of the Cordova Historical Society, C467-2-6.

The first motorized vehicle traveled the Valdez-Fairbanks Trail in 1913. Its route would later be designated as the Richardson Highway. The driver is Bobby Sheldon of Fairbanks. Courtesy of the Anchorage Museum of History and Art, B62.1A.83; Hunt photo P203.

⁂ McCarthy-May Creek Road (Route 57) ⁂

The Alaska Road Commission built the twenty-mile road between McCarthy and May Creek in 1925 to serve the Nizina and Bremner mining districts, particularly for traffic to Dan and Chititu Creeks. A pack trail was built about the same time to give travelers better access to the Bremner area. Pedestrians still use the Young Creek Bridge, but the grander Nizina Bridge, the largest road bridge in Alaska at the time of its construction in 1914, is in ruins. The first bridge was replaced by a steel span and concrete foundations in 1923. Flooding in the early 1930s destroyed this bridge, which was rebuilt in 1935, then ruined again some years later.

⁂ The Slana-Tok Cutoff ⁂

The Tok Cutoff was built in 1942 by the U.S. Army. The Alaska Highway, also built that year, carried traffic to Fairbanks, but the cutoff was intended to provide a shorter route from the highway west to the Copper River basin and Anchorage.

⁂ Nabesna and Nabesna Road ⁂

The forty-five-mile road from Slana to Nabesna was built to service the Nabesna Mine (see Chapter 4). The mine is closed, but a lodge nearby accommodates hunters and other visitors.

⁂ Glenn Highway ⁂

The Glenn Highway was a 1940–1942 wartime construction project to provide a link from the Richardson Highway to Anchorage via Chickaloon and Palmer. Holly Sterling was chief highway engineer for the district in 1940 when it was decided to build a road from the

The Nizina Bridge, September 1935. Like earlier bridges across the torrent, this one was eventually taken by the river. Courtesy of the Alaska State Library, Alaska Road Commission Collection, PCA 61-5-165.

Freighting on the Chitina River. Courtesy of the Anchorage Museum of History and Art, B72.32.292.

Richardson Highway at mile 116 to Chickaloon. Ben Woods, Harry Heintz, and Bill Trims were among those who gathered horses and equipment and set to work. Progress was slow and difficult, according to local historian Mrs. M. R. Clayton. "It was a wet summer and the going was rough. The horses floundered around and bogged down to their bellies in the mud. The mosquitoes were very hungry." Sterling sent Trims back to mile 116 with the horses while he and the other men continued the survey on foot. "Several weeks later they all arrived at Chickaloon in a rather poor and ragged condition."

Construction began in earnest in October when a cat and freight sleds were available to push a trail through. Soon after work started snow fell to impede progress, then men fell ill after drinking swamp water. After six weeks they reached Nelchina Creek near the present Eureka and stopped work for the winter.

In 1941 the highway engineers had a big crew ready. Some 300 men from all parts of Alaska worked on the job, including Johnny Billum (whose ancestor was the pioneer ferry operator on the Copper River during the gold rush era), John Paulson, Walter Rinerson, Gus Johnson, Harry Johns, Harry Hobson, Oscar Craig, and Jerome Luebke—who later settled in Glennallen.

The work continued in 1942. Since all the supplies had to come from Valdez and Thompson Pass had been closed over the winter, spring work was delayed until supplies could be trucked in. Moose Creek became a construction camp that season, called Glennallen. Early in winter 1942 the construction parties completed the pioneer road all the way to Palmer.

❋ Maritime Transport ❋

A number of shipping companies served Prince William Sound before the gold rush. The Pacific Steam Whaling Company and others served salmon canneries primarily. Regular steamship service from Pacific Coast ports to Valdez commenced with the gold rush. Cordova became a port of call when the town developed incidentally to Kennecott's production. Ship lines included those operated by the Northwestern Commercial Company, founded by John Rosene and other Seattle businessmen; the Pacific Steam Whaling Company, which had promoted the superiority of the Copper River route to the Klondike in its advertisements and owned the salmon cannery near the modern Cordova; and others. The Pacific Steam Whaling Company was taken over by the Pacific Packing and Navigation

Gracie and the snow bird. Gracie Strandberg was a nurse at the Kennecott Hospital. Courtesy of the Alfonse Nikolaus Collection.

Company, which failed in 1904. Subsequently, John Rosene's Northwestern Commercial Company took over their ships and got in on the Valdez traffic.

The syndicate wished to control the transport of its copper all the way to the smelter, so it acquired Rosene's company. At the same time the syndicate provided more business for its ships by acquiring a number of canneries in the region. By 1908, as railroad construction began the syndicate founded the Alaska Steamship Company, which boasted fifteen steamers—the largest fleet in Alaska. The company thrived until Kennecott closed, then survived for several decades longer under other ownership until finally folding in the early 1970s.

* Conclusion *

All major transportation routes in Alaska derived from other economic developments or in anticipation of them. This pattern is certainly apparent within the Wrangell-St. Elias region, where most routes emanated from expansion of the mineral industry. Declines in the industry meant reduction of trail and road maintenance and abandonment of rail and other routes. Construction of the Copper River and Northwestern Railway gave an important transport route and promised a general acceleration of the region's population. But the forecasts of the boomers fell short because the railroad was not built into the Yukon country and because no one found resources that invited further development. When Kennecott quit mining, the railroad stopped running. Everyone agreed that it was great country, but there was only one Kennecott.

The Chitina Auto Railer at Kennecott. Courtesy of the McCarthy-Kennicott Historical Museum, No. 000340.

Yakutat, Alaska. Courtesy of the Alaska
State Library, Kayamori Collection, PCA
55-368.

Chapter 10

❊ ❊ ❊

Towns and People

McCarthy and Chisana are the only permanent communities within park boundaries. A few homesteaders, miners, guides, and others live at various places within the region, particularly along the Chitina-McCarthy and Nabesna Roads and in the Dan Creek-May Creek area. Communities adjoining Wrangell-St. Elias Park and Preserve, including Yakutat, Cordova, Chitina, Copper Center, Glennallen, Gulkana, Gakona, Chistochina, and Slana share a common history with it.

❊ Yakutat ❊

After the destruction of the Russian colonists by the Tlingits in 1805, the Russian American Company traders did not return to Yakutat. White traders did not locate there permanently until some years after Alaska's purchase by the United States in 1867. They may have been discouraged somewhat by the reputation of the Yakutats as "treacherous and warlike and have committed a number of murders merely for plunder," according to Alaska expert William H. Dall, who went on to warn: "Navigators in small trading vessels who may be visited by them should therefore be on their guard and never allow them to spend the night on board."[1]

In 1886 there was a small stampede of miners from Juneau after discovery of gold in beach sands near Yakutat. A similar find occurred at about the same time at Lituya Bay, but quantities proved small at both places. Although one Yakutat miner got $40 to each ton of sand, mining declined after thousands of dogfish washed ashore, covering the sands with their decaying remains. Tides cleaned the beaches after a few years, and by 1890 some forty or fifty miners were trying their luck. None earned much, as the shallow diggings had been nearly exhausted in the first season. An estimated $3,000 was the total take for 1891.

The area's history since United States purchase has received the most attention from anthropologists, particularly Frederica de Laguna, whose comprehensive study, *Under Mount Saint Elias: The History and Culture of the Yakutat Tlingit*, was published in three large volumes in 1972. She recounts arrival of the first missionaries, Adolph Lydell of the Swedish Free Mission Church in 1887 and Karl Hendrickson a year later. Hendrickson built a sawmill and school.

Yakutat's fishing industry boomed in the 1880s. Several canneries operated for years, then fishing slacked off in the 1920s. Considerable capital investment was made by F. S. Simpson and others from Seattle in 1930. They established a lumber company, cannery, sawmill, store, and the Yakutat and Southern Railroad. The tiny railroad served the fish-hauling needs of the cannery. It no longer operates, nor does another one built to haul fish from the Akwe River to the mouth of Dry Bay. About 500 people reside in the region today, most of them in the town of Yakutat. The economy depends upon its fisheries, wood products industry, tourism, and oil and gas exploration activities. Sport hunting and fishing attracts outsiders, as hunting opportunities are good and some of the area's streams are famed for salmon and steelhead runs. Other tourist attractions include "flight-seeing" over Russell Fiord, the Hubbard and Malaspina Glaciers, and Icy Bay.[2]

❖ Cordova ❖

Valdez did not fade away for lack of a railroad, but Cordova developed into a substantial town because of one. By 1909, a year after its founding, Cordova had 1,500 people and ten stores, two hotels, two lumber yards, three churches, ten saloons, and a school. Cordova's interests were bound to the Guggenheim syndicate that formed the Kennecott Corporation and constructed the Copper River and Northwestern Railway to mine copper and bring it to market. As the terminal for the railroad, Cordova was assured of continuing commercial importance. Nominally, Cordova was an independent community, but it resembled a company town in many respects. George C. Hazelet, the developer of the townsite, worked for Kennecott, and he differed from the usual town promoter in his restraint about the town's future. He told a reporter in 1909 that Cordova eventually would have a population of 5,000 to 10,000 people supporting the mining and transportation industries, but he thought that 1,500 was plenty at the time: "No greater misfortunes could befall the town than a large influx of people before this is warranted by the permanent development of the country."[3]

Cordova had been the site of the old Indian village of Eyak and a cannery location before it was designated the railroad terminal. Its features included a good natural harbor, plenty of level ground for construction, and a location only twenty miles from the mouth of the Copper River. The town's newspaper supported the syndicate and attacked anyone who criticized the Kennecott Company. As in other mining towns, the editors endlessly boosted Cordova and pumped up the economic potential as boundless. Cordova is and was a pleasant place to live. Even when the town was in its raw beginnings, there were some amenities. One was the club room of the Episcopal Church, which was supervised by Eustice P. Ziegler, later a famed painter. Men could play cards, shoot pool, smoke, drink coffee, and read magazines without any obligation to attend church services.

Among the residents closely associated with earlier events was photographer Eric A. Hegg. Hegg's images of the Klondike stampede are among the best-known photographs of that event. After the Klondike rush, Hegg went Outside for a time, but returned as photographer of the construction of the Copper River and Northwestern Railway. Then he opened a studio in Cordova.

Cordova, Alaska. Courtesy of the Washington State Historical Society.

Camp 42 along the Copper River & Northwestern Railway. Courtesy of the Washington State Historical Society.

Cordova, of course, survived the closing of the Kennecott operations and the end of its railroad. It was not entirely dependent on copper mining, although the shutdown was a severe blow. Today the fisheries of Prince William Sound and the Copper River provide much of the income for the town's nearly 3,000 residents. Salmon run from May to September and fishermen take black cod and king and tanner crab during winter. Cordova's economy also benefits from recreation and tourism. The natural environment offers spectacular mountain, river, and ocean scenes and wilderness experience opportunities. Visitors increasingly include birdwatchers, who come to view the millions of shorebirds passing through the Hartney Bay and Copper River delta area—dunlins, western sandpipers, black-bellied plovers, trumpeter swans, Canada geese, and other species. Sports fishermen, kayakers, and hikers also flock to Cordova during summer. As Cordova has no connection to the Alaska highway system, visitors must travel by air or sea. The town is served by the ferries of the Alaska Marine Highway, which also call at Valdez, Whittier, and Seward.

❊ McCarthy ❊

McCarthy, though not plotted until 1912, developed into a small community in 1908, serving the railroad and Kennecott mining interests 150 miles inland from Cordova. The town, established on John E. Barrett's homestead, superseded Nizina on the Nizina River as the regional hub. Traders from Nizina and Blackburn, two miles north of McCarthy, moved to the new town when the railroad built maintenance facilities there. McCarthy lies about four miles from Kennecott, and its facilities provided for mine and mill workers who preferred recreation away from the company town of Kennecott. McCarthy grew at a lively pace. Its first newspaper was the *Copper Bee*. Briefly in 1916 the town supported a weekly journal, the *Avalanche*, succeeded by the *McCarthy Weekly News*, published sporadically by different owners from 1917 to 1927. The town's peak population in the 1920s was 127, but area newspapers served Kennecott's population of 500 as well. A number of commercial establishments, stores, saloons, and other businesses prospered. Prostitutes lived on "the Row," an alley east of Kennecott Avenue.

The town was only about one year old in 1913 when the Chisana gold stampede gave it a strong economic boost. For some years miners continued to pass through McCarthy and helped sustain the economy. Besides activities related to mining and the railroad, support services for hunters and other travelers have been the only other long-term commercial activity. Grain and hay production in the area peaked on fifteen farms that operated in the 1920s. Dating a town's decline from a vital community to a marginal one often relates to closure of vital services, such as the school. In December 1931, while Kennecott was still operating, the commissioner of education closed the McCarthy school, which then had only two pupils. The post office closure in 1943 was an official recognition that the once bustling railroad/mining center was on its last legs.

McCarthy lives on. It survived the fading of the Chisana boom and the more significant closing of Kennecott, existing in ghostly fashion into modern times. The town even survived the loss of the bridge that linked it to the Edgerton and Richardson Highways. From the time of its founding McCarthy was connected across the Kennicott River to the road to Chitina by a bridge, which had to be rebuilt after many spring breakups and floods from glacial outburst lakes. The last bridge built by the state in 1974, was reduced to a footbridge after one season and finally washed out in 1981.[4] With the establishment of Wrangell-St. Elias National Park and Preserve, the gradual "improvement" of the McCarthy Road, and the general increase in tourism to Alaska, the area now attracts thousands of visitors annually.

❊ McCarthy of Margaret Harrais ❊

As one of only two towns within park boundaries, the history of McCarthy deserves particular attention. Fortunately, one of the town's last schoolteachers, Margaret Harrais, wrote about the place in detail. She traveled there in 1923 with her husband, Martin, to live in a three-room log cabin on the edge of town. As Martin left after a week to return to his prospecting work for Kennecott, she was pleased that the cabin had all the amenities, including a sewing machine, screened porches, and "a marvelous view of snow-capped mountains and glaciers, the light and shade on them forever changing. . . . The great Kennicott Glacier sweeps in a majestic curve from the foot of Mt. Blackburn and shoves its foot right in our faces."[5]

Valdez, Alaska. Courtesy of the Museum of History and Industry, Seattle, 92.7.6.37; Guy Cameron photo.

This bridge across the Tonsina River was built in 1899 entirely without metal fittings. Courtesy of the Valdez Museum, P1986.117.44; Miles brothers photo 591.

Margaret was not so pleased with the moral tone of the town, which served the recreation center for the 1,600 Kennecott Mine workers: "Everything that is outlawed on their private grounds thrives here in McCarthy, to the shame of the government. The big company insists that they must have McCarthy as a 'playground for their men'; and $278,000,000 [Margaret's estimate of the company's worth] does not have to shout, it need only whisper." Martin did not believe that the Alaska president of the Woman's Christian Temperance Union could hold a teaching job long once company officers became aware of her attitude, but she determined to do her best for the eleven children in her charge.[6]

McCarthy had an unusual teacher in Margaret Harrais. Soon after graduating from teachers' college in Ohio, she headed west to teach in eastern Washington and Idaho, where she also served as the county superintendent of schools. After other varied experience, she took a job as principal of schools at Skagway in 1914, quitting after two years because Skagway seemed too much like a Seattle suburb. She moved to Fairbanks as city school superintendent and found the interior more to her liking. There she met Martin, a miner who had made money in the Klondike and Fairbanks, but invested it in the doomed town of Chena near Fairbanks and lost his stake. He took a job prospecting in the upper Chitina district for Kennecott, and she went Outside for her health. After some time in Colorado Springs and San Diego, the couple married in 1920. For several years she remained in California while he spent the mining season in Alaska. She took the job at McCarthy in 1923 to end this seasonal separation.

Harrais was interested in everything that went on in McCarthy. She attended a trial in the U.S. commissioner's log courthouse to see how the jurors behaved. Women had recently attained the right to sit as jurors and showed that they "would not be any more prone to vote their prejudice and emotions than men."[7]

As her first winter passed, Harrais came to know most of the town's one hundred residents, if you included "all that head in and out of the town for mail and supplies and a few of the oldest and best loved huskies of the streets." There was no church within 200 miles, but "the little white and green schoolhouse set in their midst proclaims it to be an organized community of homes." The territory did well by its students, providing all necessary equipment and libraries beyond the standard of schools in Ohio and the Northwest. "Here Uncle Sam spends $241.53 a year for the education of each and every child, no matter what its race or color, and here the program of living service was planned and fostered."[8]

Margaret did not mind being without mail for three months on a summer expedition into the wilderness, but in McCarthy she appreciated its regularity. "The weekly mail," she observed, "is like an oasis to a desert traveler." The mail sometimes failed, as when the much anticipated Christmas mail did not arrive because of the shipwreck of the *Northwestern*. Mail from the next ship to arrive at Cordova was delayed when a glacier lake in the Miles Glacier broke and washed out miles of the Copper River and Northwestern Railway track. Later in the season another railroad delay resulted when water flowed over sections of track, then froze in a thin sheet of ice that had to be chipped away. When workers pick-axed three miles of track, "another sheet of ice froze over the cleared track and it all had to be done all over again." No mail reached McCarthy for forty-two days.[9]

In June 1927 Margaret accompanied Martin, who no longer worked for Kennecott, on a three-month horseback expedition into the upper Chitina country. Once beyond the Nizina mining district, they left the "government trail" behind and followed the river as best they could. Many channels and a wayward course caused delays. At times they had to cut their way "through virgin forest where the river swung to our side and forced us to leave the bars for higher ground." Even with two axemen toiling ahead, the party was fortunate to make six miles a day in the wooded areas. Travel was easier once they were out of the forest, and the scenery was marvelous as they rode toward what seemed to be the Eternal Source of things. Imagine riding for two whole days into the heart of an amphitheater, the mountains rising higher and ever higher, their crowns growing whiter and ever whiter, great glaciers descending the canyons on both sides, and Mt. St. Elias and Mt. Logan forming an incomparable background straight ahead![10]

Several times they crossed Short River, which carried the main discharge of the Barnard Glacier. The passages gave Margaret uneasy moments as the horses plunged across the torrent. Up the valley they approached the "great Chitina Glacier—nine miles in width,"and found their home for the summer, a knoll surrounded on three sides with tall spruce, yielding a "perfect view of Mt. St. Elias." Swiftly the men built a log cabin "that was completely in harmony with its environment, picturesque enough to satisfy the most artistic eye.[11]

The U.S. Geological Survey made its first investigation of the upper Chitina Valley area in 1915. Fred Moffit led a party from McCarthy to the Chitina Glacier via the valley of Young Creek. Several copper signs had been noted between Canyon Creek and the glacier, about sixty-five miles from McCarthy, and it was Moffit's report that induced Harrais to try mining there. In 1926 he staked his claims, including an area just north of the glacier terminus, where the limestone showed the presence of copper minerals.

In 1930 Margaret decided to fly in for the first time. In a mere forty minutes she soared over a route never covered before "in less than five long gruelling days." Flying seemed far less dangerous than the overland passage, even though it included landing on a "home-made" airfield from which large boulders had been removed. She had been a little apprehensive about landing, "but you can't get away from pioneering up here and get anywhere. We simply had to have that first flight up here to flag the attention of the Territory to our need." The pilot of this first flight was Harold Gillam, a legend in the region.[12]

The season was an important one for the Harrais couple because Martin brought in mineral surveyors so that they could claim legal title to their ten claims. Gaining title was not a bargain counter transaction. First, there must be $500 worth of work done on every claim; then the Territory takes $20 a claim for its land office fee; the surveyor charges $100 a claim for his work; the newspaper takes several hundred dollars for advertising; lastly, the federal government takes $100 a claim for its fee.[13]

He had done most of his work on claims along the canyon of what he named Margaret Creek, blasting the surfaces on the canyon walls and running six drifts, from three to thirty feet in length into the limestone of the west wall. He also did some blasting and sampling about a quarter mile west of Margaret Creek on Dry Gulch. He built a water reservoir and an aqueduct to provide the necessary water system.

Living in a remote section of Alaska did not protect the Harraises from the impact of the depression. In 1932 they lost their savings when a Seattle bank failed and their investment in Seattle business property when tenants could no longer pay rent. Suddenly, "the little old school job, that previously had been more a diversion than a task," became the major source of family income. But as Kennecott employment declined, fewer pupils attended school in McCarthy, and the school was closed when enrollment did not meet the required number. "The school was so small that I moved the equipment over to my cabin, and school went on as usual except the salary."[14]

When this third disaster struck, Martin was at their mining camp and out of contact. Margaret, forced to make quick decisions on her own, concluded that further mining develop-

A prize dog team in Chitina. Courtesy of the Sheldon Museum and Cultural Center, Haines, Alaska.

ment was impossible for the present, so she sold back to Kennecott a consignment of explosives. This sale provided all the cash they had to leave McCarthy and find other means of making a living. "Youth was gone, enthusiasm was gone; all that remained was one another and a grim determination to keep our chins above water and be self-sustaining." It was even worse than they realized at the time because the railroad shut down a few years later, ending hopes of reopening their mine or selling it to others.[15]

From McCarthy the couple went to Cordova, where Martin managed a lumber mill briefly before the depression forced its closure. Next, Margaret took a teacher's job at Ellamar, an Indian village on the coast between Cordova and Valdez. Ellamar had once been the site of a copper mine, but it had shut down in 1920. They never got back to McCarthy. Martin died in 1936 while mining at Mineral Creek, and Margaret succeeded him as U.S. commissioner at Valdez. For some years she served the public with distinction in law, welfare, and education in Valdez. She died in the 1954 earthquake when the Valdez city dock she was standing on capsized into Valdez Bay.[16]

(*Above*) *Aerial view of McCarthy and the Kennicott Glacier; August 12, 1937. Courtesy of the Archives, Rasmuson Library, University of Alaska Fairbanks; Washburn Collection, 504N.*

(*Right*) *The railroad tunnel linking Chitina with the Copper River. Courtesy of the Archives, Rasmuson Library, University of Alaska Fairbanks; Mears Collection, 84-75-403N, Hunt photo.*

In 1962 the U.S. Geological Survey undertook its first investigation of the upper Chitina region in nearly fifty years. Government geologists had received permission from Margaret to use her cabin as a base for their work. The cabin and food cache were in good shape, although the water system no longer functioned. Geologist James F. Seitz did not find favorable copper prospects in the area where the Harraises had worked so hard.[17]

Other families and individuals shared the expectations of Martin and Margaret Harrais in local mines. Asa C. Baldwin, who had been involved in the Boundary Survey from 1907 and had done mineral surveys for Kennecott and others in the region for years, had claims of his own in the Bremner Mountains. He invested money and labor in his Yellow Band Gold Mine for several years. Baldwin died in 1942, but his daughter recently recalled visiting Chitina and McCarthy in 1938 when Asa still had high expectations. She is sad that the mining stock for Yellow Band is now considered an amusing relic:

In that stock lay the dreams of many people. What prevented them from coming into reality was no failure of the mine. I am sure the gold is still there . . . when the war ended, wages had skyrocketed but the price of gold remained low for years. . . . Now the mine is permanently encased in a National Park Wilderness and the equipment is still there, slowly disintegrating. It would have been lovely to be a gold mine heiress, but I am glad to see the land that my father loved so much and dedicated his life to, preserved the way he knew it.[18]

❋ Chitina ❋

Chitina, one hundred miles inland from Cordova on the Copper River, was another railroad town. Chitina townsite lots were first put on the market in August 1910. Buyers selected lots near the railroad and business section or on Chitina Heights behind the business section. The town's population was never large, but it served as the regional hub for mining, trading, and guiding. It gained some amenities, including a school for residents and one in the nearby Native village for youngsters there, a hotel, and various stores. An important transfer point, travelers could take a stageline to the Willow Creek Junction on the Valdez Trail, then on to Fairbanks, 305 miles away. The government built a wagon road from the Valdez Trail at Willow Creek to Chitina after funds were raised from Cordova businessmen and from railroad and poll tax receipts. The cut-off gave travelers from Cordova to the interior the advantage of traveling the railroad as far as Chitina and then the Ed S. Orr Stage Company or other means to continue on into the interior. According to a magazine writer in 1910, the Chitina-Willow Creek stretch:

. . . is one of the best pieces of road en route. . . . It runs along the dry benches and is through timber all the way, with road houses every few miles. Recently a party came through from Fairbanks in seven days . . . and this time will be lessened when the winter trails are at their best.[19]

The railroad-trail route to the interior raised hopes that the day would come when the Copper River and Northwestern Railway or another railroad would be extended to the Yukon-Tanana interior because the Chitina transfer route did not serve much traffic. Chitina's lifeline and reason for being was the traffic to Kennecott, and the town could not survive once this flow stopped.

Winter travel by train was sometimes difficult because of heavy snowfalls. Trains operated only during daylight hours, so the usual run was to Chitina for an overnight stop before continuing on to McCarthy and Kennecott. The train had two sections, the first consisting of a rotary snowplow pushed along by two locomotives, an oil-burner and a coal-burner, and sleeping and cooking cars for train crews. Following behind were a locomotive, four or five gondola cars for copper ore, and a combination passenger and baggage coach. It could be a cold passage, as D. J. McKenzie, a railroad shopman at Cordova observed on a December 1917 journey:

As the train proceeded towards the mountains, the snow got deeper and deeper, the thermometer went lower and lower, and I got colder and colder . . . There was a pot-bellied stove in the passenger compartment but, I discovered to my sorrow, it was far too small to keep the coach warm in extremely cold weather.°

McCarthy, Alaska. Courtesy of the Rasmuson Library Archives, University of Alaska Fairbanks; Fairbanks Collection, 68.69.1369.

At mile 55 the train stopped for a lunch of sandwiches and coffee shared by crew and passengers, then pushed on into deep snow. "It was a beautiful sight to ride close behind the first section and watch the arc of new snow as it lifted clear of the tracks, reflecting all the colors of the rainbow in the sunshine," McKenzie said. At times the train barely moved as the frozen snow slowed the rotary of the plow which was pushed against the snowbanks by the combined might of the two locomotives. When the snowbanks were higher than the rotary, the plow would back away while the banks were broken down by hand.[21]

McKenzie found things pretty lively at Chitina because local Indians were coming into town for a big potlatch. "This was the time for selling furs, trading or selling horses and dogs, dancing, feasting, and generally having a good time." The railroad man stayed at the little hotel in comfort and warmth, continuing on the next day to McCarthy via Strelna, the coldest place along the way. Most descriptions of Chitina were left by travelers who passed through. The residents, of course, knew it as home. White residents worked for the railroad or one of the stores. Natives trapped and hunted and some worked at hauling and other wage jobs. Life became less isolated as radio reached the region and air travel commenced. The first airplane landed in town on January 17, 1931. The premier issue of the *Chitina Weekly Herald*, a little newspaper published by grade school students and their teacher, recorded the event. Bush pilot Harold Gillam had guided his Swallow TP down onto the ice of Town Lake. Otto A. Nelson, treasurer of Gillam Airways, had built a beacon fire to show him the way. All the residents turned out to celebrate the occasion, including Melvin Chase of the Chitina Cash Store; Louis G. Hinckel of the Hubbard-Elliott Mining Company of Strelna; and William Frame of the Richardson Highway Transportation Company.[22]

Later issues of the *Herald* reported on myriad community happenings—residents treated at Kennecott hospital; ship arrivals at Cordova; freight-hauler Carl Carlson's purchase of a Snow Bird, described as "a car on skis in front;" snow and rockslides along the railroad; and the travails of various truckers. The paper also editorialized about various social concerns: "CAUTION: In order to help protect our small population from being cut down too much this winter we will supply all moonshiners and bootleggers who apply at our office with the following labels: POISON."[23]

The entire 31 December 1931 issue was the work of students of Chitina's Native school, who reported on snaring rabbits and other local events of interest to them. Eight-year-old Freda Joe wrote about the season's first snow: "Last Tuesday afternoon Mother Frost shook her bed and covered ground with white feather. We were so glad that we thinking we could sleigh down the hill, and it give us water to wash our clothes and bathing."[24]

Once the railroad shut down, population declined rapidly. In the 1940s the population numbered about forty, mostly Native, although a few more people drifted in each summer. Most buildings deteriorated, and Chitina was soon classified as a ghost town.

Otto A. Nelson, a pioneer of the region, became the leading resident of the town after the railroad quit. He had given up teaching school in Missouri to come to Alaska and take up railroading in 1908. Initially a surveyor with the Copper River and Northwestern Railway, he gradually assumed other engineering jobs. He made his home in Chitina, where he and his wife raised a family. Forty years after his arrival he was one of the few residents left. In his later years Nelson often reminisced about life in Chitina. He recalled watching the breakup of ice destroy the wooden trestle bridge over the Copper River each spring. After 1939, however, this annual sideshow ceased as the bridge was never again rebuilt.

Since the railroad stopped running, Chitina has changed little. Today the town has a handful of residents, two restaurants, a gas station, and a park ranger station. Things liven up during the salmon dip-netting season on the Chitina River. Tourists drive the Edgerton Highway in the summer, and some venture down the gravel road from Chitina to McCarthy. Chitina Village, one mile south of Chitina, developed as an Indian village after railroad construction. In 1928 the Bureau of Indian Affairs built a school for the village, which survived until the late 1950s, and a small hospital.

The McCarthy Drug Store. Courtesy of the Museum of History and Industry, Seattle, no. 18947.

✳ Slana ✳

Once an Indian village on the north bank of the Slana River, Slana occupies an area near the northwest corner of the boundary of the Wrangell-St. Elias National Park and Preserve and the Nabesna Road. For many years the only settlers were the owners of the roadhouse and a few homesteaders, many of whom worked at seasonal jobs to keep things going. Recently the population in the area has grown to about 150. Most of the newcomers took advantage of the Bureau of Land Management's offering of free land to homesite settlers in

(Above) The Kenny Lake Roadhouse. Courtesy of the Valdez Museum.

(Below) Downtown Glennallen, Alaska, about 1950. Courtesy of the Rasmuson Library Archives, University of Alaska Fairbanks; Machetanz Collection, 73-75-861.

September 1983. In all, some 350 eager land seekers claimed five-acre sites. The land made available for staking consisted of 10,250 acres of black spruce bog interspersed with patches of dry ground. Unfortunately, many of those who migrated to Alaska under this program knew little about actual conditions. They assumed the land was suitable for farming, that subsistence game could be readily gathered in the area, and that local employment would provide them with some income until their land flourished. "But instead of the American dream," as an Anchorage newspaper observed in January 1985, "those hundreds found a wet, boggy land—a place lacking in jobs, game, sufficient firewood, even the possibility of subsistence."[25] Against formidable odds, some of the tougher members of the community hung on and found means of supporting themselves. Over time a scattered community has formed.

❊ Chistochina ❊

Chistochina is located on the Tok Cutoff approximately forty-two miles north of Glennallen. First settled as a fish camp, the village was named for a U.S. Army telegraph station established there in 1903. The most traditional of all Copper basin communities, subsistence hunting, fishing, and gathering remain the mainstay of the village's economy.

❊ Gakona ❊

Dating from 1905, the village of Gakona is situated on the Tok Cutoff at the junction of the Gakona and Copper Rivers. Gakona is also the name of an old roadhouse located near the village on the Gakona River. Another roadhouse, a modern structure, is located where the Tok Cutoff branches from the Richardson Highway. Jim Doyle, the first homesteader in the region, built the first roadhouse in 1902. He cleared about eighty acres and raised grain for his horses and vegetables for himself. He built a number of buildings with timber from his land, including his home, which later became the lodge, a barn, icehouse, warehouse, and blacksmith shop. Doyle later expanded his house to accommodate those traveling to and from Eagle or Dawson. Mike Johnson, a local fur trader, took over the lodge in 1912 and started a store. J. M. Elmer, manager of the Slate Creek Mining Company, bought it in 1918. The mining company failed in 1925, and Arne Sundt took over operation of the lodge still in use today. In 1934 he added a liquor store. Sundt died in 1946, but his wife, Henra, and his son carried on until 1975.[26]

Copper Center, Alaska, about 1910. Courtesy of the Anchorage Museum of History and Art, B62.1.2261; Hunt photo C2426.

❊ Gulkana ❊

Gulkana is at mile 204 Richardson Highway. Its population is about fifty-three, consisting of a Native village, stores, and the Gulkana Airport, located twelve miles away. The airport, like the Alaska Highway and Tok Cutoff, was a World War II construction project. A Federal Aviation Administration station and the Wrangell-St. Elias National Park and Preserve air service and ranger facilities also are located at the airport.

❊ Glennallen ❊

Glennallen got its name from two gold-rush-era U.S. Army explorers, Capt. Edwin F. Glenn and Lt. Henry T. Allen. The town originated as a construction camp for the Glenn Highway in the early 1940s. Construction parties completed a pioneer road from the Richardson Highway to Palmer in early winter 1942. As time passed the region gained telephone lines, an electrical plant, and other amenities. The Reverend Vince Joy and his family moved to Glennallen in 1946 and built a church. Construction of a hospital, begun in 1948, was completed in 1956. A high school was built in 1962, and the town became headquarters for all schools in the district. By 1966 the former construction camp had a population of 600, and it has been growing steadily ever since. As a center for a mission church, hospital, schools, and government and commercial facilities, Glennallen has become a town of importance.[27]

✳ Copper Center ✳

Copper Center developed as a gold rush camp during the 1898 stampede from Valdez. Gold seekers tramped over Valdez Glacier and down the Klutina River to its confluence with the Copper River. Gold-rush-era sources do not evidence the presence of an Indian village at the site, although there may have been one in prehistoric times. The nearest Indian village noted in the area was five miles south of present-day Copper Center. During the height of the stampede prospectors set up tent camps along both the Copper and Klutina Rivers, but the first cabins were built on a west bank site, one-half mile west of the Copper. Another camp sprang up at what was called Copper Ferry, where a ferry crossed the river to Millard Trail. The area got a boost as a goldfield service center in June 1898 when Benjamin F. Millard pioneered a trail from the east bank to the mouth of the Slana River. The east bank site of Old Copper Center apparently was settled in 1901–1902 by prospectors intent on investigating mineral prospects on that side of the river. Its days as a mining center were short lived, but it did draw a Native population and existed for some time as a village.

Copper Center, poorly located to continue as a mining center after the stampede, did survive as an important roadhouse and supply center. Several government facilities, notably the telegraph and agricultural stations were located there. Construction of the Valdez Trail through Copper Center insured permanence. Soon after it gained a post office and a school.

The Copper Center Roadhouse, originally established by Andrew Holman in 1898, was the first roadhouse and store site in the Copper River Valley. The present lodge, built on the original site in 1932 by Florence Barnes, was taken over by George and Florence Ashby in 1948. It remains an important stop for visitors en route to the park, who also enjoy the Copper Center Historical Museum housed next door.

✳ Chisana ✳

Today's Chisana residents, including Ivan Thorall, a miner and guide knowledgeable about local history, Ray McNutt, Terry Overly, Iver Johnson, and others have a keen sense of the town's past. Johnson and his wife Dot now winter in Sequim, Washington, but still enjoy summers at Chisana. Iver settled there in 1946, prospecting for gold and sustaining himself by hunting moose and other game. In 1956 he helped build the expansive airstrip there for Cordova Air. Johnson and Thorall greatly admired N. Peter Nelson, one of the original discoverers of gold at Chisana, who continued to live there for many years. Nelson died Outside at the age of ninety-six, and Thorall and Johnson arranged to return his ashes to his town. They built a monument to Nelson on a hill overlooking Bonanza Creek.

Old-timers still vividly remember Nelson and other local folks. They point out the First Avenue cabin once owned by Sidney "Too Much" Johnson, the dogsled freight and express musher, who carried up to 200 pounds of freight and mail from the railroad over the seventy-three-mile stretch into Chisana. He earned his nickname, and the dissatisfaction of

Gulkana, Alaska, about 1910. Courtesy of the Alaska State Library, Alaska Road Commission Collection, PCA 61-3-126.

his customers, when he found the going too tough on the Nizina and Chisana glaciers and had to unload freight that was "too much" to continue with on the sled.

Anthony J. Dimond, the gold-rush-era U.S. commissioner in Chisana and later Alaska's congressional delegate, was succeeded by Anthony McGettigan, who served from 1914 to 1920, then was a postmaster until 1937. Aaron E. Nelson was the last commissioner and served from 1920 to 1930.

Yearly gold production statistics for the 1913–1940 period effectively tell the area's economic/mining history. As the town declined in the 1930s and 1940s, most Native residents left their nearby village and moved to another site downstream and across the Chisana River. The few remaining Indians moved to Northway or Nabesna in 1951. Chisana had only one store by the 1930s, operated by Charles A. Simons. The post office relocated to Nabesna in 1939. Now the mail arrives by air from Tok, and on a summer day one might find most of the town's residents along the airstrip, chatting as they await the mail plane.[28]

✳ Conclusion ✳

Old towns within the park, McCarthy and Chisana, saw little activity after the decline of mining and the railroad. In the 1960s, regional population and service centers moved outside of what is now the Park and Preserve to communities on the Richardson and Glenn Highways. Because communities within the park faded, the road and trail network also declined. Recently, with an increase in visitors to the area, McCarthy's summer population has grown. The area's residents are currently struggling with how to maintain their unique lifestyle in the face of growing tourism pressures.

A hunter on snowshoes. Note his traditional
squirrel-skin parka. Courtesy of the
Washington State Historical Society.

Chapter 11

✳ ✳ ✳

Making a Living

Making a living in or near the Wrangell-St. Elias National Park and Preserve has always involved vigorous exploitation of rather limited opportunities. Outfitting and guiding hunters and fishermen has recently become a lively industry, but little demand existed for such services earlier. The memoirs of a handful of venturesome outdoorsmen provide some insight into their unique lifestyle. Hardy Trefzger was a hunter, trapper, trader, prospector, and guide and, as U.S. commissioner, the most important government official in the Yakutat area. He and a partner voyaged north in 1911 to prospect for copper. They carried traps with them as a cover for their true purpose—discovering a fortune. They dug numerous unproductive holes without finding any good prospects and gave up on copper. Later they found a little gold on Khantaak Island and on Logan Bluff, but the setting was richer in natural beauty than in mineral wealth. "A prospector's life is full of hope and much disappointment and despair," Trefzger reflected. "But he lives with nature and enjoys the breathtaking scenery, and the ever-changing of its color. The Fairweather and St. Elias ranges are the most beautiful mountains in Alaska."[1]

Yakutat was an Indian village of about 300 Natives and a dozen whites when Trefzger arrived. He became intrigued by Native life, customs, and language, "and I was astonished at their ingenuity and efficiency. They practically lived off the country. They bought very little in the village store to supplement their diet." For greens they gathered and dried seaweed in summer for winter use, In spring they picked wild celery and devil's club shoots and took sap from the hemlock trees. In summer and early fall they gathered berries, including strawberries, blueberries, and cranberries. The shore provided clams and mussels, which they strung up on willows to dry. From the ocean depths they caught halibut on homemade hooks and then dried the fish for later use. They pulled devilfish from under the rocks with poles tipped with iron hooks. Seal hunting in front of Hubbard Glacier was a major spring event for the entire community according to tradition. After successful hunts, the women and older children skinned the animals and rendered oil from the flesh. The young skins were kept by the women for moccasins and the rest sold to Mr. Beaseley, the storekeeper, at fifty cents each. In my time I have baled many thousands of skins for shipment. They fished salmon for the cannery where some of the women also worked on the packing line, and for their own consumption—each family put up 300 to 500 pounds of smoked salmon. Their few store needs included flour, tea, rice, baking powder, gun powder, outing flannel and calico for clothing, and coal oils.[2]

Trefzger did not entirely live off the land, but he did take advantage of trapping, hunting, fishing, and, later, working as a storekeeper. Catching fish for the cannery in the summer could be profitable, even though he was paid only one cent each for pink salmon, four cents for cohos, and seven to eight cents for sockeyes. In his 1963 writing he marveled at recent inflation in prices: "Little did I dream in the early days of my travels in Alaska that humps [pinks] would one time bring forty to fifty cents, and sockeyes one and a quarter dollars each."[3]

For a couple of years in the early 1920s Trefzger tried fox farming on Kriwoi Island. He also took a fling at oil prospecting at Lituya Bay. In the 1940s and 1950s interest in hunting bears in the region by outsiders induced Trefzger to offer his services as a hunting guide. An encounter with a brown bear almost cost him his life. While he was photographing bears, he was attacked by a sow with cubs: "She let out a grunt and charged me at once. I dropped the camera and reached for the rifle, about eight feet away. By the time I had the safety off and had straightened up, she was in front of me on my hind legs." The encounter climaxed with the bear biting Trefzger's head and leaving him for dead. He managed to get to his lodge at Dry Bay. The timely arrival of a bush pilot got him to Yakutat for emergency treatment, and he was flown to Seattle for extended care and recuperation.[4]

⁎ Trophy Hunting ⁎

Sport hunting in the Wrangell-St. Elias region mostly went unrecorded, but George O. Young published an account of his 1919 expedition that has since become a classic in hunting narrative literature. Young and a few others set out from McCarthy to hunt in the territories tributary to the Donjek and Generc Rivers in the Yukon Territory by way of White River. Young liked what he saw of McCarthy despite high prices there and learned that the town survived in large part by providing recreation for Kennecott miners:

We were surprised to find that the village supported an ice plant, notwithstanding [that] an immense glacier, containing no doubt millions of tons of ice, extended to the limits of the village, although the ice from it was probably unfit for domestic use. Labor is an object in that country and we were told that ice could be manufactured cheaper than a clean natural ice of good quality could be collected.

He also noted that the town was well supplied with liquor despite the prohibition laws.[5] Young paid $50 for his Alaska hunting license, which permitted him to take two bull moose north of the sixty-second parallel; three bull caribou; three mountain sheep (rams only); three goats; and a limited number of bears, depending upon the region. Restrictions on game in the Yukon Territory were comparable. Young's outfitter, Charley Baxter, had his base on Kluane Lake, but in McCarthy he did meet a famed local guide, Capt. J. P. Hubric, who was also well-known as a regional photographer. Hunting over the planned distance required a small caravan of packhorses and several men, including experienced Natives, to manage the animals. The party moved up the Nizina, then crossed Nizina Glacier. Young was impressed by the vastness of the icefield. "The glaciers of Switzerland are known throughout the world, yet the entire glacial area of that country is not equal to some of the single, larger glaciers of Alaska." Before his journey was completed, Young made tedious crossings of several glaciers with pack animals.[6]

Young's first hunt for goats required a climb of the slopes above the Nizina. After three hours he and his Native guides got within range of a flock, but Young found he could barely position himself securely enough on the precipitous slope to risk a shot. Bracing himself with the help of his guide's shoulder, Young set his sights on his prey:

The goat presented a wonderful sight as he gazed down upon us, his head, neck and right shoulder showing plainly. He appeared as white as snow in contrast to the color of his surroundings. I aimed carefully at his right shoulder and fired, whereupon he plunged forward, just grazing a slight projection on the cliff only a few feet below the shelf where he stood; then down he came, turning over and over, a sight that I shall never forget. Nor did he once strike the side of the granite walls in his descent . . . It lodged perhaps fifteen hundred feet down the incline, where it was not so steep. . . . What an experience it was! Perhaps no hunter ever witnessed a more spectacular sight in securing a trophy . . . I had fully expected the horns to be damaged, but saw to my surprise they were

Bill Slimpert and his trophy Dall sheep. Courtesy of the Mike Sullivan Collection.

intact. The Indian said it was one of the largest goats that he had ever seen. We estimated his weight to be three hundred and fifty pounds, while his horns were ten and a half inches in length.[7]

Along the way Young observed the peculiarities of the weather as well as the beauty of the country, quoting another hunter who referred to the Skolai Pass as:

. . . the battleground of the elements. It is nearly always stormy on the south side of the Pass and clear on the north, as the mountains change the climate entirely. Skolai being the lowest pass in this section, it appears that the winds funnel through this pass and bring all the storms up from the coast. There they wear themselves out against the mountains and appear to rise, for as soon as you cross the Russell glacier and get on the north side, you encounter an entirely different climate.[8]

In crossing Russell Glacier Young had a chance to observe the skills of another guide, Harry Boyden, an Englishman who was leading a scientific party from a California museum. Boyden moved across the glacier without hesitation, ignoring the willow sticks other travelers had shoved in crevasse cracks to mark the trail when snows obscured the route. Young was amused when their party met another one on the glacier, a grizzled freight packer leading his eight animals from Chisana on his regular route to McCarthy. For the hunters meeting someone was an event—the only such traffic encountered that summer, but Boyden and the freighter took it lightly: " 'Hello, Shorty,' said Boyden as they met. 'Hello, Harry, colder than hell, ain't it?' And they continued on the way without stopping."[9]

Young learned that a freighter needed two weeks to travel between Chisana and McCarthy and could understand why living in the mining town was expensive. The summer packing rate was forty cents a pound. Winter rate, when dogs replaced horses, was thirty-five cents. After crossing Russell Glacier in the fast time of seven hours, Young and his party noted that they had crossed the great divide of the St. Elias:

We came within sight of the great White River. It derives its name from the fact that the river bar and mountain sides are almost covered with white volcano ash for a distance of fifty miles, giving it the appearance of snow. The river bar is almost two miles wide at the foot of the glacier where many of the channels emerge

Unidentified early bear hunter. Courtesy of the McCarthy-Kennicott Historical Museum.

from beneath the big ice field. The width of the bar increases to about five miles further down. . . . Before us lay a section of the country considered to be one of the greatest game fields on the American continent.[10]

Young and his party took other game, including bear, moose, and mountain sheep, before crossing the boundary into Canada. They suffered severe mishaps, however, including the loss of a number of trophies when their boat sank in White River. This hunting expedition did not begin a trend in the region. According to one of the guides who was contacted before a second edition of Young's book was published in 1947, no such extended trips occurred again after 1919. Harry Boyden, and perhaps others, led parties from McCarthy to the headwaters of White River on occasion, but they did not continue on into the Yukon Territory.

Young considered the Wrangell-St. Elias region expedition as the great adventure of his life. He became very involved in wildlife conservation projects in his native West Virginia and more interested in photographing game animals than in shooting them. The sentiments he expressed in the concluding words of his book catch the impact of the country upon him:

We had gone far beyond the beaten trail and looked upon a great wilderness undefaced by the hands of man. I trust that I may be able always to retain in my mind the picture of that wilderness; the majestic mountains and valleys; the yawning chasms; the great rivers and the monstrous glaciers which feed them; that I will always keep fresh the memory of the Northern Lights, the azure skies, the glorious sunsets, and the beautiful mountain sheep as they grazed so peacefully on plots of green, or wound their way over lofty crests.[11]

✳ Smithsonian Specimens ✳

Science and sport were served in 1924 when Frank C. Baldwin and Milton B. Medary made a fifty-day expedition to the northern slope of the Wrangell Mountains. A Seattle newspaper noted that the secretary of agriculture had granted a special permit allowing the hunters to exceed the bag limit on grizzly bears, caribou, mountain sheep, and goats: "They will collect specimens for the United States Biological Survey that will go to the Smithsonian Institution."[12]

The hunters took the train to McCarthy to meet their guide, the ubiquitous Andy Taylor, and Jimmy Brown, a long-time packer and wrangler in the area. Medary's lively diary of the trip recorded everything of interest, including his impressions of McCarthy:

The Alaska House is kept by Kate, an ex-dance-hall 'lady,' who has kept about 80 thousand dollars of her earnings. The town is full of husky dogs and women of easy virtue, and most of the money earned by the workers in the Kennecott mines is left in McCarthy.[13]

As the party moved towards Russell Glacier, it did some hunting for camp food, and Medary got some experience climbing for sheep. They camped on the ninth day at the Skolai Basin Camp, "a little relief hut built by the government, as several persons have starved to death or been frozen here in winter . . . located just at the foot of the moraine of the Russell Glacier." The trail between their Chitistone camp and Skolai had been full of interest. Altogether about forty sheep were seen that day. The scenery was wonderful, looking down dizzy precipices to canyons without bottoms, and down glaciers and snow, and up almost vertically to immense peaks of rock, some of which have never been scaled.[14] Smaller-scale sights also delighted the eye:

The trail passed through the little basins in the rocks full of lovely green pasture where the sheep graze. These little basins in the hot summer sun seem so far above rivers of solid ice. They are very beautiful, as they are full of brilliant flowers, whole acres of dog-tooth violets of wonderful deep blue and twice as large as any I have ever seen, but the beauty spots were little clumps of beautiful fresh forget-me-nots, bigger and purer and fresher than in a florist's. Every few yards a little bunch would seem to be traveling down the trail to meet me and as it passed by the horse's head each seemed to call from everyone I ever loved or cared for not to be forgotten.[15]

On August 9 the party reached the headwaters of the White River and spent the night in an abandoned log cabin that earlier had been a roadhouse on the gold rush trail to Chisana. Eventually they reached Chisana, "a collection of 452 log cabins in which one man lives alone." Charles A. Simons, the old town's sole resident, was storekeeper and postmaster for miners who still worked about twenty claims about eight miles from town and lived in cabins near their workings. A few miles from Chisana the hunters came on a small Upper Tanana village near Cooper Creek. A week later the hunters crossed the divide to the headwaters of the Nabesna:

Immediately the character of the country changed. The peaks came closer together and in another mile we were in a narrow solemn quiet canyon, with Willow Creek, clear as crystal flowing and leaping among the rocks at the bottom, with the solid rock of the mountain walls rising higher and steeper on both sides. The trail led along among the rocks and water at the bottom, and finally led straight into a clear blue lake filling the bottom of the canyon from wall to wall in marvelous blue purity. The only sign of life was a flock of wild duck swimming down the lake. The floor of the canyon sloped gently into the depths, and the walls dropped sheer into it.[16]

On steep trails the hunters came to appreciate the wariness of their horses. Sometimes they saw the bleached bones of horses that had failed to keep to the trail. But, of course, the ruggedness of the country contributed to its scenic grandeur, and the travelers appreciated it fully. When Medary reached the floor of the Willow Creek Canyon, he noted a lovely mountain brook "between majestic walls of rock covered on their lower slopes with mossy green and purple and white flowers, still far above the timber line."[17] Such tranquil scenes could have as much impact as grander ones: "In this land, I am learning that any expression in its whole aspect must be nobly big and sublimely simple, and that its detail must be as exquisite as a snow-flake, a mountain-brook, a wild-flower or a featherless bird."[18] The hunters got the trophies they sought in the White River and Nabesna country, then started for civilization in early September. One stop was at DeWitt's trading station near the Slana River. DeWitt had been a fur trader in the area for eight years:

He travels among the Indians and many of them come to him. . . . DeWitt is a typical moving-picture type of lantern jawed westerner and everything about his place |including pens for foxes, one pair of which he sold for $1300| is the real storybook atmosphere.[19]

At Chistochina the hunters heard an unusual bear story that concerned the trader there, Earl Hirst. A grizzly had taken a swipe at Hirst as he was riding in the middle of a string of pack horses, knocking him to the ground and biting his head, leaving his scalp hanging over his eyes. When the bear attacked Hirst's companion, the trader managed to regain his feet, throw his scalp back on his head, and shoot the beast. The hunters did not complain that they had not experienced anything so grisly in their bear hunting.

The party moved on to Tolsona, another trading post, then to Gakona, "the outfitting point for the Slate Creek gold mines." Mike Johnson and his wife ran the roadhouse. As she was an excellent cook and Mike told good stories of the gold rush era, the hunters ended their trip on a pleasant note and drove with Johnson by auto to Chitina and the railroad. At Chitina they reported their game trophies to the game warden, and saw Jimmy Brown off for his return trip to Nabesna. Brown, who spent his winters among the Indians near the Nabesna Glacier, advised the hunters that "we had been only the third hunting party to enter it since it was known to the outside world."[20]

The hunters were pleased about their trip. They were told that only one other scientific party, one hunting specimens for the Brooklyn Museum, had preceded them into the Nabesna region. "There have only been 24 parties in this part of Alaska, but only three who have gone as far as we did and only one which has made as long a trip through this region."[21] Medary confirmed his belief that they had traveled in some relatively unexplored areas by conversations aboard ship from Cordova to Seattle with Alfred H. Brooks and other members of the U.S. Geological Survey. "They tell us we have been through the wildest of the virgin country, some of which Sargent has never been in and Brooks only knows from the exploring party which went through it about 25 years ago."[22]

✳ Andy Taylor ✳

Medary was impressed with their guide, Andy Taylor, a Canadian who had been a boatman on the Stikine River when the Klondike gold rush began, and who then ran a pack train over White Pass from Skagway to Dawson. About 1900 he first ventured into White River country and soon made it his own. From his base at Dawson, he prospected in the region, guided the boundary survey parties and mounting climbing expeditions, and was in on the big Chisana strike in 1913. According to legend, Taylor did not take much care with his Chisana riches. "He paid his debts, bought more supplies, then celebrated for a couple of days and gave away, threw away and spent his share of the gold."[23] Eventually, Taylor shifted his base from Dawson to McCarthy, and he was based there when Medary met him. Medary described Taylor as:

. . . wiry, straight, his eyes are very fine. . . . He looks out through his eyes from his deeper self and looks into you searching for something beyond your eyes; born in Canada, educated in Portland, Maine; he has been in every kind of life; made and spent $80 to $100 thousand dollars in the Dawson fields.

Taylor was very much his own man and was not too outgoing:

He is disliked by many, but I find him full of a deep soul. He reads all the time and has read lots of good stuff. He has been in Siberia and knows the whole political story of Russia and its effect on the labor move-ment in England. He sees everything and often when the pack-train comes in, I have seen him tie up two or three of the horses and reshoe them. He makes wonderful pie and puddings and is a far better cook than men who make their living by it. I like to be out with him because he thinks and talks about interesting things.[24]

✳ Chisana as Hunting Center ✳

Some hunting had been done in the Chisana area before the 1913 gold rush led to the estab-lishment of a town, but sport hunting sustained a number of residents after most miners quit the place. The old gold town provided a good base for hunting from the 1930s when air service became available. Lou Anderton established himself as a guide and storekeeper at Chisana in 1925, using buildings in the western portion of the townsite and building a corral for his pack animals on what had once been First Avenue. His commercial interests kept some of the buildings, including those formerly occupied by the U.S. commissioner as his dwelling and his court, in repair. After Anderton's death in 1961 his Pioneer Outfitters service was conducted by the Overly family. About 1969 the Overlys moved to a new site a mile out of town and nearer the Chisana River where they acquired a homestead. Other long-time guides in the area have included Ray McNutt, whose homestead includes the eastern part of the Chisana townsite. Chisana is still an important outfitting and hunting center and the commercial guides

Trout fishing on Eyak lake near Cordova about 1910. Courtesy of the Museum of History and Industry, Seattle, 92.7.4.58, Hegg photo.

share an interest with the Park Service in preserving the old gold town.

❊ Hunting ❊
Controversies

Resident and nonresident hunting regulations became more controversial after World War II. Sport hunting increased in popularity among a population that had grown dramatically in the 1940s. Among the sportsmen were military personnel granted resident hunting rights during the war. The increase in hunters coincided with the reduction of the cost of hunting in remote regions such as the Wrangell-St. Elias with the availability of small aircraft for transport. Over a relatively short time span, what had been an expensive, elitist venture become a sporting experience available to almost any-one. Outfitters and guides in Wrangell St. Elias exercised considerable influence on the state's game management policies in the 1970s. By 1975 some 250 guides worked in the region, including two master guides and twelve registered guides holding permanent territories. Strife among the guides over territories was sometimes violent, despite state efforts to mediate disputes. Native and non-Native subsistence hunters within the region resented the increases of sport hunting. Subsistence hunters and fishermen were prominent in the Yakutat region, the western portions of the Copper River Valley, along the western slopes of Mounts Drum and Stanford, and along the salmon-bearing rivers. Non-native subsistence use had developed during the mining era and after, as miners and homesteaders provided some of their needs from the land. In the 1970s most such users lived in the Chitina Valley near McCarthy, May and Dan Creeks, and along the Nabesna Road. These individuals, as Michael Lappan's administrative history of Wrangell-St. Elias indicates, also resented the creation of the park, fearing an interference with their hunting, trapping, and fishing. Controversies over subsistence rights continue to rock the state. Conflict among hunters and game managers are perennial public issues and continue to affect game regulations.

❊ Hunting Today ❊

With the division of Wrangell-St. Elias reserved lands into park and preserve regions in 1980, guided sport hunting has been restricted to the preserves. This division provides the same protection for game animals in the affected region as that introduced by Canada with the establishment of the Kluane Game Sanctuary within the Kluane National Park in 1943. Hunting in the Park has been restricted to subsistence hunting by local, rural residents only.

❊ Fisheries ❊

Sport fishing is allowed in both the preserve and the park but generally is not very productive. Many streams are fast flowing and silt laden in summer and flow little during winter. Within the Wrangell-St. Elias complex only the Beaver Creek system north of the White River; Hanagita and Tebay Rivers south of the Chitina Valley; and rivers in the Yakutat Forelands have clear water streams. Those near Yakutat nourish major salmon runs; those farther north support grayling [Beaver Creek] and rainbow trout [Hanagita and Tebay]. . . .

Trapper at Solo Creek. Courtesy of the National Park Service. Photo by K. Mullen, 1982.

Fishing in both Hanagita and Tebay rivers is considered excellent but because of difficult access, is only lightly pursued.[25]

Red and king salmon runs on the Copper River are important for subsistence and sports fishermen. Fishwheels are active on the Copper from Chitina to Chistochina, and dip-netting at Chitina also attracts a good deal of interest. State officials supervising the salmon take close the recreational fishery at times to protect escapement, a call that is never popular with sports fishermen. Lake fishing in the interior includes that at Tanada, Copper, Ptarmigan, and Rock Lakes for ling cod, grayling, and trout. Most fishermen fly in by float-plane during the summer, although all-terrain vehicles can reach Tanada Lake from the Nabesna Road. There is some ice fishing on Tanada and Copper Lakes during winter, and both are readily accessible by snow machine. Commercial recreational fishing camps are located on these major lakes as well as on lakes in the Chitina Valley and the Hanagita and Tebay River drainages, where fishermen come in by floatplane.[26]

❋ Farming and Fur Raising ❋

There have always been some individuals willing to raise grain or other crops in the Copper River Valley and sometimes within the current boundaries of the park. Despite the tendency of early nineteenth-century boosters to proclaim the area's suitability for agriculture, the growing season is too short and subject to unseasonal frost for sustained success. Along the rail line farmers were assured of an easy, inexpensive transit to market so there was some small production during the rail era. During the same period of 1910–1938 some farmers doubled as fur raisers, developing fox breeding operations. It was the general belief that fur raising was particularly appropriate to the long winters of the region, which may have been true, but other economic factors dictated the industry's profits. By 1920 there were several fox farms, including one near the confluence of the Sanford and Copper Rivers. Blue foxes were in demand for fur coats until 1933 when the price of pelts fell from $500 to $18.50 over a few months, thus making fox raising unprofitable. Among the part-time fur farmers were Chitina storekeeper Billy Tibbs and Andy Taylor.

* Tourism *

Visitors touring Alaska in the late nineteenth and early twentieth centuries did not usually venture beyond the towns of Southeastern, which they reached on ships plying the Inside Passage. Interior tourist facilities were scarce, and the primitive means of transport did not encourage pleasure travel. The situation changed with construction of the Copper River and Northwestern Railway. The railroad advertised the scenic wonders of its route from 1909, extolling the spectacular Miles and Childs Glaciers, the "million dollar" bridge across the Copper River, and the superlative mountain scenery. Many of the tourists were content to take the train from Cordova for a half-day trip to the Miles and Childs Glaciers, then return to their ships. At the glaciers tourists heard about the desperate race by railroad builder Mike Heney and his forces to build the famed bridge before the onset of winter doomed their efforts. Tourists exclaimed about the noise from the glaciers and enjoyed the opportunity to follow a short trail leading toward the Childs. As one brochure described the experience: "You may loll at ease by the river bank on a carpet of flowers while the glacier splits with a noise like a canon shot, or the staccato reports of small arms and watch avalanche after avalanche start 300 feet above."[27]

In time a longer trip became popular. Tourists took the railroad to Chitina, then transferred to a road stage line for conveyance to Willow Creek near the Richardson Highway (old Valdez Trail). Once on the Richardson, they returned to the coast at Valdez. This loop tour was first offered by the Alaska Steamship Company in 1925. Another option travelers had was to continue on into the interior to Fairbanks (270 miles) or some other point. Once the Alaska Railroad was completed, tourists could return to the coast at Seward via the railroad. To encourage hunters' use of the line, the Copper River and Northwestern Railway provided a hotel at Chitina (where guests could admire a huge copper nugget placed outside the door), a facility at Strelna, and hunting cabins along the Kuskulana Road. But there were few hunting parties, and other tourists did not patronize the railroad to the extent that encouraged rail operation after the Kennecott mines shut down in 1938. There were few tourists in the region from 1938 until after the war. Gradually during the 1950s and 1960s the scenic and other recreational possibilities of the region became better known, and tourism increased.

* Conclusions *

The historical pattern of activities reviewed in this chapter shows some sharp transitions. Guided hunting and fishing has increased in popularity since the 1960s. As the park begins to draw increasing numbers of people, interest in recreations such as guided adventure travel and flightseeing will likely increase. The impact of all of the activities discussed here has not been so profound as in most other regions of Alaska because of the wilderness nature of much of the land. It was for this reason that the region was selected as a park and the designation assures that the wilderness character will be largely preserved.

Cordova Air flying over Wrangell-St. Elias region. Courtesy of the National Archives and Records Administration, Washington, D.C.

Endnotes

✳ ✳ ✳

Key to Abbreviations

AHL: Alaska Historical Library, Juneau, Alaska

NPS: National Park Service-Alaska Region

ARL: Alaska Resources Library, Anchorage, Alaska

RG: Record Group

GPO: Government Printing Office, Washington, D.C

UAF: University of Alaska Fairbanks, Fairbanks, Alaska

NA: National Archives, Washington, D.C.

USGS: United States Geological Surve

WRST: Wrangell-St. Elias National Park and Preserve, Copper Center, Alaska

Introduction

1. Richter, Donald H., et al., *Guide to the Volcanoes of the Western Wrangell Mountains, Alaska—Wrangell-St. Elias National Park and Preserve*, USGS Bulletin, no. 2072 (Washington: GPO, 1995), 3.

2. Ernest Gruening to Harold L. Ickes, November 7, 1938, copy in historical files, WRST files.

3. Harry J. Liek and John D. Coffman, "Report on Proposed Alaska National Park," September 1, 1938, copy in WRST files.

4. President Franklin D. Roosevelt to Harold L. Ickes, January 21, 1941, copy in WRST files.

5. Alaska Native Claims Settlement Act, Pub. L. no. 92–203, 85 stat. 688 (December 18, 1971), sec. 17(d)(2).

Chapter 1

1. James VanStone, "Report of a Brief Archaeological Survey of the Copper River in the Chitina Region," typescript, November 2 1952, historical files, NPS.

2. A. V. Grinev, "The Lost Expedition of Dmitri Tarkhanov on the Copper River," *Sovetskaia Etnogragia* 4 (1987): 15–16. Copy in WRST files is a typescript translation by Richard Bland.

3. Ibid, 16.

4. Ibid, 17–18.

5. Kaj Birket–Smith and Frederica de Laguna, *The Eyak Indians of the Copper River Delta* (Kobenhavn: Levin & Munksgard, 1938), 8.

6. Ibid, 149.

7. Ibid, 361.

8. Grinev, "The Lost Expedition," 19.

9. Ibid, 18.

10. Frederica de Laguna and Catharine McClellan, "Ahtna," in *Handbook of North American Indians*, vol. 6 (Washington: Smithsonian Institution, 1981), 641.

11. Ibid, 656.

12. Ibid.

13. Ibid, 661.

14. Ibid.

15. Ibid, 646.

16. Ibid, 656.

17. Robert A. McKennan, *The Upper Tanana Indians* (New Haven: Yale University Department of Anthropology, 1959), 3.

18. Ibid.

19. Ibid, 26.

20. James A. Ketz, *Paxson Lake: Two Nineteenth Century Ahtna Sites in the Copper Basin, Alaska* (Fairbanks: Cooperative Park Studies Unit, 1983), 83–84.

21. Birket–Smith and de Laguna, *The Eyak Indians*, 151.

22. Ibid, 73–76.

23. Ibid, 78.

24. An excellent study of the trader and his region was done by Michael Brown, *Indians, Traders, and Bureaucrats in the Upper Tanana District: A History of the Tetlin Reserve* (Anchorage: U.S. Bureau of Land Management, 1984).

25. Ketz, *Paxson Lake*, 83.

26. McKennan, *The Upper Tanana Indians*, 86.

27. Ibid.

28. Brown, *Indians, Traders and Bureaucrats*, 109–10.

29. Ibid, 111.

30. *Cordova Star*, September 21, 1947.

31. Holly Reckord, *Where the Raven Stood: Cultural Resources of the Ahtna Region* (Fairbanks: Cooperative Park Studies Unit, 1983); see also Reckord, *That's the Way We Live; Subsistence in the Wrangell-St. Elias National Park and Preserve* (Fairbanks: Cooperative Park Studies Unit, 1983).

32. Froelich G. Rainey, *Anthropological Papers of the American Museum of Natural History: Archaeology in Central Alaska*, vol. 36, pt. 4 (New York: American Museum of Natural History, 1939), 355.

33. Ibid, 358.

34. Reckord, *Where Raven Stood*, 12.

35. Anne D. Shinkwin, *Archaeological Report: Dekah De'nin's Village: An Early Nineteenth Century Ahtna Village, Chitina, Alaska* (Fairbanks: Cooperative Park Studies Unit, 1974).

36. Reckord, *Where Raven Stood*, passim.

37. James Kari, *Ahtna Place Names Lists* (Fairbanks: Copper River Native Association and Alaska Native Language Center, 1983), 8.

38. James Kari, ed., *Tatl'ahwt'aenn Nenn'. The Headwaters People's Country* (Fairbanks: Alaska Native Language Center, 1986).

39. Reckord, Where Raven Stood, 4.

Chapter 2

1. Sven Waxell, *The American Expedition* (London: William Hodge and Company 1952), 105. There is some complication in that the log book of the St. Peter indicates the date of the sighting as the 17th, which was not St. Elias Day. Elias is the Greek name for Elijah who, according to legend, "went up by a whirlwind into heaven." Thus, the use of Elijah's name seems appropriate for the lofty mountain to which the name moved from the island when charts were made some years later. It remains customary to credit Bering with naming the mountain even though the evidence does not confirm it.

2. Hubert H. Bancroft, *History of Alaska, 1730–1885* (Darien, Conn.: Hafner Publishing Co., 1970), 2.

3. Georg Wilhelm Steller, *Journal of a Voyage with Bering 1741–1742* (Palo Alto: Stanford University Press, 1988), 65. Among useful secondary accounts is Glynn Baratt, *Russia in Pacific Waters 1715–1825* (Vancouver: University of British Columbia, 1981).

4. Ibid, 70–71.

5. Ibid, 71.

6. Ibid, 72, 77.

7. Jean F. de Galaup La Perouse, *Voyages and Adventures* (Honolulu: University of Hawaii Press, 1964), 27.

8. Capt. George Dixon, A Voyage Round the World (London: George Goulding, 1789), 171.

9. Ibid, 172.

10. Tomas de Suria, Journal of Tomas de Suria of His Voyage with Malaspina to the Northwest Coast of America in 1791 (Fairfield, Wa.: Ye Galleon Press, 1980), 38.

11. Ibid, 47.

12. Alaska Geographical Society, "Yakutat," 14. The best secondary account of the Malaspina and other Spanish voyages is by Warren L. Cook, Flood Tide of Empire: Spain and the Pacific Northwest, 1543–1819 (New Haven, Conn.: Yale University Press, 1973).

13. George Vancouver, A Voyage of Discovery to the North Pacific Ocean (London: Hakluyt Society), 1552.

14. The tsar acted in order to provide more control over Alaska matters and better protect the Natives. Shelikov had long protested the abuses of other traders. See his petition of Oct. 15, 1793 in Documents of the Russian American Company, edited by Richard A. Pierce (Kingston, Ontario: Limestone Press, 1976), 46–59.

15. James W. VanStone, "Exploring the Copper River Country," Pacific Northwest Quarterly (October 1955): 115; the Putrov–Kulikalov message to headquarters is from Alaska Geographic Society, "Yakutat," 17.

16. Gregorii Shelikov to Alexander Baranov, August 9, 1794, in P. A. Tikhmenev, A History of the Russian American Company, vol. 2, Documents, edited by Richard A. Pierce and Alton S. Donnelly (Kingston, Ontario: Limestone Press, 1979), 54–55.

17. Ibid, 55–56.

18. Ibid, 56.

19. Ibid, 56–57.

20. Richard Pierce, Russian America: A Biological Dictionary (Kingston, Ontario: Limestone Press, 1990), 405. For another account of the Russian colony's history, see Alaska Geographic Society, "Yakutat," 17–21.

21. Tikhmenev, History, 151–52.

22. William S. Hanable, Alaska's Copper River. The 18th and 19th Centuries (Anchorage: Alaska Historical Society, 1982), 17–18.

23. Grinev, "The Lost Expedition," 1–19.

24. VanStone, "Exploring the Copper River Country," 115.

25. Fred John, Sr. and Katie John, as told to B. Stephen Strong, "The Killing of the Russians at Batzulnetas Village," Alaska Journal 3, no. 3 (summer 1973): 147–48.

Chapter 3

1. Morgan Sherwood, Exploration of Alaska (New Haven, Conn.: Yale University Press, 1965), 40.

2. Quoted in Israel C. Russell, "An Expedition to Mount St. Elias, Alaska," National Geographic Magazine (May 1891): 71.

3. Ibid.

4. Ibid, 6.

5. Lt. William R. Abercrombie, "A Supplementary Expedition into the Copper River Valley," in Compilation of Narratives of Exploration in Alaska, Senate Reports, 56th Cong, 1st sess., no. 1023 (Washington: GPO, 1900), 383.

6. Ibid, 387.

7. Ibid, 388.

8. Ibid.

9. Lt. Henry T. Allen, Report of an Expedition to the Copper, Tanana, and Koyukuk Rivers (Washington: GPO, 1887), 34.

10. Ibid, 40.

11. Ibid, 33.

12. Ibid, 48.

13. Ibid, 49.

14. Ibid, 50.

15. Ibid, 49.

16. Ibid, 51.

17. Ibid.

18. Ibid, 57.

19. Ibid.

20. Ibid, 58.

21. Ibid.

22. Ibid, 59.

23. Ibid.

24. Ibid.

25. Ibid, 61.

26. Ibid, 63.

27. Ibid.

28. Ibid, 64.

29. Ibid, 65.

30. Ibid.

31. Ibid, 67.

32. Ibid, 68.

33. Ibid, 69–70.

34. Ibid, 72.

35. Ibid, 73.

36. Sherwood, Exploration of Alaska, 116.

37. Charles Willard Hayes, "An Exploration through the Yukon District," National Geographic Magazine 4 (May 15, 1892): 119.

38. Ibid, 120–23.

39. Ibid, 123–24.

40. Ibid, 124–25.

41. Ibid, 125–26.

42. Ibid, 120.

43. Capt. William R. Abercrombie, "Copper River Exploring Expedition, 1899," in Compilation of Narratives of Exploration in Alaska, Senate Reports, 56th Cong, 1st sess., no. 1023 (Washington: GPO, 1900), 382.

44. Ibid, 387.

45. Ibid, 388.

46. Oscar Rohn, "Report of Oscar Rohn on Exploration in Wrangell Mountain District," in Alaska 1899. Copper River Exploring Expedition, Capt. William R. Abercrombie, ed. (Washington: GPO, 1900), 112–30.

47. Fred H. Moffit and A. G. Maddren, Mineral Resources of the Kotsina-Chitina Region, Alaska, USGS Bulletin, no. 745 (Washington: GPO, 1909), 20.

48. Fred H. Moffit and Adolph Knopf, Mineral Resources of the Nabesna-White River District, Alaska, USGS Bulletin, no. 417 (Washington: GPO, 1910), 13–20.

49. Quoted in Cole, Historic Use of the Chisana and Nabesna Rivers, 5.

50. Ibid.

51 Stephen R. Capps, The Chisana–White River District, Alaska, USGS Bulletin, no. 630 (Washington: GPO, 1916), 11.

52. Ibid, 7.

Chapter 4

1. For a general history of mining in the Yukon and Alaska, see William R. Hunt, Golden Places (Anchorage: National Park Service, 1990).

2. Addison M. Powell, Trailing and Camping in Alaska (New York: Wessels & Bissel, 1910), 3, 7.

3. Charles A. Margeson, Experiences of Gold Hunters in Alaska (Hornellsville, N.Y.: Charles Margeson, 1899), 103–34.

4. George Hazelet's diary, 32, 38–39. A typescript of the diary is in the ARL.

5. Ibid, 39.

6. Ibid, 45.

7. Ibid, 104.

8. Philip S. Smith, *Past Placer Gold Production from Alaska*, USGS Bulletin, no. 857–B (Washington: GPO, 1933), 96.

9. Frank C. Schrader, "A Reconnaissance of a Part of Prince William Sound in 1898," in United States Geological Survey, *Twentieth Annual Report* (Washington: GPO, 1899), 62–63, for this and following quotes including the mileage chart.

10. Levensaler credited Jack and Bill Williams as co-discoverers with Kane. L. A. Levensaler to Ralph McKay, July 21, 1968, McKay Collection, UAF. See also Robert L. Spude, "Dan Creek Mining Operations," notes on Wrangell-St. Elias, NPS files.

11. Donald J. Orth, *Dictionary of Alaska Place Names*, USGS professional paper no. 567 (Washington: GPO, 1967), 898; Robert L. Spude, "Notes on the History of the Chititu Creek Mining Operations," NPS files.

12. Walter C. Mendenhall and Frank C. Schrader, *Mineral Resources of the Mount Wrangell District, Alaska*, USGS professional paper no. 15 (Washington: GPO, 1903), 59–62.

13. L. A. Levensaler to Ralph McKay, July 21, 1868, McKay Collection, UAF.

14. *Chitina Leader*, October 21 1913; Alfred H. Brooks, *Mineral Resources of Alaska: Report on the Progress of Investigations in 1913* (Washington: GPO, 1914), 61.

15. Robert Spude, "Notes on Chititu Creek," NPS files.

16. William Stroecker, "A Partial Biography of Edward H. Stroecker," passim, typescript, Robe Collection, UAF.

17. Cited in Mary Mangusso, "Anthony J. Dimond" (unpublished Ph.D. dissertation, Texas Tech University, 1978), 27–28.

18. Orth, *Alaska Place Names*, 692, 898; Harold E. Smith, "Chititu Gold," *Alaska Sportsman* (September 1964): 46.

19. *Fagerberg v. Fagerberg*, court record, case C45, RG21, NA, Alaska Region, Anchorage, Alaska.

20. Smith, *Past Placer Gold Production*, 47.

21. *Charles Malander v. Frank Kernan*, court record, case 95, RG21, NA.

22. *John E. Andrus v. Frank Kernan and Charles Schlosser*, court record, case 910, RG21, NA.

23. Pierre Berton, *Klondike Fever* (New York: Alfred A. Knopf, 1974), 59, 400–401, 417; *Frank Kernan v. John Andrus*, court record, case 926 C, RG21, NA.

24. Quoted in Terrence Cole, *Historic Use of the Chisana and Nabesna Rivers* (Anchorage: Alaska Department of Natural Resources, Division of Lands, 1979) 33–34.

25. Ibid, 34.

26. Ibid, 35.

27. *Valdez News*, September 12 1903.

28. Cole, *Chisana and Nabesna Rivers*, 36.

29. *Valdez News*, October 3 1905.

30. *Dawson Daily News*, October 3, 1905.

31. Ibid.

32. Carl Whitham to President Franklin Roosevelt, August 7, 1933, Nabesna Mining Company Collection, AHL, Juneau, Alaska.

33. Philip R. Holdsworth, "Nabesna Gold Mine and Mill" (unpublished B.S. thesis, University of Washington, 1937), passim.

Chapter 5

1. *Copper River Mining Company v. R. F. McClellan*, 2 Alaska Reports, 134. The case was appealed to the U.S. Supreme Court. Published depositions of all parties involved including Major William R. Abercrombie are part of the file for case 200006, NA.

2. William C. Douglass, "A History of the Kennecott Mines," 4, typescript, NPS files.

3. Ibid.

4. W. E. Dunkle, "Economic Geology and History of the Copper River District," paper presented at Alaska Engineers Meeting, Juneau, Alaska, 1954, 3–5, McKay Collection, UAF.

5. Douglass, "Kennecott Mines," 8.

6. Alfred H. Brooks, *Mineral Resources of Alaska: Report on the Progress of Investigations in 1919*, USGS Bulletin, no. 714 (Washington: GPO, 1921), 194–96.

7. Melody Webb Grauman, "Big Business in Alaska: The Kennecott Mines, 1898–1938" (Fairbanks: Cooperative Park Studies Unit, 1977), 37.

8. Robert L. Spude and Sandra M. Faulkner, "Kennecott, Alaska" (Anchorage: National Park Service, 1987), 7.

9. Grauman, "Big Business in Alaska," 38.

10. "General Points of Interest on the Kennecott Mother Lode Mines," July 15, 1924, Kennecott Collection, UAF.

11. Contract of June 7, 1923, McCracken Collection, UAF.

12. Douglass, "School Days," Douglass Collection, UAF.

13. Ralph McKay memoirs, McKay Collection, UAF.

14. Grauman, "Big Business in Alaska", 45–46.

15. Ibid, 47.

16. *Ernest Vande Vord v. Kennecott*, court record, case C–39, RG21, NA.

17. *Daniel S. Reeder v. Katalla Company and Copper River and Northwestern Railway*, court record, case C–42, RG21, NA.

18. *James Heney v. Copper River and Northwestern Railway*, court record, case C–49, RG21, NA.

19. *Estate of E. A. Reed v. Copper River and Northwestern Railway*, court record, case C–50, RG21, NA.

20. *J. E. Dyer v. Copper River and Northwestern Railway*, court record, case C–3, RG21, NA.

21. Philip S. Smith, *Mineral Resources of Alaska: Report on Progress of Investigation in 1933*, USGS Bulletin, no. 864 (Washington: GPO, 1936), 59.

22. Twenty–Fourth Annual Report of the Kennecott Copper Corporation, 1938, 6, Kennecott Collection, UAF.

23. Douglass, "Kennecott Mines," 11; Melody Webb Grauman, "Kennecott: Alaska Origins of a Copper Empire, 1900–1938," *Western Historical Quarterly* 9, no. 2 (April 1978): 207.

24. Fred H. Moffit and J. B. Mertie Jr., *The Kotsina–Kuskulana District*, USGS Bulletin, no. 745 (Washington: GPO, 1923), 115.

25. Department of the Interior news release, National Park Service, July 30, 1985; publications of the Geneva Pacific Corporation, NPS files; Theodore W. VanZelst to Robert Spude, November 27, 1984, NPS files.

26. *Chicago Record–Herald*, January 19, 1902.

27. Diary of unknown visitor, Kennecott Collection, NPS files.

28. *Alaska Monthly Magazine* (July 1907): 9.

29. *Elliott v. Elliott*, 3 Alaska Reports, 352–76; *Hubbard v. Hubbard*, court record, case 669, RG21, NA.

30. James Wickersham to President Warren Harding, January 6, 1921, RG 60, Letters Received, NA.

31. See Grauman, "Kennecott," 197–211; Robert A. Stearns, "The Morgan–Guggenheim Syndicate and the Development of Alaska, 1906–1915" (unpublished Ph.D. dissertation, University of California-Santa Barbara, 1967), passim; Jeannette P. Nichols, Alaska (Cleveland: Arthur Clark and Company, 1924), passim; William R. Hunt, Alaska: A Bicentennial History (New York: W. W. Norton and Company, 1976), 135–66; U. S. Senate, Investigation of the Department of the Interior and of the Bureau of Forestry (Washington: GPO, 1911), passim.

32. C. L. Andrews, "Viewing the Copper River Spectacle," Alaska-Yukon Magazine (October 1910): 237.

33. Archie E. Shiels, The Kennecott Story, 8, typescript, AHL.

34. L. W. Storm, "Chitina Copper Region in Southern Alaska," Engineering and Mining Journal (November 19, 1910): 10–11.

35. James Wickersham diary, April 30, 1910, Wickersham Collection, UAF.

36. John Carson to David Jarvis, May 6, 1908, Keystone Canyon Collection, microfilm 140, UAF.

37. John Boyce, Appointments File, RG60, NA.

38. S. McNamara to Attorney General, February 11, 1911; Elmer Todd to attorney general, April 14, 1911, Keystone Canyon Collection, microfilm, 140, UAF.

39. Lone E. Janson, The Copper Spike, 64; James Wickersham diary, June 24, 1911, with clipping of New York Times story of the same date, UAF.

40. Margaret Harrais, "Alaska History Manuscript," Chapter 28, 3, Harrais Collection, UAF.

41. Ibid, 7.

42. Nichols, Alaska; Robert A. Stearns, "Alaska's Kennecott Copper," Alaska Journal (Annual Edition 1975): 130–39; Stearns, "The Morgan-Guggenheim Syndicate," passim.

43. Grauman, "Kennecott," 210.

44. For this and following quotes see Ocha Potter, "Excerpts from an unpublished manuscript entitled 'Alaska,' " NPS files.

Chapter 6

1. Unidentified clippings, Fonda Scrapbook, University of Washington, Seattle, Washington (hereafter cited UW).

2. Fred Best to parents August 27, 1912, Best Collection, AHL.

3. Fred Best diary, July 1913, Best Collection, AHL.

4. Fairbanks Weekly Times, July 21, 1913.

5. Ibid.

6. Ibid.

7. Chitina Leader, July 22, 1913.

8. Ibid, July 29, 1913.

9. Ibid, August 5, 1913.

10. Ibid, August 12, 1913.

11. Ibid, July 18, 1913.

12. Fairbanks Weekly Times, July 26, 1913.

13. Ibid.

14. Ibid, July 12, 1913.

15. Ibid, July 13, 1913.

16. Ibid, August 7, 1913.

17. Chitina Leader, August 19, 1913.

18. Fairbanks Weekly Times, August 25, 1913.

19. Ibid.

20. Quoted in M. J. Kirchhoff, "Shushanna," 44, typescript, NPS files.

21. Ibid.

22. Ibid.

23. Fairbanks Weekly Times, September 1, 1913.

24. Seattle Post–Intelligencer, October 8, 1913.

25. Ibid.

26. Fairbanks Weekly Times, September 6, 1913.

27. Ibid, September 14, 1913.

28. Ibid, September 15, 1913.

29. Ibid.

30. Seattle Post–Intelligencer, October 15, 1913.

31. Ibid, June 15, 1914.

32. Ibid.

33. Fred Best diary, November 26, 1918, and other scattered entries, Best Collection, AHL.

34. Chitina Leader, February 24, 1914.

35. Fred Best to parents, April 1, 1914, Best Collection, AHL.

36. Ibid.

37. Ibid.

38. Ibid.

39. Fred Best diary, May 12, 1914, Best Collection, AHL.

40. Ibid, July 3, 1914.

41. Undated, unidentified clipping, probably a Seattle paper, c. August 1914, NPS files.

42. Repler to Harold Waller, October 31, 1914, Waller Papers, UAF.

43. Chitina Leader, September 23, 1913.

44. Mangusso, "Anthony J. Dimond," 39.

45. Ibid.

46. Hazelet diary, October 14, 1913, ARL.

47. Ibid, November 25, 1913, ARL.

48. Chitina Leader, May 18, 1915.

49. Ibid, November 11, 1913.

50. Fairbanks Weekly Times, September 29, 1913.

51. Chitina Leader, April 14, 1914.

52. Archie A. Clongier v. A. H. Findlason, court record, case C75, RG21, NA.

53. Sutherland v. Purdy, court record, case C73, RG21, NA.

54. Chitina Leader, December 16, 1913.

55. Ibid, July 27, 1915.

56. Ibid, August 12, 1915.

57. Ibid, May 12, 1914.

Chapter 7

1. Thomas Riggs Diary, June 1907, Riggs Family Collection, Library of Congress, microfilm 66, UAF. For a recent general history of the survey see Lewis Green, The Boundary Hunters (Vancouver: University of British Columbia Press, 1982).

2. Thomas Riggs diary, UAF.

3. Thomas Riggs Jr., "Surveying the 141st Meridian," National Geographic 23 (July 1912): 687.

4. Ibid, 685.

5. Ibid, 713.

6. International Boundary Commission, Joint Report Upon the Survey and Demarcation of the International Boundary between the United States and Canada (Ottawa and Washington: GPO, 1918), 45.

7. Thomas Riggs diary, UAF.

8. Ibid.

9. Ibid, August 1909.

10. International Boundary Commission, Joint Report, 46.

11. Ibid, 78.

12. Ibid.

13. Ibid, 81.

14. Ibid, 82.

15. Ibid, 96.

16. Asa C. Baldwin, "Surveying the top of Mount St. Elias," draft of an article, Asa Baldwin Papers, MS 36, AHL.

17. Ibid.

18. *Seattle Post–Intelligencer*, September 13, 1913.

19. The UAF microfilm contains the Riggs diary. Other materials on his career and personal life are among his correspondence and other material in the Riggs Family Papers, Library of Congress, Washington:

20. Asa C. Baldwin Papers, MS 36, AHL.

Chapter 8

1. Orth, *Alaska Place Names*, 825.

2. Lt. Frederick Schwatka, "Two Expeditions to Mount St. Elias," Century (April 1891): 870.

3. Ibid, 871–72.

4. Ibid, 872.

5. William Williams, "Climbing Mount St. Elias," *Scribner's Magazine* (April 1889): 387.

6. Ibid, 393.

7. Ibid, 400.

8. Ibid.

9. Ibid, 403.

10. Ibid.

11. Mark B. Kerr, "Mount St. Elias and Its Glaciers," *Scribner's Magazine* (March 1891): 361.

12. Israel C. Russell, "The Expedition of the National Geographic Society and the U.S. Geological Survey," *Century* (April 1891): 872.

13. Ibid, 872–73.

14. Ibid, 874.

15. Kerr, "Mount St. Elias," 363–64.

16. Ibid, 366.

17. Ibid.

18. Ibid, 369.

19. Ibid, 372.

20. Russell, "The Expedition," 884.

21. Israel C. Russell, "Mount St. Elias Revisited," *Century* (June 1892): 200.

22. Ibid, 201.

23. Ibid, 203.

24. Ibid.

25. C. L. Andrews diary, June 25 and 28, 1897.

26. Robert Dunn, "Conquering Our Greatest Volcano," *Harper's Monthly Magazine*, 18 (March 1909): 497.

27. Ibid, 498.

28. Ibid, 503.

29. Ibid, 504.

30. Ibid, 509.

31. Dora Keen, "First Up Mount Blackburn," reprinted in *Alaska Geographic Society*, "Wrangell-St. Elias: International Mountain Wilderness," *Alaska Geographic* 8, no. 1 (1981): 10.

32. Ibid, 119.

33. Ibid.

34. Ibid.

35. J. Vincent Hoeman, "Wrangell Range," *American Alpine Journal* 15 (1945): 121–22.

36. H. F. Lambert, "The Conquest of Mount Logan," *National Geographic Magazine* 49, no. 6 (June 1926): 631.

37. Allen Carpe, "The Ascent of Mount Bona," *American Alpine Journal* 1 (1931): 253–54.

38. Terris Moore, "Mt. Sanford: An Alaskan Ski Climb," *American Alpine Journal* 3 (1933): 265–73.

Chapter 9

1. Capt. William R. Abercrombie, "Copper River Exploring Expedition, 1899," in *Compilation of Narratives of Exploration in Alaska*, Senate Reports, 56th Cong, 1st sess., no. 1023 (Washington:: GPO, 1900), 381.

2. John C. Rice, "From Valdez to Eagle City," typed transcript of government report, Valdez Trail Collection, UAF.

3. Ibid.

4. Ibid.

5. Ibid.

6. Addison Powell, *Trailing and Camping in Alaska* (New York: Wessels & Bissell, 1910), 214.

7. Rice, "From Valdez to Eagle City," Valdez Trail Collection, UAF.

8. Ibid.

9. Joseph Kerr to cousin, October 12, 1900, Oregon Historical Society, Portland, Oregon.

10. J. M. Clapp, *Wagon Road from Valdez to Fort Egbert*, U.S. House, 58th Cong., 3rd sess., document 192 (Washington: GPO, 1905), 5–6.

11. Ibid.

12. Lynn Smith, "A Hard Trip," unpublished manuscript, Smith Papers, UAF.

13. Ibid.

14. Ibid.

15. Ibid.

16. James Wickersham, *Old Yukon: Tales, Trails, and Trials* (Washington: Washington Law Book Company, 1983), 443.

17. Ibid, 444–45.

18. Ibid, 445.

19. Ibid, 448.

20. Ron Lautaret, "You Can't Catch Bootleggers with Sunday School Teachers," *Alaska Journal* (Anchorage: Alaska Northwest Publishing Co. 1981), 43.

21. Ibid.

22. Claus–M. Naske, *Paving Alaska's Trails: The Work of the Alaska Road Commission* (Lanham, Md.: University Press of America, 1986), passim.

23. Ibid, 185–245.

24. Ibid, 245.

25. E. J. E. Schuster, "The Reynolds System," *Anchorage Daily News*, "Alaska Living," July 30, 1967, 7–9.

26. George Hazelet to Edward Hasey, September 2, 1907, Keystone Canyon Collection, microfilm 140, UAF.

27. George Perry to James Lathrop, September 16, 1907; Lathrop to Perry, September 19, 1907, Keystone Canyon Collection, microfilm 140, UAF.

28. E. P. McAdams to John Wilkie, March 18, 1908, Keystone Canyon Collection, microfilm 140, UAF.

29. Wilford Hogatt to Secretary of Interior, October 26, 1907, Keystone Canyon Collection, microfilm 140, UAF; James Wickersham diary, March 27, 28, April 1, 1908, AHL. Wickersham attributed Harlan's behavior to grief caused by his son's death.

30. Theodore Roosevelt to Attorney General, December 27, 1907, February 10, 1908, Bonaparte Papers, Library of Congress, Washington, D.C.

31. E. P. McAdams to John Wilkie, March 20, 1908, Keystone Canyon Collection, microfilm 140, UAF.

32. John Ostrander to Tom Donohue, March 8, 1908, Donohue-Ostrander Collection, 200, UAF.

33. John Ostrander to Tom Donohue, April 12, 1908, Donohue-Ostrander Collection, UAF; the district court record is the U.S. *v. Hasey*, case 545B, RG21, NA.

34. Woodrow Johansen, "The Copper River and Northwestern Railroad," *Northern Engineer* 7, no. 2 (summer 1975): 19–31.

35. Carlyle Ellis, "The Winter's Crucial Battle on Copper River," *Alaska-Yukon Magazine* (June 1910): 27–35; Sidney D. Charles, "The Conquering of the Copper," *Alaska-Yukon Magazine* (December 1910): 365–70; E. C. Hawkins's report, copy in NPS files.

36. Robert DeArmond, "Sternwheel Steamboats on the Copper River," *The Sea Chest: Journal of the Puget Sound Maritime Historical Society* 22, no. 2 (December 1988): 48–56.

37. Johansen, "The Copper River and Northwestern Railroad," 25.

38. Quoted in John Kinney, "Copper and the Settlement of South–Central Alaska," *Journal of the West* 10, no. 2 (April 1971): 311.

Chapter 10

1. Frederica de Laguna, *Under Mount St. Elias: The History and Culture of the Yakutat Tlinglit* (Washington: Smithsonian Institution, 1972), 181.

2. *Alaska Geographic Society*, "Yakutat," 66.

3. Mary Grinnell, "Cordova," *Alaska Magazine* (August 1909): 326.

4. *Anchorage Daily News*, September 3, 1983.

5. Margaret Harrais, "Alaska Periscope," 124, unpublished manuscript, Harrais Collection, UAF.

6. Ibid, 126.

7. Ibid, 127.

8. Ibid, 128, 129.

9. Ibid, 137, 152.

10. Ibid, 141, 142.

11. Ibid, 145.

12. Ibid, 163.

13. Ibid, 166.

14. Ibid, 171.

15. Ibid, 172.

16. Sylvia F. Munsey, "Margaret Harrais," *Alaska Journal* (Summer 1975): 144–52.

17. *Contributions to Economic Geology of Alaska*, USGS Bulletin, no. 1655 (Washington: GPO, 1963), 63–68.

18. Sylvia W. Baldwin, "My Memories of Alaska," *Copper River Country Journal* (March 2, 1989): 2.

19. Sidney D. Charles, "Cordova, The New Gateway Metropolis," *Alaska–Yukon Magazine* (December 1910): 396.

20. D. J. McKenzie, "Freeze-Out At McCarthy," *Alaska Sportsman* (September 1964): 35.

21. Ibid.

22. *Chitina Weekly Herald*, January 18, 1931.

23. Ibid, December 6, 1931.

24. Ibid, December 31, 1931.

25. *Anchorage Daily News*, September 20, 1985.

26. *Copper River Valley Visitors Guide*, 1983, 3.

27. Mrs M. R. Clayton, "A History of Early Glennallen, Alaska," typescript, UAF.

28. Interviews with Chisana residents, NPS files.

Chapter 11

1. Hardy Trefzger, *My Fifty Years of Hunting, Fishing, Prospecting, Guiding, Trading, and Trapping in Alaska* (New York: Exposition Press, 1963), 21.

2. Ibid, 22.

3. Ibid, 101.

4. Ibid, 153.

5. George O. Young, *Alaskan-Yukon Trophies Won and Lost* (Huntington, W.V.: Standard Publications, 1947), 24.

6. Ibid, 57.

7. Ibid, 78.

8. Ibid, 88.

9. Ibid, 90.

10. Ibid, 93.

11. Ibid, 273.

12. Typescript of unidentified newspaper clippings, Medary Collection, UAF.

13. Milton Medary diary, 1, Medary Collection, UAF.

14. Ibid, 4.

15. Ibid, 5.

16. Ibid, 17.

17. Ibid.

18. Ibid, 17–18.

19. Ibid, 54–55.

20. Ibid, 62.

21. Ibid, 63.

22. Ibid, 68.

23. "Andy Taylor—A Man of the Region," Alaska Geographic Society, *Wrangell-St. Elias: International Mountain Wilderness*, 107.

24. Milton Medary diary, 42, Medary Collection, UAF.

25. Alaska Geographic Society, *Wrangell-St. Elias: International Mountain Wilderness*, 126.

26. Ibid, 126–27.

27. Frank Norris, *Gawking at the Midnight Sun: The Tourist in Early Alaska* (Anchorage: Alaska Historical Commission, 1985), 96.

Regional Bibliography

✳ ✳ ✳

I. Archival Collections

Alaska State Archives: Juneau
Corporation Papers.
Governors of Alaska, various papers.
U.S. Commissioners Records. Record Group 305.
U.S. District Court of Alaska. Record Group 505.

Alaska State Library: Juneau
Fred Best Collection.
Klondike Mining Collections.
Nabesna Mining Company Collection.
Newspaper Collections.

Anchorage: National Archives and Records Administration
Alaska District Court Records. Record Group 21.

Anchorage: University of Alaska Archives
Chititu Mining Company Collection.
Fred W. Fickett Collection.

Library of Congress: Washington:
Gifford Pinchot Collection.
Key Pittman Collection.
Riggs Family Collection.

National Archives and Records Administration: Washington:
Adjutant General. Alaska Trails. Record Group 94. Files 307198,
30929, 355877, 362888, and 423757.
Department of Justice. Appointments Files. Letters Received
from Alaska. Record Group 60.
Department of the Interior. Central Classified File. Alaska
Congressional and Investigation. Ballinger-Pinchot
Controversy. Record Group 48. File 1-108, 2-24, 2-39, and 10-3.

University of Alaska Archives: Fairbanks
Alaska Commercial Company Collection.
Alaska Mining Collection.
Alfred H. Brooks Collection.
Stephen Capps Collection.
Thomas Donohue-John Ostrander Collection.
William Douglass Collection.
Margaret Harrais Collection.
Martin Harrais Collection.
Keystone Canyon Collection (microfilm 140: a compilation made
by Claus-M. Naske of Department of Justice Records,
Record Group 60, National Archives).
Kennecott Copper Company Collection.
Ralph McKay Collection.
L. V. Ray Collection.
Dan Sutherland Collection.
Harold H. Waller Collection.

University of Oregon Library: Eugene
Kirke Johnson Collection.

University of Washington Archives, Suzzallo Library: Seattle
John E. Ballaine Collection.
Charles E. Hubbell Collection.
William T. Perkins Collection.
Minor Roberts Collection.
John Rosene Collection.

University of Wyoming Archives: Laramie
William Douglass Collection.
Mining Collection.
USGS: Denver

II. Theses, Dissertations, and Government Reports

Brown, Michael. Indians, *Traders and Bureaucrats in the Upper
Tanana District: A History of the Tetlin Reserve.* Anchorage Bureau of
Land Management, 1984.

Brown, William. Gaunt Beauty, *Tenuous Life. Historic Resources
Study for the Gates of the Arctic National Park.* Anchorage:
National Park Service, 1988.

Bureau of Land Management. *Settlement Opportunities in Alaska:
Central Copper River Basin,* 1950.

Cole, Terrence. *Historic Use of the Chisana and Nabesna Rivers, Alaska.*
Anchorage: Department of Natural Resources, Division
of Lands, 1979.

Douglass, William C. "A History of the Kennecott Mines,"
typescript, 1964.

Dunkle, W. E. "Economic Geology and History of the Copper River
District." Paper given at Alaska Engineers Meeting, Juneau,
1954. McKay Collection, UAF.

Field, William O., ed. "Mountain Glaciers of the Northern
Hemisphere." Vol. 2. Alaska and Adjacent Canada. Hanover,
N.H.: Cold Regions Research and Engineering Laboratory,
June 1975.

Grauman, Melody Webb. "Big Business in Alaska: The Kennecott
Mines, 1898–1938." Fairbanks: Cooperative Park Studies Unit,
occasional paper no. 1, March 1977.

Gudgel-Holmes, Dianne. *Ethnohistory of Four Interior Alaskan
Waterbodies.* Anchorage: Alaska Department of Natural
Resources, 1979.

Heiner, Virginia Doyle. "Alaska Mining History: A Source Document."
Anchorage: Division of Parks, Office of History and Archeology,
1977.

Holdsworth, Philip R. "Nabesna Gold Mine and Mill." Unpublished
B.S. thesis, University of Washington, 1937.

Hunt, William R. *Golden Places: The History of the Alaska-Yukon
Mining With Particular Reference to National Park Lands.*
Anchorage: National Park Service, c. 1990.

Ketz, James A. "Paxson Lake: Two Nineteenth Century Ahtna Sites
in the Copper River Basin, Alaska." Fairbanks: Cooperative Park
Studies Unit, occasional paper no. 33, 1983.

Lappan, Michael Anthony. "Whose Promised Land? A History of
Conservation and Development Management Plans for the
Wrangell and Saint Elias Mountains Region, Alaska (1938-1980)."
Unpublished master's thesis, University of California-Santa Barbara,
1984.

Logsdon, Charles, et al. "Copper River Wrangells: Socioeconomic
Overview." Anchorage Institute for Social and Economic Research,
University of Alaska, n.d.

Mangusso, Mary. "Anthony J. Dimond: A Political Biography."
Unpublished Ph.D. dissertation, Texas Tech University, 1978.

Norris, Frank, *Gawking at the Midnight Sun: The Tourist in Early Alaska*. Anchorage: Alaska Historical Commission, 1985.

Reckord, Holly. "That's the Way We Live: Subsistence in the Wrangell-St. Elias National Park and Preserve." Fairbanks: Cooperative Park Studies Unit, occasional paper no. 34, 1983.

_____. "Where Raven Stood: Cultural Resources of the Ahtna Region." Fairbanks: Cooperative Park Studies Unit, occasional paper no. 35, 1983.

Shiels, Archie W. "The Kennecott Story." Typescript. Bellingham, Wash., 1967. Copy at AHL.

Shinkwin, Anne D. "Archeological Report: Dekah De'nin's Village: An Early Nineteenth Century Ahtna Village, Chitina, Alaska." Fairbanks: Cooperative Park Studies Unit, 1974.

Spude, Robert L. "Chilkoot Trail: From Dyea to Summit with the '98 Stampeders." Fairbanks: Cooperative Park Studies Unit, occasional paper no. 26, 1980.

_____. and Sandra M. Faulkner. "Kennecott, Alaska." Anchorage: National Park Service, 1987.

Stearns, Robert A. "The Morgan-Guggenheim Syndicate and the Development of Alaska, 1906-1915." Unpublished Ph.D. dissertation, University of California-Santa Barbara, 1967.

Twenty-Fourth Annual Report of the Kennecott Copper Corporation. New York: Kennecott Copper Corporation, 1938.

III. Public Documents

U. S. Government Documents—By Author or Title

Abercrombie, Capt. William R. "A Military Reconnaissance of the Copper River Valley, 1898." In *Compilation of Narratives of Exploration in Alaska*. Senate Reports, 56th Cong., 1st sess., No. 1023 (1900) (Serial 3896), 563–90.

Abercrombie, Lt. William R. "A Supplementary Expedition into the Copper River Valley." In *Compilation of Narratives of Exploration in Alaska*. Senate Reports, 56th Cong., 1st sess., No. 1023 (1900) (Serial 3896), 383–410.

_____. Alaska, 1899. Copper River Exploring Expedition. Washington: GPO, 1900.

Allen, Lt. Henry T. Report of an Expedition to the Copper, Tanana, and Koyukuk Rivers, in the Territory of Alaska, in the Year 1885. Washington: GPO, 1887.

_____. "A Military Reconnaissance of the Copper River Valley, 1885." In *Compilation of Narratives of Exploration in Alaska*. Senate Reps., 56th Cong., 1st sess., no. 1023 (1900) (Serial 3896), 411–88.

Brooks, Alfred H. *Mineral Resources of Alaska: Report of Progress of Investigations in 1909*. USGS Bulletin 442. Washington: GPO, 1910.

_____. *Mineral Resources of Alaska: Report on Progress of Investigation in 1913*. USGS Bulletin 662. Washington: GPO, 1914.

_____. *Mineral Resources of Alaska: Report on Progress of Investigation in 1916*. USGS Bulletin 662. Washington: GPO, 1918.

_____. *Mineral Resources of Alaska: Report on Progress of Investigations in 1919*. USGS Bulletin 714. Washington: GPO, 1921.

Capps, Stephen R. *The Chisana-White River District, Alaska*. USGS Bulletin 630. Washington: GPO, 1916.

Clapp, J. M. *Wagon Road from Valdez to Ft. Egbert*. U.S. House, 58th Cong., 3rd sess., doc. 192. Washington: GPO, 1905.

Cobb, Edward H. *Placer Deposits of Alaska*. USGS Bulleton 1374. Washington: GPO, 1973.

Compilations of Narratives of Exploration in Alaska. Senate Reports, 56th Cong., 1st sess., no. 1023. Washington: GPO, 1900.

Contributions to Economic Geology of Alaska. USGS Bulleton 1655. Washington: GPO, 1963.

Glenn, Capt. Edwin F. and Capt. William R. Abercrombie. *Reports of Explorations in the Territory of Alaska, 1898*. Washington: GPO, 1899.

Mendenhall, Walter C. and Frank C. Schrader. *Mineral Resources of the Mount Wrangell District, Alaska*. USGS professional paper no. 15. Washington: GPO, 1903.

Moffit, Fred H. and J. B. Mertie, Jr. *The Kotsina-Kuskulana District, Alaska*. USGS Bulletin 745. Washington: GPO, 1923.

Orth, Donald J. *Dictionary of Alaska Place Names*. USGS professional paper no. 567. Washington: GPO, 1967.

Richter, Donald H., et al.. *Guide to the Volcanoes of the Western Wrangell Mountains, Alaska—Wrangell–St. Elias National Park and Preserve*. USGS Bulletin 2072. Washington: GPO, 1995.

Schrader, Frank C. "A Reconnaissance of a Part of Prince William Sound and the Copper River District in 1898." In USGS, *Twentieth Annual Report*. Washington: GPO, 1899.

Schwatka, Frederick. *Report of a Military Reconnaissance in Alaska, Made in 1883*. Senate Ex. Doc., 48th Cong. 2nd sess., no. 2 (1885) (Serial 2261).

Smith, Philip S. *Mineral Resources of Alaska: Report on Progress of Investigation in 1933*. USGS Bulletin 864. Washington: GPO, 1936.

_____. *Mineral Resources of Alaska : Report on Progress of Investigation in 1936*. USGS Bulletin 897. Washington: GPO, 1938.

_____. *Past Placer Gold Production from Alaska*. USGS Bulletin 857-B. Washington: GPO, 1933.

U.S. Government Documents — General

International Boundary Commission. *Joint Report Upon the Survey and Demarcation of the International Boundary between the United States and Canada*. Ottawa and Washington: GPO, 1918.

U.S. Alaska Railroad Commission. *Railway Routes in Alaska*. House Ex. Doc., 62nd Cong., 3rd sess., no. 1346. Washington: GPO, 1913.

U.S. Senate. Committee on Public Lands. *Government Railroad and Coal Lands in Alaska*. 62nd cong., 2nd sess. Washington: GPO, 1912.

_____. Committee on Territories. *Conditions in Alaska*. Senate Reps., 58th Cong., 2nd sess., no. 282 Pt. 2. Washington: GPO, 1904.

_____. Committee on Territories. *Construction of Railroads in Alaska*. 63rd Cong., 1st sess. Washington: GPO, 1913.

_____. *Investigation of the Department of the Interior and of the Bureau of Forestry*. Senate Doc. 719, 61st Cong., 3rd sess. Washington: GPO, 1911.

U.S. Department of Agriculture, Forest Service, Alaska Region. *Kayak Island 1741–1981.* Leaflet no. 158. Washington: GPO, 1981.

U.S. Department of the Interior. *Annual Report of the Governor of Alaska to the Department of the Interior, 1890–1935.*

_____. Annual Report(s) of the Secretary of the Interior, 1885–1920.

IV. Newspapers

Alaska Prospector, 1902–1903.

Alaska Weekly, 1923–35.

Chitina Leader, 1913–15.

Chitina Weekly Herald, 1931–35.

Cordovan Daily Alaskan, 1909–1910.

Fairbanks Daily News, 1913–14.

Fairbanks Weekly Times, 1913.

Valdez News, 1903.

Weekly Star (Whitehorse, Yukon), 1913–14.

V. Books

Archibald, Margaret. *Grubstake to Grocery Store: Supplying the Klondike, 1897-1907.* Canadian Historic Sites no. 26. Ottawa: Parks Canada, 1983.

Atwood, Evangeline. *Frontier Politics.* Portland: Binford and Mort, 1979.

_____. and Robert N. DeArmond. *Who's Who in Alaska Politics.* Portland: Binford and Mort, 1977.

Bancroft, Hubert H. *History of Alaska 1730–1885.* Darien, Conn.: Hafner Publishing Co., 1970.

Beach, Rex. *The Iron Trail.* New York: Harper and Brothers, 1913.

_____. *Personal Exposures.* New York: Harper and Brothers, 1940.

Beaglehole, J. C. *The Voyages of Captain James Cook on His Voyages of Discovery.* Vol. III. *The Voyage of the Resolution and the Discovery 1776–1780.* Cambridge, England: Hakluyt Society, 1972.

Berton, Pierre. *Klondike Fever.* New York: Alfred A. Knopf, 1974.

Birket-Smith, Kaj and Frederica De Laguna. *The Eyak Indians of the Copper River Delta.* Kobenhavn: Levin & Munksgard, 1938.

Brooks, Alfred H. *Blazing Alaska's Trails.* College: University of Alaska Press, 1953.

Copper Handbook. Vol. 5. Houghton, Mich.: Horace J. Stevens, 1975.

Copper River Joe [Charles H. Remington]. *A Golden Cross (?) on Trails from the Valdez Glacier.* Los Angeles: White-Thompson Publishers, 1939.

Crandall, Faye E., ed. *Into the Copper River Valley. The Letters and Ministry of Vincent James Joy Pioneer Missionary to Alaska.* Taylors, S.C.: Faith Printing Company, Inc., 1994.

Davidson, George. *The Alaska Boundary.* San Francisco: Alaska Packers Association, 1903.

Day, Beth. *Glacier Pilot. The Story of Bob Reeve and the Flyers Who Pushed Back Alaska's Air Frontiers.* New York: Holt, Rinehart and Winston, 1957.

De Laguna, Frederica. *Under Mount Saint Elias: The History and Culture of the Yakutat Tlingit.* Washington: Smithsonian Institution, 1972.

Dietz, Authur A. *Mad Rush for Gold in Frozen North.* Los Angeles: Times-Mirror Printing and Binding House, 1914.

Goulet, Emil Oliver. *Rugged Years on the Alaska Frontier.* Philadelphia: Dorrance and Company, 1949.

Green, Lewis. *The Boundary Hunters.* Vancouver: University of British Columbia Press, 1982.

Gruening, Ernest. *State of Alaska.* New York: Random House, 1968.

Hanable, William. *Alaska's Copper River. The 18th and 19th Centuries.* Anchorage: Alaska Historical Society, 1983.

Heller, Herbert L., ed. *Sourdough Sagas.* New York: Ballantine Books, 1967.

Helm, June, ed. *Handbook of North American Indians: Subarctic.* Vol. 6. Washington: Smithsonian Institution, 1981.

Hunt, William R. *Alaska: A Bicentennial History.* New York: W. W. Norton & Co., 1976.

_____. *Arctic Passage: The Turbulent History of the Land and People of the Bering Sea 1897–1975.* New York: Charles Scribner's Sons, 1975.

_____. *Distant Justice: Policing the Alaska Frontier.* Norman: University of Oklahoma Press, 1987.

_____. *North of 53: The Wild Days of the Alaska-Yukon Mining Frontier 1870–1914.* New York: Macmillan Publishing Co., 1974.

James, James Alton. *The First Scientific Exploration of Russian America and the Purchase of Alaska.* Northwestern University Studies in Social Science no. 4. Chicago: Northwestern University, 1942.

Janson, Lone E. *The Copper Spike.* Anchorage: Alaska Northwest Publishing Co., 1975.

_____. *Mudhole Smith: Alaska Flyer.* Anchorage: Alaska Northwest Publishing Co., 1981.

Kari, James. *Ahtna Place Names Lists.* Fairbanks: Copper River Native Association and Alaska Native Language Center, 1983.

_____, ed. *Tatl'ahwt'aenn Nenn'. The Headwaters People's Country.* Fairbanks: Alaska Native Language Center, 1986.

_____, ed. *Athna Athabaskan Dictionary.* Alaska Native Language Center, 1990.

Kitchener, L. D. *Flag Over the North: The Story of the Northern Commercial Company.* Seattle: Superior Publishing Co., 1954.

La Perouse, Jean F. de Galaup. *Voyages and Adventures.* Honolulu: University of Hawaii Press.

McKennan, Robert A. *The Upper Tanana Indians.* New Haven: Yale University Department of Anthropology, 1959.

McQuesten, Leroy N. *Recollections of Leroy N. McQuesten of Life in the Yukon, 1871–1885.* Dawson: Yukon Order of Pioneers,1952.

Margeson, Charles A. *Experiences of Gold Hunters in Alaska.* Hornellsville, N.Y.: Charles Margeson, 1899.

Mertie, Evelyn. *Thirty Summers and a Winter.* Fairbanks: Mining Industry Resources Lab, University of Alaska, 1982.

Mining in Alaska's Past: Conference Proceedings. Publication Number 27. Anchorage: Alaska Division of Parks, 1980.

Naske, Claus-M. *Paving Alaska's Trails: The Work of the Alaska Road Commission.* Lanham, Md.: University Press of America, 1986.

_____. and Herman Slotnick. *Alaska: A History of the 49th State.* Norman: University of Oklahoma, 1987.

Nichols, Jeannette Paddock. *Alaska.* Cleveland: Arthur Clark and Co., 1924.

Penlington, Norman. *The Alaska Boundary Dispute: A Critical Reappraisal*. Toronto: McGraw-Hill Ryerson, 1972.

Peterson, Knut D. *When Alaska Was Free*. Port Washington, N.Y.: Ashley Press, 1977.

_____. *The Lost Frontier*. Port Washington, N.Y.: Ashley Press, 1980.

Pierce, Richard A. *Russian America: A Biographical Dictionary*. Kingston, Ontario: Limestone Press, 1990.

Polk's Alaska Yukon Gazetteer. 1907–1924.

Potter, Jean. *The Flying North*. New York: Macmillan Co., 1945.

Powell, Addison M. *Trailing and Camping in Alaska*. New York: Wessels and Bissel, 1910.

Rainey, Froelich G. *Anthropological Papers of the American Museum of Natural History: Archaeology in Central Alaska*. Vol. 36, pt. 4. New York: American Museum of Natural History, 1939.

Remley, David A. *Crooked Road: The Story of the Alaska Highway*. New York: McGraw-Hill Book Co., 1976.

Ricks, Melvin B. *Alaska Bibliography*. Stephen W. and Betty J. Haycox, eds. Portland: Binfords and Mort, 1977.

_____. *Directory of Alaskan Post Offices and Postmasters*. Ketchikan: Tongass Publishing Co., 1965.

Roden, Henry. *Alaska Mining Law*. Juneau: Henry Roden, 1913.

Schwatka, Frederick. *Along Alaska's Great River*. New York: Cassell and Co., 1885.

Sherwood, Morgan. *Alaska and Its History*. Seattle: University of Washington Press, 1967.

_____. *Exploration of Alaska*. New Haven: Yale University Press, 1965.

Soberg, Ralph. *Bridging Alaska. From the Big Delta to the Kenai*. Walnut Creek, Calif.: Hardscratch Press, 1991.

Tarr, Ralph Stockman and Lawrence Martin. *Alaskan Glacier Studies of the National Geographic Society in the Yakutat Bay, Prince Wiliam Sound and Lower Copper River Regions*. Washington: National Geographic Society, 1914.

Tower, Elizabeth A. *Big Mike Heney. Irish Prince of the Iron Trails*. Anchorage: self-published, 1988.

_____. *Ghosts of Kennecott. The Story of Stephen Birch*. Anchorage: self-published, 1990.

Transportation in Alaska's Past. Anchorage: Alaska Historical Society, 1982.

Trefzger, Hardy. *My Fifty Years of Hunting, Fishing, Prospecting, Guiding, Trading and Trapping in Alaska*. New York: Exposition Press, 1963.

Twitchell, Heath, Jr. *Allen: The Biography of an Army Officer, 1859–1930*. New Brunswick: Rutgers University Press, 1974.

Webb, Melody. *The Last Frontier*. Albuquerque: University of New Mexico Press, 1985.

Whiting, F. B., M.D. *Grit, Grief and Gold. A True Narrative of an Alaska Pathfinder*. Seattle: Peacock Publishing Company, 1923.

Wickersham, James. *Old Yukon: Tales, Trails, and Trials*. Washington: Washington Law Book Co., 1938.

Wolff, Ernest. *Handbook for the Alaska Prospector*. Ann Arbor, Mich.: Edward Brothers, 1969.

Wright, Allen B. *Prelude to Bonanza: The Discovery and Exploration of the Yukon*. Sidney, B.C.: Gray's Publishing Co., 1976.

Young, George O. *Alaskan-Yukon Trophies Won and Lost*. Huntington, W.V.: Standard Publications, 1947.

Young, Otis E. *Western Mining: An Informal Account of Precious-Metals Prospecting, Placering, Lode Mining, and Milling on the American Frontier from Spanish Times to 1893*. Norman: University of Oklahoma Press, 1970.

VI. Articles and Serial Publications

Alaska Geographical Society. "Prince William Sound." *Alaska Geographic* 2, no. 3 (1975).

_____. "Yakutat: The Turbulent Crescent." *Alaska Geographic* 2, no. 4 (1975).

_____. "Wrangell-St. Elias: International Mountain Wilderness." *Alaska Geographic* 8, no. 1 (1981).

_____. "Alaska's Glaciers." *Alaska Geographic* 9, no. 1 (1982).

_____. "Alaska Steam: A Pictorial History of the Alaska Steamship Company." *Alaska Geographic* 11, no. 4 (1984).

_____. "The Tanana Basin." *Alaska Geographic* 16, no. 3 (1989).

_____. "The Copper Trail." *Alaska Geographic* 16, no. 4 (1989).

Agosti, Dona. "Reliving on the Chitistone Goat Trails." *This Alaska Sports* 6, no. 4 (September/October 1983).

Andrews, C. L. "Viewing the Copper River Spectacles." *Alaska-Yukon Magazine* 10, no. 4 (October 1910): 231–37.

Baldwin, Sylvia Wells. "My Memories of Alaska." *Copper River Country Journal*, March 2, 1989.

Benson, Carl. "Glacier-Volcano Interactions of Mt. Wrangell, Alaska." *Annual Report 1977–78*. Geophysical Institute. University of Alaska. Fairbanks: University of Alaska, 1978, 1–26.

_____. and Anthony B. Follett. "Application of Photogrammetry to the Study of Volcano-Glacier Interactions on Mount Wrangell, Alaska." *Photogrammetric Engineering and Remote Sensing* 52, no. 6 (June 1986): 813–27.

Beerman, Eric. "Spanish Admiral Antonio Valdez and Valdez, Alaska." *Alaska Journal* (Spring 1979): 38–45.

Carpe, Allen. "The Ascent of Mount Bona." *American Alpine Journal* 1 (1931): 245–54.

Charles, Sidney D. "The Conquering of the Coppers." *Alaska-Yukon Magazine* (December 1910): 365–70.

_____. "Cordova, the New Gateway Metropolis." *Alaska-Yukon Magazine* (December 1910): 396.

DeArmond, Robert N. "Sternwheel Steamboats on the Copper River." *The Sea Chest: Journal of the Puget Sound Maritime Historical Society* 22, no. 2 (December 1988): 48–56.

_____. "Tale of the Phantom Steamer." *Alaska Magazine* (August 1988): 25–26.

De Laguna, Frederica and Catharine McClellan. "Ahtna." In *Handbook of North American Indians*, vol. 6, June Helm, ed. Washington: Smithsonian Institution, 1981, 641–63.

Dunn, Robert. "Conquering Our Greatest Volcano." *Harper's Monthly Magazine* 18, no. 706 (March 1909): 497–509.

Ellis, Carlyle. "The Winters Crucial Battle on Copper River." *Alaska-Yukon Magazine* (June 1910): 27–35.

Farquhar, F. P. "Naming Alaska's Mountains: Some Accounts of Their First Ascent." *American Alpine Journal* 11 (1959): 211–32.

Grauman, Melody Webb. "Kennecott: Alaska Origins of a Copper Empire, 1900–1938." *Western Historical Quarterly* 9, no. 2 (April 1978): 197–211.

Grinnell, May. "Cordova." *Alaska-Yukon Magazine* (August 1909): 326-31.

Grinev, A. V. "The Lost Expedition of Dmitri Tarkhanov on the Copper River." *Sovetskaia Etnogragia* 4 (1987): 88–180.

Hayes, C. Willard. "An Expediton through the Yukon District." *National Geographic* 4 (May 15, 1892): 117–62.

————. "Copper River as a Route to the Yukon Basin." *American Geographical Society Bulletin* 30 (1898): 127–34.

Hoeman, J. Vincent. "Wrangell Range." *American Alpine Journal.* 15: 121–22.

Johansen, Woodrow. "The Copper River and Northwestern Railway." *Northern Engineer* 7, no. 2 (Summer 1975): 19–31.

John, Fred and Katie (as told to B. Stephen Strong). "The Killing of the Russians at Batzulnetas Village." *Alaska Journal* 3, no. 3 (Summer 1973): 147–48.

Keen, Dora. "First Up Mount Blackburn," reprinted in "Wrangell-St. Elias: International Mountain Wilderness." *Alaska Geographic* 8, no. 1 (1981).

Kerr, Mark Brickell. "Mount St. Elias and Its Glaciers." *Scribner's* (March 1891): 361–72.

Kinney, John. "Copper and the Settlement of South Central Alaska." *Journal of the West* 10, no. 2 (April 1971): 307–18.

Lambert, H. F. "The Conquest of Mount Logan." *National Geographic* 49, no. 6 (June 1926): 597–631.

Lautaret, Ron. "You Can't Catch Bootleggers with Sunday School Teachers." *Alaska Journal.* Anchorage: Alaska Northwest Publishing Co., 1981, 40–43.

Lee, Timothy E. "Environmental Effects and Monitoring of Abandoned Drilling Muds: The Wrangell-St. Elias Approach." *Park Science*: A *Resource Management Bulletin* 9, no. 4 (Summer 1989): 8–9.

McKenzie, D. J. "Freeze-Out at McCarthy." *Alaska Sportsman* (September 1964): 34–35.

Moore, Terris. "Mt. Sanford: An Alaskan Ski Climb." *American Alpine Journal* 3 (1933): 265–73.

Munsey, Sylvia Falconer. "Margaret Harrais." *Alaska Journal* (Summer 1975): 144–52.

Nielsen, Lawrence. "The Valdez and Klutina Glaciers, Alaska." *Appalachia* 33 (1960–61), magazine nos. 130, 131, 132, 133.

Riggs, Thomas. "Surveying the 141st Meridian." *National Geographic* 23 (July 1912): 687–90.

Russell, Israel. "An Expedition to Mount St. Elias, Alaska." *National Geographic* 3 (May 1891): 59–64.

————. "The Expedition of the National Geographic Society and the U.S. Geological Survey." *Century* (April 1891): 872–84.

————. "Mount St. Elias Revisited." *Century* (June 1892): 190–203.

Schuster, E. J. E. "The Reynolds System." In "Alaska Living." *Alaska Daily News,* June 30, 1967, 7–9.

Schwatka, Frederick. "Two Expeditions to Mount St. Elias." *Century* (April 1891): 665–84.

Seton-Karr, H. W. "Explorations in Alaska and North-west British Columbia." Proceedings of the Royal Geographical Society and Monthly Record of Geography (February 1891): 65–86.

Shepard, Thomas R. "Placer Mining Law in Alaska." Reprint from the *Yale Law Journal* (May 1909). New Haven: S. Z. Field, n.d.

Sherwood, Morgan. "Science in Russia America, 1741 to 1865." *Pacific Northwest Quarterly* (January 1967): 33–37.

Smith, Harold E. "Chititu Gold." *Alaska Sportsman* (September 1964): 38, 46–48.

Solie, Dan. "Icing on Fire: A Season on the Summit of Mount Wrangell." *Alaska Journal* 14, no. 4 (Autumn 1984): 8–15.

Stearns, Robert A. "Alaska's Kennecott Copper." *Alaska Journal* (1975 Annual Edition). Anchorage: Alaska Northwest Publishing Co., 1975, 130–139.

Storm, L. W. "Chitina Copper Region in Southern Alaska." *Engineering and Mining Journal* (November 19, 1910): 565–67.

VanStone, James. "Exploring the Copper River Country." *Pacific Northwest Quarterly* (October 1955): 115–23.

————. "Report of a Brief Archaeological Survey of the Copper River in the Chitina Region." Typescript, November 2, 1953. National Park Service files.

————. "Russian Exploration in Interior Alaska." *Pacific Northwest Quarterly* (April 1959): 37–47.

Williams, William. "Climbing Mount St. Elias." *Scribner's Magazine* (April 1889): 387–403.

Index

❊   ❊   ❊

222

About the Author

❄   ❄   ❄

William R. Hunt is Professor Emeritus of History at the University of Alaska Fairbanks. He was a Research Historian with the National Park Service when he wrote this park history, "as interesting and enjoyable as anything I have ever done" including the awesome experience of "spending practically a full day touring the perimeter of the park by air. From the air I could only imagine the thoughts of surveyors and boundary fixers who traversed park borders on foot and horseback. What might they say of "grandeur" at the end of their daily treks? Perhaps park visitors do not and should not so much address themselves to "grandeur" as to more modest words describing their modest uses of the land. We go to look and to enjoy quiet pleasures and recreations, observing grand and small according to our interests and the keenness of our impressions. There is so much to observe in the Wrangell-St. Elias of past human activities and the natural world."

Hunt is the author of *Alaska: A Bicentennial History* (Norton); *To Stand at the Pole: The Admiral Peary-Doctor Frederick Cook Controversy* (Stein & Day); *Distant Justice: Policing the Alaska Frontier* (University of Oklahoma); *North of 53*; *Alaska Yukon Mining Frontier* (Macmillan); among other titles. He is currently working on *The Trail of Lonely Hearts: True Tales of Alaskan Romances*.